Japan and Bri
An Aesthetic Dialogue 1850

美味 滋養 葡萄酒

赤玉ポートワイン

Japan and Britain
An Aesthetic Dialogue 1850 - 1930

Edited and with texts by
Tomoko Sato and Toshio Watanabe

With essays by
Sir Hugh Cortazzi, Shuji Takashina and Ellen P. Conant

Lund Humphries, London
in association with
Barbican Art Gallery and the Setagaya Art Museum
1991

Cat.161
KATAOKA TOSHIRO
AND INOUE MOKUDA
Akadama Port Wine, 1922

BP has enjoyed a long standing relationship with Japan dating back to the 1950s when its business was primarily sales of crude oil. An office was opened in Tokyo in 1960 and currently BP has around fifty employees there with others elsewhere in Japan. Between 1968 and 1976 BP built twenty very large crude carriers in Japanese yards.

Japan is now a significant market for BP with sales of crude oil, oil products, liquefied natural gas, bulk chemicals and coal being the main activities. For its part, BP is a purchaser of Japanese services, goods and materials, and Japanese shipyards are once more constructing vessels for BP. Tokyo is also one of the major financial centres of the world and therefore an important source of finance for BP, whose shares were first listed in 1987 on the Tokyo Stock Exchange.

Over the years BP has established business links with many Japanese corporations and now has partnerships and joint ventures with Japanese corporations not just in the Asia Pacific Region but in other parts of the world, including Great Britain.

BP is recognised as a leading corporate sponsor of the Arts. Because of our long association with Japan, its people and its institutions we have been delighted to support The Japan Festival 1991 and to sponsor this Exhibition, which depicts the artistic exchanges between our two countries over the period 1850-1930.

Robert Horton, Chairman
The British Petroleum Company p.l.c.

This exhibition is about dialogue. It illustrates, through its very realisation, how a deeper understanding of the art and culture of our two countries has led to closer and more fruitful communication. It reflects in all senses a collaboration between two cultures.

Such an ambitious project, however, could not have been undertaken without generous assistance from a group of supporters in Japan. We would like to thank the following companies for their generous contribution.

The Yasuda Fire & Marine Insurance Company Limited
Asahi Breweries, Ltd.
The Dai-ichi Kangyo Bank, Ltd.
The Fuji Bank, Ltd
The Meiji Mutual Life Insurance Co.
The Mitsubishi Bank, Ltd.
The Mitsubishi Trust and Banking Corporation
Nippon Life Insurance Co.
Orient Corporation
The Sumitomo Bank, Ltd.
The Sumitomo Trust and Banking Co., Ltd.
Suntory Limited
Yamatane Corporation

Yoshio Tsubouchi, Chairman   Philip Willoughby, Chairman
The Setagaya Art Promotion Foundation   Libraries, Art Galleries, Record Committee
                                          Corporation of London

Copyright © 1991
Barbican Art Gallery, Corporation of London,
the Setagaya Art Museum, Tokyo,
and the authors

First edition 1991
Published by
Lund Humphries Publishers Ltd
16 Pembridge Road, London W11
in association with
Barbican Art Gallery, London
and the Setagaya Art Museum, Tokyo

British Library Cataloguing in Publication Data
A catalogue record for this book is available from
the British Library

ISBN 0 85331 596 5

Edited by
Charlotte Burri and John Taylor
with the assistance of
Jane Alison, Penny Ashford, Carol Brown,
Judy Digney, John Hoole, Sonya Larsen,
Donna Loveday, Anna Parker,
Tomoko Sato, Toshio Watanabe

Designed by
Kono Communications Design LONDON/TOKYO
John Hoole and Tomoko Sato

Made and printed in Great Britain by
BAS Printers Ltd, Over Wallop, Stockbridge,
Hampshire

This catalogue accompanies the exhibition
Japan and Britain:
An Aesthetic Dialogue 1850 - 1930
at Barbican Art Gallery
17 October 1991 - 12 January 1992
Organised by Barbican Art Gallery, London
and the Setagaya Art Museum, Tokyo

Exhibition Selectors:
Tomoko Sato, Toshio Watanabe

Exhibition Organisers:
Tomoko Sato, Nozomi Endo, Masako Shimizu

Exhibition Co-ordinators:
Donna Loveday, Denna Jones Anderson

Exhibition Administration:
John Hoole, Judy Digney, Carol Brown,
Nathalie Compton-Roberts

Education Programme:
Anna Parker, Christine Stewart

Exhibition Design:
Andy Creed-Miles,
Kono Communications Design LONDON/TOKYO
David Stracy

Cat.23 GOUNTEI SADAHIDE (1807-?)
Dinner at a Foreign Merchant's House

CONTENTS

Cat.300
AUBREY BEARDSLEY
(1872-1898)
*J'ai baisé ta bouche
Iokanaan*, 1893

FOREWORD

This exhibition has been timed to coincide with the Japan Festival 1991, a major event that celebrates the 100th anniversary of the foundation of the Japan Society in London and which provides the perfect occasion for an exhibition about the cultural interchange between our two countries.

The establishment of the Society itself in 1891 was a symptom of the countries' closening ties that had developed following Lord Elgin's mission to Japan in 1858. With the subsequent treaty and the opening up of Japan, Japanese *objets d'art* began to pour into Britain. The impact of Japanese style upon late Victorian taste has been documented by many books and exhibitions. However, the cultural cross-fertilisation that was engendered by these links has never been fully appreciated.

Japan and Britain: An Aesthetic Dialogue 1850 - 1930 illustrates the constant appeal that 'things foreign' have for members of the human race. The two-way traffic of information and influences that was established between Japan and Britain during this period has ultimately fostered a greater understanding between our two, comparatively alien, cultures. This exhibition should not therefore be seen just as a study of a cultural period isolated in time and space, but also a reflection upon the process that still goes on as strongly today and, hopefully, continues to encourage an improved understanding between our two countries, just as between all our international neighbours.

As evidence of the two-way process at work, this exhibition is a product of Anglo-Japanese museum collaboration, researched by Japanese scholars based in Britain, in consultation with their compatriots in Japan, and organised by both our organisations, with the object of showing the exhibition in London and Tokyo. Further to this, an exhibition of this scale can only be realised if substantial financial support can be found, and we are very pleased that the efforts of our two organisations to mount this display have received the support of sponsors in both our countries, The British Petroleum Company plc, The Yasuda Fire & Marine Insurance Company Limited, Asahi Breweries, Ltd., The Dai-ichi Kangyo Bank, Ltd., The Fuji Bank, Ltd., The Meiji Mutual Life Insurance Co., The Mitsubishi Bank, Ltd., The Mitsubishi Trust and Banking Corporation, Nippon Life Insurance Co., Orient Corporation, The Sumitomo Bank, Ltd., The Sumitomo Trust and Banking Co., Ltd., Suntory Limited and Yamatane Corporation. We are also grateful for the assistance of Nikkei and the Japan Foundation, as well as the Museums and Galleries Commission.

In Tokyo, our grateful thanks go to Yoshio Tsubouchi, the President of the Setagaya Art Promotion Foundation, and Ambassador Yamazaki, whose persuasive efforts to secure support for the exhibition have made the whole project feasible, and the staff of the Setagaya Art Museum, in particular Nozomi Endo and Masako Shimizu, who have guided the exhibition to its successful realisation.

In London, major credit is due to Tomoko Sato of Barbican Art Gallery and Dr Toshio Watanabe of the Chelsea College of Art and Design, who have selected the exhibition and written the catalogue. They have received much advice from Sir Hugh Cortazzi, former British Ambassador to Japan and Chairman of the Japan Society, London, who agreed at an early stage to be a patron of the exhibition, subsequently lending works from his private collection and contributing an illuminating essay to this publication.

Such an extensive display of objects from our two countries could not have been mounted without the willingness and cooperation of the many museums and private collectors that have lent exhibits. To all such participants in this venture, we give grateful thanks.

John Hoole, Curator   Seiji Oshima, Director
Barbican Art Gallery   Setagaya Art Museum

PREFACE

This exhibition charts for the first time the intercultural relationships between Japan and Britain in art. Why has such an exhibition never been mounted before?

One crucial reason is due to the way in which our perception of Modern Art has changed. The conventional view of 'Modern Art' was that it developed almost exclusively in Paris from the mid-nineteenth century until immediately after World War II, when New York was seen to take on the mantle of 'the mainstream'. Everything else was relegated to the sidelines, including British Victorian and Edwardian art. The study of Japonisme only gained ground during the 1960s and 1970s, and then mainly because it provided an insight into the 'mainstream' Impressionists and Post-Impressionists who were inspired and affected by it.

The methodology of these earlier Japonisme studies was centred on the investigation of canonical works by modern masters such as Manet, Degas and van Gogh, and tried to find isolated sources for particular paintings. What was seen to count was the linear progress of Modern Art, from Courbet to Manet and Degas, from Monet and Renoir to the four giants of Post-Impressionism and then to Picasso and Matisse. The significance of Japanese art was reduced to individual motifs or formal devices which formed part of a vast reservoir of heterogeneous motifs, from which Western masters could pick and choose. When a formal device, such as the use of flat colours in van Gogh, was seen to contribute to the inexorable way forward of Modern Art, that was judged a good choice, but when Monet painted his wife in a gaudy kimono, this use of a Japanese motif was regarded as superficial and the artist was castigated for being old fashioned.

A change in direction became noticeable from the late 1970s. 1 Scholars turned their attention to the Japonisme of countries other than France, to the period after 1900 and to areas other than painting, such as design, architecture, and photography. Above all, Japonisme was now seen as a more integrated cultural phenomenon, affecting not only paintings in isolation but a whole society. This exhibition is part of the same trend. We hope to show that Japonisme was a significant cultural phenomenon not just in Paris, but also in Britain. It did not stop at 1900 and clearly manifested itself not just in painting but in architecture, interior design, ceramics, metalwork, theatre design, book design, and printmaking.

How did the Japanese perceive their own Modern Art from the same period? The story is very similar. Those artists from the Meiji (1868-1912) and Taisho (1912-1926) periods who achieved canonical status were mostly either Japanese-style painters or Paris-trained oil painters based in Tokyo. More recently, this perception has also been challenged, though there is still a long way to go and the study of the art of nineteenth-century Japan is nothing like as advanced as its British counterpart. 2 One positive effect of the mushrooming of provincial art museums in Japan is their search for artists born or active in their area. This means that many unjustly neglected artists, not hitherto seen as part of the mainstream, are receiving more serious attention. Retrospective exhibitions of these artists are being mounted and catalogues published. Organisations such as the Tokyo National Research Institute for Cultural Properties (Tokyo Kokuritsu Bunkazai Kenkyujo) and the Meiji Art Studies Society (Meiji Bijutsu Gakkai) are actively pursuing documentary research and casting their net ever wider. Without the result of these recent research activities, this exhibition would not have been possible.

Nevertheless, there are still two areas of Meiji and Taisho art where more attention is urgently needed. The first is the history of the design of this period. Attention is still concentrated on one-off masterpieces produced by craftsmen rather than on product design, graphic design or design related to popular culture. The second is the Japanese lack of interest in issues of gender and art during our period. 3

Cat.260
SHIMOMURA KANZAN
(1873-1930)
*Copy of J.E. Millais's
Knight Errant*, c.1904

11

Initially, when we conceived this exhibition, we divided it into two clear sections: one for British Japonisme and another for the British influence on Japan. However, the more our research progressed, the more untenable this plan became. Eventually we abandoned it in favour of a loose chronological framework intermingling the two, so that the comparisons would emerge more clearly. The mutual influence of these two countries does not constitute two separate phenomena, but one intricate relationship. Take, for example, the role played by one Englishman, Josiah Conder (1852-1920). He was taught by the Japanophile William Burges and was employed by the Japanese government to build Western-style architecture in Japan, where he created, among other designs, a Japonisme interior in pure Aesthetic Movement style in the middle of Tokyo. This same Conder studied Japanese painting under Kawanabe Kyosai (1831-1889) and even won a prize for his painting at a Japanese exhibition. He went on to publish books on Japanese flower arrangement (1891), Japanese gardens (1893) and Kawanabe Kyosai (1911), which were widely read and strongly affected British artists and designers. One of the gardens illustrated in his book was recreated in Bitchet Green, Kent in the early part of this century. 4 With Conder, we have the exemplary Japonist, whose work blended into the two-way process of cultural contact and information dissemination, while involved in developments in both countries.

This exhibition is also intended as a contribution to the debate on the interactions between two cultures. Since Edward W. Said published his book *Orientalism* in 1978, the issue of Eurocentrism has been much discussed. It has been suggested that if Picasso received inspiration from an African sculpture, he was considered clever, but if an African artist receives inspiration from Picasso he is a mere copyist. A Westerner who judges the Japanese painter Aoki Shigeru to be simply copying Burne-Jones might not dream of looking at Whistler's painting *Nocturne: Blue and Gold - Old Battersea Bridge* (Cat. 68) and levelling the same charge at him with regard to Hiroshige. The relationship of Aoki to Burne-Jones and Whistler to Hiroshige can be only understood within a larger cultural context, which this exhibition is trying to provide.

Harold Bloom has argued, in his book *The Anxiety of Influence*, that poetic influence proceeds by a misreading of the prior poet, 'an act of creative correction that is actually and necessarily a misinterpretation'. 5 While we are not restricting ourselves to the consideration of artistic giants, as Bloom did, this notion could profitably be transferred to our context. Most, if not all, our examples seem to be based on some kind of misreading or misinterpretation, but these created new possibilities.

The aesthetic dialogue between Britain and Japan has led to a rich, complex and organic whole, where the two nations no longer remain two separate cultural entities, but have become two strongly interrelating ones that grow progressively closer through mutual understanding.

Toshio Watanabe

NOTES
1 For the analysis of the historiography of Japonisme in the West and in Japan see Watanabe 1991b, pp.13-52.
2 A recent and particularly innovative attempt at a revisionist exhibition was *Nihon Bijutsu no Jukyu Seiki* (19th century Japanese Art) which took place at Hyogo Prefectural Museum of Modern Art in Kobe in 1990.
3 Thomas Rimer makes a similar point in his article, 'Tokyo in Paris/Paris in Tokyo', in Takashina et al. 1987, pp.33-79; p.79.
4 We are grateful to Dr Christopher Thacker for this information.
5 Bloom 1973, p.30

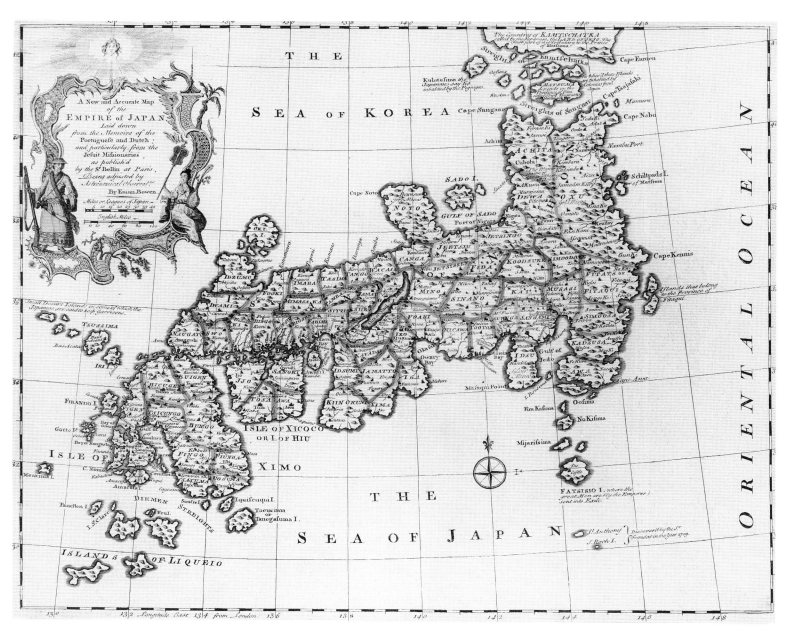

Cat.5 EMANUEL BOWEN
A New and Accurate Map of the Empire of Japan, 1747

13

The Aesthetic Dialogue Examined
JAPAN AND BRITAIN 1850 - 1930

Tomoko Sato and Toshio Watanabe

THE TREATY OF EDO

In August 1858, the British battleship, *HMS Furious*, was approaching Edo (today's Tokyo). It was the first British ship to enter Edo Bay since Japan had been closed in the early seventeenth century. 1 Lord Elgin, the British envoy who had just succeeded in opening China with the Treaties of Tientsin, was on board and now charged with making a treaty with Japan. One of the three escorting vessels was the *Emperor*, a steam yacht which was to be presented to the Shogun as a gift from Queen Victoria. 2

When Japan and Britain began a dialogue during that summer, their political and cultural conditions were markedly different. In 1858, Britain commanded a world-wide empire, with an established parliamentary system and the most advanced technology in the world. Advocating free trade, the empire and its markets were expanding towards the Far East. On the other hand, Japan was still a feudal society, which had been virtually isolated from the rest of the world for more than two hundred years by a self-enforced isolation policy called 'sakoku'. Only recently had Japan reluctantly opened some of its ports to the West when threatened by the arrival of Americans in 1853 with modern warships which the Japanese called 'Black Ships'. National opinion was sharply divided over the question of the opening up of Japan, and this accelerated the disintegration of the Tokugawa Shogunate whose decline was already evident in the early nineteenth century. By 1858 a strong current of political change was under way in Japan.

The Treaty of Edo was signed on 26 August 1858, sealing diplomatic and commercial relationships between Japan and Britain. Its clauses included the opening of three ports, 'most-favoured-nation' status and the freedom to trade with private individuals. 3 In the same year, Japan also signed commercial treaties with the United States, Holland, France and Russia.

The news of the Treaty of Edo was welcomed by the British press and merchants both at home and abroad. The culture of Japan and its potential as a British market were covered in major press articles at the time. The leading British firm in Hong Kong, Jardine, Matheson and Company, and their fellow merchants in China wrote enthusiastically to Lord Elgin, thanking him 'for the opening of commercial relations with the rich and interesting Empire of Japan', and saying that they believed the treaty would create 'substantial advantages on [sic] the commerce of the world.' 4

Indeed, the event was to have a great impact on the commerce of the world from that time onwards, but it was also the beginning of a full-scale cultural dialogue between Japan and Britain. While the arrival of Europeans and Americans began to change the cultural ambience of Japan, an influx of Japanese goods and information inspired Western artists and collectors. Their enthusiasm for Japan was to develop into a wider and deeper phenomenon called 'Japonisme', a 'taste for things Japanese', 5 which spread across Europe and the United States during the last four decades of the nineteenth century and beyond. The term was first used in 1872 by the French art critic and collector Philippe Burty (1830-1890) in his article in *La Renaissance littéraire et artistique* (May 1872). 6 The term was introduced to Britain in 1875 when Burty's article, entitled 'Japonism', appeared in *The Academy*, where the term was defined as 'the study of the art and genius of Japan'. 7 By that time, London, alongside Paris, was also a centre for the vogue of Japan.

Cat.21 C. CAPTAIN F. B. BEDWELL, RN
Exchange of Full Powers between the British Ambassador
and the Japanese Commissioners, Yeddo, 1858

In Japan, after the fall of the Tokugawa Shogunate in 1867, the new Meiji Government began to carry out a full-scale Westernisation programme, necessary, in their opinion, to distance the feudal past and to help Japan catch up quickly with the leading nations of the world. Britain was its principal model. Although it was the United States which initially opened up Japan in 1853, after the Treaty of Edo Britain quickly established its position in Japan. As soon as the foreigners' quarters became ready in Yokohama in 1859, Jardine, Matheson and Company moved into Building No.1, later known as 'Ei Ichiban Kan' (British Building No.1), and at that time the majority of Western residents in Yokohama were British. Britain quickly dominated Japanese trade and diplomatic links in the formative years of modern Japan.

NOTES
1 Checkland 1988, p.156
2 Fox 1969, p.42
3 Ibid, pp.43-4
4 Parliamentary Papers, Houses of Commons, 1859, xxxiii, p.487 : Jardine, Matheson & Co. et al to Lord Elgin, Hong Kong, 14 March 1859, quoted by Fox, ibid., p.45
5 This definition of 'Japonisme' was given by Gabriel P. Weisberg in Meech and Weisberg 1990-91, p.7
6 G.P. Weisberg, 'Philippe Burty and Early "Japonisme"', from *Japonisme in Art*, 1980, p.116
7 P. Burty, 'Japonism', *The Academy*, August 7, 1875, p.150; quotation taken from ibid., p.116

It was during the 1850s, especially after the Treaty of Edo, that great waves of cultural influence began to reach the shores of Japan and Britain. In fact there had been contact much earlier, starting in 1600 when William Adams (1564-1620) drifted ashore in the south of Japan with the Dutch ship, *De Liefde*. Given the Japanese name, Miura Anjin, Adams was employed by the first Tokugawa Shogun, Ieyasu (1542-1616), as a consultant for overseas affairs. Subsequently a station for the British East India Company was founded in 1613 at Hirado, a small island in Kyushu, through which Japanese goods were exported to Britain and other European countries.

However, this commercial link was terminated in 1623. By that time, foreigners' activities in Japan had been severely limited and persecution of Christians had begun to intensify. In this political climate, the British left Japan voluntarily, mainly because of economic difficulties. By the early 1640s, Japan's only link with Europe was the Dutch, who were allowed to continue commercial activities under limited conditions at Dejima, the artificial island created in Nagasaki Bay. Until the mid-1850s, the Dutch monopolised Japanese trade in the West. Information about world affairs reached the Japanese government mainly through an annual account submitted by the Dutch.

Japan and its culture were first introduced to Britain by means of the commercial contacts of the British East India Company in the early seventeenth century, which apparently brought about a Jacobean vogue for lacquerware. 1 In the English language, 'Japan' became synonymous with lacquer-work in general, and soon the term 'japanning' began to refer to imitation lacquer. In 1688 John Stalker and George Parker published a DIY guide, *A Treatise of Japanning and Varnishing*, one of the earliest books

Cat.13
MARTIN CARLIN
(?-1785)
Lady's Writing Desk, c.1780

Cat.10 WORCESTER PORCELAIN COMPANY
Vase with Cover, 1765

Cat.12 JAPANESE AND ENGLISH
Lacquer Cabinet with Carved Wood Stand, c.1680

in Europe about the Japan-inspired lacquer technique. At this early stage the authors were already emphasising the beauty of Japanese art: 'Let not the Europeans any longer flatter themselves with the empty notions of having surpassed all the world beside in stately Palaces, costly Temples, and sumptuous Fabricks; Ancient and modern Rome must now give place: The glory of one Country, Japan alone, has exceeded in beauty and magnificence all the pride of the Vatican at this time, and the Pantheon heretofore...' 2

From about the mid-seventeenth century, porcelain joined lacquer as an important export item. Despite the national isolation policy, Japanese manufacturers began to produce export wares to meet growing Western demand. In 1660 alone, Arita produced 11,530 pieces destined solely for Holland. 3 The Dutch traders played the role of intermediaries selling the porcelain wares to Britain and the rest of Europe.

Certain styles of Japanese porcelain had a strong appeal for Western aesthetics and the most influential of all was the Kakiemon style. The term 'Kakiemon' derived from Sakaida Kakiemon in Arita, the legendary developer of a red enamelling technique following Chinese examples. Kakiemon ware was in general decorated in pictorial styles, delicately painted in red, blue, turquoise and yellow over a milky white glaze. Alongside the blue and white ware, the Kakiemon style was widely imitated by English craftsmen and eventually became incorporated into the repertoire of English bone china.

Lacquer and porcelain became fashionable in aristocratic circles and remained popular throughout the seventeenth and eighteenth centuries. Examples can be seen in many stately homes today, such as Burghley House in Stamford, Lincolnshire. 4 This vogue for Japanese objects was the extension of a larger current of fashion in Europe at that time called 'chinoiserie', which was a manifestation of fanciful European dreams and curiosity about the exotic East. However it took a long time before Japan was clearly acknowledged as a separate entity by the West, Japanese items being included, as late as 1851, in the Chinese section in the Great Exhibition held at the Crystal Palace. 5

NOTES
1 Irwin 1953
2 John Stalker and George Parker, *Treatise of Japanning and Varnishing* (Reprint of 1688 ed.), London 1971, p.xv
3 Oliver Impey, 'The Trade in Japanese Porcelain', in Ayers et al. 1990, pp.15-24; pp.18-19
4 The Burghley House collection is particularly valuable because of its 1688 inventory, which includes many identifiable Japanese porcelain pieces.
5 *The Official Catalogue of the Great Exhibition of the Works of Industry of All Nations, 1851* shows a considerable number of Japanese items in the Chinese section. They range from screens and lacquer works to silks and specimens of copper. The exhibitors included private collections and importing firms in London.

JAPONISME AND MID-VICTORIAN PAINTING

For the development of Japonisme in Britain, the International Exhibition held in London in 1862 was undoubtedly the greatest landmark. 1 The event provided the largest display of Japanese art ever seen at that time in Europe: the official catalogue of the exhibition recorded a total of 623 items, ranging from Japanese prints and books to bronzes, porcelain and lacquer-works as well as enamelled wares. The exhibits were drawn mainly from the collection of Rutherford Alcock, the first British Consul-General in Japan, and therefore represented a cross-section of Japanese goods more appealing to the Western eye.

The Japanese work shown at the 1862 exhibition had a great impact on artists, and above all on the medieval revivalists of the 1860s who saw a direct parallel between the ideal medieval society that they sought to invent and the newly revealed contemporary Japan.

From this point on, a surprising number of Victorian artists collected Japanese art of one sort or another. 2 From the 1870s onwards it was probably unusual for an artist not to have any Japanese objects in his house or studio. This applies even to those who expressed negative opinions on Japanese art, such as William Morris, who seems to have owned two Japanese paintings. 3 The prevalence of Japanese objects gives an important aesthetic context for the discussion of Victorian Japonisme.

The majority of British painters were attracted to the decorative quality of Japanese motifs and objects and included them in their work without regard to their proper context. However, it was James McNeill Whistler (see Section III) who introduced the strong elements of Japanese composition and provided a link between Japanese art and the then current British movement in painting. Whistler was unusual in starting to use Japanese compositional devices before depicting Japanese objects, and this probably reflected his great interest in composition *per se*.

Whistler's Japonisme evolved from the artistic milieu of Paris and London, both of which he was involved with in the early 1860s. By around 1860 he was friendly with the Parisian avant-garde artists, including Fantin-Latour, Bracquemond and Manet, all admirers of Japanese art. At that time, the style of Whistler's work reflected the influence of the French Realists, especially Courbet. His subjects were drawn from urban life, including middle-class homes and the Thames docklands. At the same time he was struggling to move towards a position in which the pictorial space was radically tampered with. In both of these endeavours Whistler found a kindred spirit in Hiroshige. In the prints of this Japanese master, the city life of Edo was depicted by means of a striking formal language, quite unlike anything to be found in the West. For instance, an object in the foreground was startlingly juxtaposed with one far away, major motifs in the composition were cut off at the picture's edge, and radical asymmetry was combined with an exaggerated linear perspective. All devices were used to depict the everyday life of a lively city, especially that of the river. Among Whistler's etchings of the Thames dated 1861 (Cats 72 and 73; also see Cat.74) can be seen for the first time a coherent group of works which show a clear response to Japanese art. Here, Whistler was not intent upon the exotic - there are no fans or kimonos in these etchings - but rather used Japanese compositional devices as the basis for pictorial experiments using Realist subject-matter.

During 1863 Whistler finally settled in London, where he became the neighbour of Rossetti in Chelsea. He joined Rossetti's circle, including Simeon and Rebecca Solomon, Frederick and Emma Sandys, Burne-Jones and Swinburne. Under Whistler's influence, the cult of Japan began among them. By that time Rossetti, like Whistler, was a keen collector of blue and white porcelain, and his growing taste for Oriental art

Cat.65
JAMES MCNEILL WHISTLER
(1834-1903)
The Artist's Studio, 1865

was fuelled by Whistler's enthusiasm, which was more focused on Japan. Rossetti's brother and art critic, William Michael Rossetti, who was perhaps the most persistent lover of Japanese art, recorded: 'It was Mr Whistler, who first called my brother's attention to Japanese art: he possessed two or three woodcut books, some coloured prints, and a screen or two.' 4

It is not clear when and how Rossetti and his circle first became acquainted with Japanese art, but it was possibly known by them before their friendship with Whistler. Rossetti had been a school friend of William Burges, an ardent promoter of Japanese art, after the International Exhibition of 1862. Furthermore, it is worth noting that before the 1862 exhibition Rossetti had developed a design scheme using crests and a simple combination of vertical and horizontal lines. This can be seen in his book design (see Cat.166), 5 and the sofa designed for Morris, Marshall, Faulkner & Company (The Fitzwilliam Museum, Cambridge), which was itself exhibited at the 1862 exhibition. Whatever the source of such design principles, these examples show that the aesthetic direction that Rossetti was following was akin to Japanese design in spirit.

Cat.80
FREDERICK SANDYS
(1829-1904)
Medea, 1868

Cat.79
DANTE GABRIEL ROSSETTI
(1828-1882)
The Beloved (The Bride),
1865-66

Whistler was also strongly affected by his new friendship with Rossetti. This is particularly evident in his so-called 'Oriental' paintings (Cats 63 and 64) from 1863 to about 1865. In these paintings, his models are no longer dock-workers and sailors, but what the Pre-Raphaelites called 'stunners', posing in an exotic setting. Japanese objects are now used not only for their aesthetic value but also to add exotic appeal. When Whistler exhibited one of his earliest of this series, *Purple and Rose: The Lange Leizen of the Six Marks* (fig.1) at the Royal Academy in 1864, William Michael Rossetti called it 'a choice piece of Orientalism.' 6

It is interesting to compare the works of Whistler and Rossetti at this time. While both drew their inspiration from exotic themes, their approaches were different. Rossetti's paintings depicted an exotic world of his own invention, while Whistler's showed a yearning for the Far East. Rossetti's main interest was in the colour and the decorative quality of Japanese objects, and this can be seen in *The Beloved* (Cat.79), in which the central female figure wears a kimono in the most un-Japanese, yet decorative, way. On the other hand, Whistler was fascinated by the Far Eastern aesthetic setting, and so filled the scene with objects to evoke China or Japan, although not hiding the fact that the true setting was London.

In 1864 Rossetti travelled to Paris, another centre of Japanese fashion, and wrote with chagrin from there after a visit to Madame De Soye's shop in the rue de Rivoli: 'I have bought very little - only four Japanese books,... but found that all the costumes were being snapped up by a French artist, Tissot.' 7 James Tissot, who was to live in London in the 1870s (see Cats 86, 87 and 88), was at that time a rival Japonist on the other side of the Channel. In the same letter, Rossetti continued: 'it seems [Tissot] is doing three Japanese pictures, which the mistress of the shop described to me as the three wonders of the world, evidently in her opinion quite throwing Whistler into the shade.'

When Rossetti became more of a recluse during the latter half of the 1860s, Whistler's relationship with him petered out, and he entered a phase of trial and error which continued until the early 1870s. In his 'Nocturnes' of the early 1870s Whistler continued the assimilation not only of Hiroshige's compositions but also of his use of colour. For instance, in his night scenes showing fireworks, monochromatic but tonal blues with golden splashes were used in a similar way to that of Hiroshige's night scenes. Indeed, Katherine A. Lochnan has shown that, before Whistler's bankruptcy sale of 1880, he owned Hiroshige's 'Fireworks, Ryogoku' (Ryogoku Hanabi), from the series *One Hundred Views of Famous Places in Edo* (Meisho Edo Hyakkei), which exactly depicts such a scene. 8

In 1865 Whistler met Albert Moore and, under his influence, began to merge classical and Japanese elements into his figurative compositions. At the same time, Whistler influenced Moore's work in which, from about 1868 onwards into the 1880s, Moore single-mindedly pursued the composition of single classical figures. For instance, *The Azaleas* of 1868 by Moore (Cat.84) shows a stylised use of flowering branches, a vertical format with a dominant standing figure, an excessively shallow space, and the decorative use of Oriental artefacts, including large vases and carpets. These devices had already been used by Whistler, for instance, in the oil study for *La Princesse du pays de la porcelaine* of 1863-64 (Cat.63).

Moore's Japonisme was also influenced by his architect friend Nesfield, who was obsessed with Japanese circular crest motifs (see Cats 110 and 111). In *The Azaleas*, Moore decorated the vase on the lower left with overlapping 'pies', which were almost certainly designed by Moore himself, but probably inspired by Nesfield. Vases with the same shape reappear in different paintings with various patterns and colours, suggesting that there may have been only a few models, and decorations were devised as appropriate. Japanese fans and books are used in the same way to harmonise with his colour scheme in an even more radical way than Whistler's.

Fig.1
JAMES MCNEILL WHISTLER
(1834-1903)
Purple and Rose:
The Lange Leizen of the Six Marks, 1864
Philadelphia Museum of Art

Cat.63
JAMES MCNEILL WHISTLER
(1834-1903)
Sketch for 'La princesse du pays
de la porcelaine', 1863-64

Cat.84
ALBERT JOSEPH MOORE
(1841-1893)
Azaleas, 1868

23

The Japanese fashion was long-lasting and far-reaching throughout the Victorian period and beyond. Even the characteristically conservative academicians were influenced by Japanese art. 9 Edward John Poynter, the arch-academician, designed a Japonist fireplace in the 1860s (Victoria and Albert Museum) and painted Lady Elcho as an aesthete surrounded by Japanese art in 1885 (Cat.90). In 1871 Alma-Tadema, known for his paintings of Roman life and exotic scenes, portrayed his wife holding a Japanese fan in an aesthetic setting (Van Gogh Museum, Amsterdam), and a recently discovered watercolour shows a woman in complete Japanese attire (Cat.288). Frederick Leighton was also a collector of Japanese art, and a Japanese screen was harmoniously incorporated in his highly decorative style in *The Mother and Child* in 1864-65 (Cat.89). Ford Madox Brown, Rossetti's friend, also used a different type of golden screen for the backdrop of his selfportrait of 1877 (Fogg Museum of Art, Cambridge, Mass.).

Cat.86
JAMES TISSOT (1836-1902)
Jeunes Femmes regardant des objets japonais
(Young Girls looking at Japanese objects), c.1869

Cat.91
JOHN ATKINSON GRIMSHAW (1836-1893)
Dulce Domum, 1876-85

The effects of the current aesthetic taste was captured by other popular painters such as Atkinson Grimshaw, who was based in Leeds until the mid-1880s. In his domestic setting as depicted in *Dulce Domum* (Cat.91), Japanese objects are shown to be essential ingredients of the fashionable interior together with peacock feathers, the symbol of the Aesthetic Movement. Certainly then, the cult of Japan reached further than Whistler, Rossetti and their circle. The level of response to Japan among these artists varied from a passing interest to a serious desire to understand its ideology, but altogether Japonisme became an essential ingredient of Victorian painting.

NOTES
1 See essay by Ellen P. Conant
2 For a more detailed discussion see Watanabe 1991b, pp.199 -244
3 The 1939 Kelmscott sale included two Japanese paintings. We are grateful to the late Basil Gray for this information.
4 *Some Reminiscences of William Michael Rossetti* (1902), vol.I, p.276
5 Tanita Hiroyuki pointed out a possible Japanese influence on Rossetti's design for his own translation of *The Early Italian Poets* (1861) and his sister, Christina Rossetti's *Goblin Market & Other Poems* (1862). See H. Tanita, 'D.G. Rossetti and Victorian Book Design', *Gareria Tsushin*, No.22 (1985), pp.12-14
6 Quoted by G. Fleming 1978, p.202
7 O. Doughty and J.R.Wahl (eds.), *Letters of Dante Gabriel Rossetti*, Oxford 1965, vol.II, pp.526-7
8 Lochnan 1984, p.179
9 For French academic art and Japan see Miura 1988

JAPONISME AND VICTORIAN DESIGN

'Good taste is no longer an expensive luxury to indulge in - the commonest articles of domestic use are now fashioned in accordance with its laws and the poorest may have cups and saucers and jugs and teapots, more artistic in form and design than were to be found twenty years ago in any homes but those of the cultured rich.'. 1 So wrote the author of an article in the periodical, *The Burlington*, in 1881. This was an effect of the artistic movement which had flourished from the late 1860s, and around this time it became more widely known as the 'Aesthetic Movement'.

The state of British design was not always assessed as favourably as this. Indeed, from the 1830s design reform was a major concern of politicians, industrialists, educationalists and designers. The poor state of British design was brought into focus by the Great Exhibition of 1851 when most commentators praised the technological developments revealed in the display but criticised the British designs as over-decorative. During the 1850s and 1860s, the efforts of reformers such as Sir Henry Cole, the first director of the South Kensington Museum (today's Victoria and Albert Museum), and the more radical William Morris, fostered a general attitude among designers for the improvement of the quality of art and life. This climate paved the way for the growth of the Aesthetic Movement.

In the 1850s medievalism was still popular. Pugin, who died in 1852, and the younger Ruskin were both strong influences towards a revival of honest design which was found, in their view, in the Gothic period. Not only designers such as Morris, Burges and Godwin, but also Rossetti and the painters of the Pre-Raphaelite circle shared this spirit.

Another growing trend at that time was Orientalism, which had been promoted as 'a fresh well of art' 2 by Cole and his fellow design reformers. At a lecture after the Great Exhibition, Cole remarked that 'it was from the East that the most impressive lesson was to be learnt.' 3

It was then that Japanese art arrived in Britain and became an integral part of the Aesthetic Movement. In the field of architecture and design, it was the Gothic Revivalists who showed the strongest interest in Japanese art during the 1860s. In reviewing the Japanese section of the 1862 International Exhibition, William Burges claimed that 'truly the Japanese Court is the real medieval court of the Exhibition.' 4 Considering that he himself with W. Slater had organised the Ecclesiological Society's Medieval Court at the exhibition, this is high praise indeed. Burges was by no means alone in this rather startling linking of Japanese art with the Middle Ages.

The Gothic Revivalists of the 1860s saw a direct connection between the contemporary Orient and the medieval world. Burges argued that the Orient was valuable for the Gothic Revivalist because it had kept a domestic life-style that had changed little since the medieval period and cited Japan as the primary example. 5 In Burges's famous Elephant Inkstand (Cats 98 and 99) he incorporated an original Japanese netsuke. This ivory piece was used unchanged and assumed a similar role to that played by antique cameos or coins on many medieval reliquaries. The foreign objects were united in one piece of work which nonetheless remained very much medieval in its overall character, thereby confirming his theory.

Both Godwin and Nesfield started as Gothicists, but then moved to a lighter less massive style leading to the 'Queen Anne' style. For both architects Japanese art seems to have been an important catalyst in this change of direction, although in Godwin's design for a country house (Cat.102) or Nesfield's design for Cloverley Hall, 6 the Japanese elements are wholly integrated into the context of the English vernacular.

Cat.95
KATE HAYLLAR (FL.1883-1898)
Sunflower and Hollyhocks, 1889

Many other designers and manufacturers also began to turn to Japanese art as a new source of inspiration. John B. Waring, one of the organisers of the International Exhibition of 1862, recommended: 'Our own manufacturers would do well to study such Japanese works, and improve their present system of decoration, which is fundamentally bad.' 7 In 1876, it was noted in *The Architect* magazine that the *Staffordshire Advertiser* had suggested the formation of Japanese museums for the benefit of local pottery schools. 8

In the dissemination of Japanese design Christopher Dresser played a vital role both as a designer and an entrepreneur. As Suzuki Hiroyuku has pointed out, Dresser negotiated the transfer to London of a hall for Shinto dance, which was exhibited by the Japanese at the International Exhibition in Vienna in 1873 and was bought for £600 by the 'Alexandra Park Company'. 9 In the same year, according to Widar Halén, Dresser founded a new importing company, the 'Alexandra Palace Company', to offer Japanese objects for sale at a Japanese village to be built in Alexandra Park in North London. 10 He also had close contact with the American company, Tiffany & Co., who commissioned him to buy Japanese art for them and he travelled to Japan in an official capacity in 1876-77.

By the late 1870s the Aesthetic Movement was in full swing, hand in hand with the cult of Japan. In 1875, Liberty's was opened in Regent Street in London, and it quickly established its reputation as a leading specialist for Japanese goods. Godwin reported the popularity of Liberty's Japanese goods in his article in 1876: 'There was quite a crowd', which according to him included well-known architects and distinguished painters, all impatiently waiting for the arrival of Japanese fans. 11

By now the Aesthetic Movement had also deeply affected Victorian interior design. The most famous and spectacular example was Whistler's 1877 'Peacock Room' (now in the Freer Gallery of Art, Washington, D.C.), which caused a sensation in London. Without the permission of his patron, Frederick Leyland, Whistler redecorated the entire room, painting over the antique leather wall covering. The interior had already been designed by another Japonist, Thomas Jeckyll, but it is Whistler's contribution which is now dominant. It is no longer the shelves, curtains or furniture which define the interior, but the colour. Though in many ways it was a unique experiment, this emphasis on a unifying colour scheme was influential and looks forward to the next generation of artists.

NOTES
1 Aslin 1981 (2nd. ed.), p.15
2 H. Cole, *Lectures on the Result of the Great Exhibition*, London 1852, p.112, quoted by Halén 1990, p.21
3 Ibid.
4 W. Burges, 'The International Exhibition', *Gentleman's Magazine*, July 1862, pp.3-12; p.11
5 W. Burges, 'The Japanese Court in the International Exhibition', *Gentleman's Magazine*, September 1862, pp.243-54; p.243
6 The drawings are in the Victoria and Albert Museum, London.
7 J.B. Waring, *Masterpieces of the International Exhibition*, London 1863, text to pl.288 of vol.III.
8 *The Architect* (December 9, 1876), p.343
9 Suzuki 1984, pp.14,16
10 Halén 1990, p.39
11 E.W.Godwin, 'A Japanese Warehouse', *The Architect* (December 23, 1876), p.363

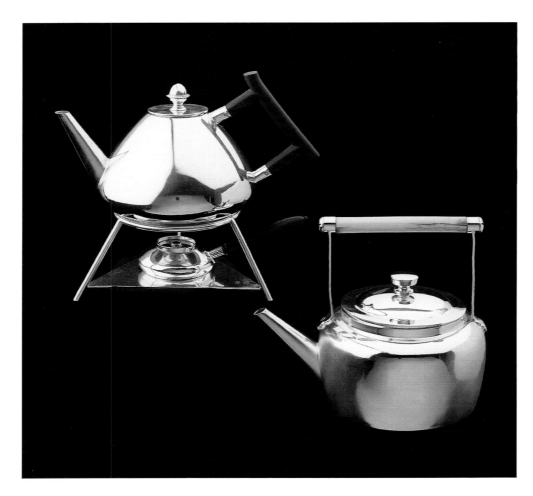

Cats 168 and 169
CHRISTOPHER DRESSER (1834-1904)
HUKIN & HEATH
Electroplated Kettles

Cat.175 MINTON & CO.
Pair of Moonflasks, c.1875

BRITAIN AND THE WESTERNISATION OF JAPAN

After the Meiji Restoration of 1868, the Japanese government saw its primary task as the modernisation of almost every aspect of Japanese civilisation and, in their eyes, modernisation meant Westernisation. To this end the government invited many foreign specialists to Japan, who came to be known as 'oyatoi' (literally meaning 'the government's official employees'). Many of them were British, 1 reflecting the Japanese view of Britain as the most advanced nation in the world.

During the Meiji period, Western-style architecture was one of the most ostentatious and potent symbols of Westernisation. The government wanted its new national Western-style institutions - universities, banks and the national mint - to function in a Western manner and to be built in Western style. Such buildings reflected economic strength and had to stand up to international comparison. Little is known of how the British architects were employed by the Japanese during the early Meiji period. However, they certainly responded vigorously to the Japanese demands.

Some of them, such as Thomas James Waters, the most important early Meiji architect before the arrival of Josiah Conder, must have had some experience in colonial architecture. His Senpukan (Cat.119) gives such an impression. Josiah Conder, who took up his post in 1877 as an official *oyatoi*, also showed a tendency towards a colonial type of architecture, using extensive verandahs and Oriental details. This emulation of the architecture of the British colonists could not have been in accordance with the precise wishes of his clients, for the Japanese government wanted a more obviously Western style.

An indication of Conder's approach to architecture can be found in the theories of his teacher Thomas Roger Smith. Smith was a well-respected architect who worked in India during the 1860s, and a writer and editor of *The Architect* magazine. 2 In India, he advocated that Western-style buildings should be built with the climatic conditions in mind. Verandahs, such as used by both Conder and Waters, were considered ideal

Cat.117
THOMAS JAMES WATERS
SHOSAI IKKEI (FL. c. 1870)
A View of the Tokyo Ginza Bricktown from Kyobashi, 1873

because they created airy shade. Smith further recommended that 'a leaning towards the peculiarities of the best Oriental styles is desirable'. 3 It is therefore understandable that Conder should apply his teacher's theories to the various buildings he was commissioned to design in Japan.

However, the situation in which Conder worked in Japan was quite different from that of Smith in India. Conder's Western-style buildings were not built by the conquerors to show off their power to the colonised. It was the 'natives' who wanted a Western style and who therefore employed experts on limited contracts to provide it. The Japanese government adopted a pragmatic approach, by engaging British professionals on short-term contracts to train Japanese students, in order to reduce reliance on experts from the West. Conder, younger and better qualified than his predecessor Waters, was given two major tasks: firstly, to design and build major Western-style public buildings immediately, and secondly, to establish training schemes for Japanese architects. However, once Conder had fulfilled these requirements, his services were dispensed with. After serving several government departments, his contract was finally terminated in 1890: permanent dependence on a Western expert was considered undesirable. However, Conder did not vanish from Japanese history, like so many other Western employees. He opened a successful private practice and settled in Japan permanently.

Cat.132
JOSIAH CONDER (1852-1920)
Rokumeikan (Deer Cry Pavilion),
1881-83

In terms of Japan's self-conscious Westernisation programme, perhaps the most extreme architectural example was Rokumeikan (Deer Cry Pavilion), which was designed by Conder and completed in 1883, to be used for entertaining foreign dignitaries. Not only was the building in a Western style but the use to which it was put illustrated the Westernisation of high society in Tokyo.

During a relatively short period regular and extravagant balls in Western dress were held in the building, and this lifestyle made an impact, however short-lived, on everyday life. This phenomenon illustrates the way in which Western manners and fashions were adopted in stylish circles. At this stage bustle dresses were still unusual and at the earlier balls there were many women who neither wore Western-style clothes nor were expected to dance. However, the Rokumeikan balls soon began to provide a

Cat.133
YOSHU CHIKANOBU (1838-1912)
*Picture of the Ladies' Charity Bazaar
at the Deer Cry Pavilion*, 1887

forum where progressive women of standing could participate in a more public life, a new development in Japanese society. A handful of these Japanese ladies had either travelled or studied abroad and played an active role, for example, in organising charity bazaars at Rokumeikan (Cat.133). Some of them adopted Western fashion and manners with ease, and in particular Lady Nabeshima (see Cats 134 and 135) was the subject of effusive comments from the French writer Pierre Loti, who saw her at one of the Rokumeikan balls. Other remarkable women, such as the Vassar College graduate, Yamakawa Sutematsu, Countess Oyama, subsequently went into women's education as teachers. They shaped a new breed of the women students, among whom the fashion for Westernised clothes and manners spread even faster.

The extent to which architectural practice altered by the turn of the century is exemplified by two buildings from students of Conder: the Bank of Japan by Tatsuno Kingo (1890-96) (Cat.126) and the Akasaka Detached Palace by Katayama Tokuma (1899-1906) (Cat.129). According to Fujimori Terunobu, Tatsuno's Bank of Japan represents three important milestones. 4 Firstly, this was the first major government building designed by a Japanese architect. Secondly, Tatsuno severed links with the traditional Japanese guilds and established a new system of construction management, based on Western models and manned by people trained by himself. Thirdly, it was the first major building built in stone rather than brick which had been introduced earlier as 'Western' building material. The choice of granite was highly unusual and the gleaming exterior, when completed, must have made a deep impression on the Japanese. When we look at Katayama's Akasaka Detached Palace, it is even more accomplished. Here the early Meiji dream had come true. Now the Japanese had a purely Western-style palace, worthy of international comparison. By this time the international standing of Japan in general had also improved immeasurably. However, as the new century began, Japanese architecture was to move in new directions.

NOTES

1 For an account of *oyatoi* in art see Conant 1990
2 For a more detailed discussion of this issue see the forthcoming article 'Vernacular Expression or Western Style?: Josiah Conder and the beginning of modern architectural design in Japan' by Toshio Watanabe, to be published by Irish Academy Press
3 T.R. Smith, 'On Buildings for European Occupation in Tropical Climates, Especially India', *RIBA Papers*, 1868, pp.197-208; p.208
4 Fujimori 1979, pp.132-35

Cat.135
JAPANESE
Portrait of Lady Nabeshima in Rome,
c.1881-82

Cat.128
TATSUNO KINGO (1854-1919)
Former Residence of Matsumoto Kenjiro,
Tobata, Kitakyushu, 1909-11
(By courtesy of Masuda Akihisa)

Cat.129
KATAYAMA TOKUMA (1853-1917)
Front Façade, Former Akasaka Detached Palace,
Tokyo, 1899-1906
(By courtesy of Masuda Akihisa)

The Images of Japan in Britain - An Effect of Westernisation

While the Cult of Japan was pervading British taste, Westernisation began to have its effect on Japanese art and exports. By the time of the International Exhibition of 1873 in London, a guide book had noted that: 'Japan is now making....rapid strides in mechanical progress, and so eagerly accepting Western ideas.' 1 The plans for the Japanese display at this exhibition had been discussed in the previous year when delegates from the new Japanese government visited the South Kensington Museum. 2 This delegation included Iwakura Tomomi (1825-83) and Okubo Toshimichi (1830-78), the principle leaders of the Meiji government, who were on a grand tour studying Western industry and technology.

In the promotion of the modern art industries of Japan in Britain, Christopher Dresser's contribution was large. Unlike most of the promoters of Japonisme at the time, his interest was not confined to collecting Japanese antiquities or adopting Japanese motifs in design, but extended to the understanding of Japanese culture and history. Following the setting up of the Alexandra Palace Company, he began to sell imported goods at the Japanese village at Alexandra Palace. Dresser was aware that in response to the spread of Japanese fashion in Europe, the Japanese art manufacturers increased output, and there was a corresponding drop in quality. The guide book to the Japanese village emphasised that the goods on offer bore a stamp of authenticity as 'the taste of Japanese work has been somewhat deteriorated by the introduction of goods of inferior workmanship, manufactured expressly for the England market'. 3 As the Westernisation programme progressed, Japanese artefacts began to include other inferior goods made by poor adoption of Western techniques. Furthermore, goods in the traditional form but made purely for the Western markets were made using colours they thought would appeal to the West.

These changes in Japanese goods began to cause disappointment among the earliest enthusiasts of Japanese art, such as Godwin. While he still maintained full admiration for Japanese art in general, Godwin commented on the decline of modern Japanese work in 1876 in *The Architect* magazine. 4 He found deterioration especially in the drawing and colours of fans and screens, and also in the artistic and printing qualities of picture books. As for the cause of this decline, he thought that 'Either the European market is ruining Japanese art, or the Japanese have taken our artistic measure and found it wanting; perhaps there is a little of both'. 5

Mortimer Menpes visited Japan in 1887-88. A disciple of Whistler, Menpes' interest in Japan was clearly influenced by his mentor's Japonisme, but is worth noting that one of the purposes of his visit was to study 'the problems which Japanese art in its latest phases present to the Western mind.' 6 When he was there, he certainly observed that Westernisation was spreading in Japanese society. He wrote: 'At the present time the Japanese are struggling to adopt all sorts of Western ideas... They want to apply our legal codes, to wear our clothes, ...and...what concerns me more nearly as painter [is that they want] to introduce English and foreign school-teachers and professors into their schools of art'. 7 He saw an exhibition of Western-style paintings by Japanese artists. He found that, in comparison with the influence of the traditional style, 'their own style', the work of Western-style artists was a 'struggle'. To his eye, 'what they did was poor and feeble; they were copying bad examples, and they copied them more or less indifferently.' 8

Nevertheless, he also found the essential characteristics of Japanese art were unchanged, and thought that this was epitomised in the work of Kawanabe Kyosai, 'the greatest Japanese painter of the day'. 9 Menpes was particularly struck by Kyosai's swift and instinctive brush drawing, and called it 'impressionistic'. He also observed that the lives of ordinary people of Japan were still little affected by Westernisation, and he

Cat.134 JAPANESE
Lady Nabeshima's Dress, c.1881

found this encouraging. 'I was resolved, as far as possible, to get at the very heart of Japanese life in so far as it appeals to the artist. With the political, the commercial, the finance of modern Japan I had nothing to do'. 10 So he chose to paint a poetic image of Japanese life, with children, traditional artisans, actors and workers, unaffected by modernisation. This was a part of the reality of Japan, but not the entire representation, as at that time Japan began to have another, notably Westernised face. However, in his view it was not how Japan should be.

Following Menpes, a large number of British and Western artists visited Japan, throughout the 1890s and the early twentieth century. These included the two Glasgow Boys, Edward Atkinson Hornel and George Henry. Neither of them depicted Westernised scenes, but chose to paint traditional aspects, such as geisha girls, young girls in Kimono, traditional ceremonial scenes, shrines, temples or natural landscapes. Hornel repeatedly painted young Japanese girls in Kimono based on a number of photographs taken in Japan. 11

In 1889, Arthur Lasenby Liberty, the founder of Liberty's and an instrument of the whole Japanese fashion, went to Japan. During his stay of three months, Liberty observed Japanese industrial arts of the day, covering all fields of manufacturers. His views on Japanese industrial arts and manufacturers were presented on his return at the Royal Society of London in 1890. In his lecture, referring to the Westernisation of Japan, he commented that 'for a while [the Japanese] failed to discriminate between material and art advantages'. 12 Surveying Japanese art industries, he discussed at length embroidery and textile manufacturers. In textiles, he noted two tendencies as a result of western influence. One was the reduction of the substance of silks, which used to be 'thicker and heavier than seemed necessary or desirable', so it was a favourable effect, and another was a deterioration in both designs and colouring. He was particularly critical about Japanese printed colour fabrics: 'The Japanese have allowed themselves to be swamped by a huge wave of retrograde influence.' 13

Cat.284
EDWARD ATKINSON HORNEL
(1864-1933)
Two Japanese Girls, 1894

However, Liberty commented on a modern Japanese device of combining printing with embroidery. This, for a given aesthetic effect saved much labour, and he recommended it to British manufacturers. 14 He also noted the efforts of the current Japanese government to 'induce their art manufacturers to conserve the spirit of past achievements' by distributing free photographs of antiquities among the principle craftsmen and manufacturers. 15 In conclusion, he claimed that despite the temporary set-back the Japanese art industries had suffered, they were now recovering and striving, and he predicted 'a renewed and broader perfection than was attained in a unique and historic past.' 16

So hoped Liberty. However, Burne-Jones's furious letter to Liberty of 1897 shows that the situation did not improve so rapidly. 17 Burne-Jones, the leading exponent of the influential Pre-Raphaelite movement, did not use Japanese motifs very conspicuously, but apparently was strongly inspired by the colours of Oriental fabrics, especially Japanese and Chinese. In that year, he returned a Kimono with a note; 'I return the Japanese Dressing Gown, ...with regret at the decadence in colour which it shows ...I cannot withhold the suppression of my deep disappointment at the level to which both have fallen, under the influence of demands made for cheapness & for assimilation to our own lower standard of beauty'. 18 According to Burne-Jones, what angered him most was, however, Liberty's shop-assistant who commented, 'they are our own colours'. Burne-Jones felt that [this attitude] accounts for the fact: it is impossible for the present time for the West to dictate colour to the East without fatal result'. 19

Despite the progress of Westernisation in Japan, and the subsequent changes in quality of Japanese work available during the 1890s, Japan was still at the height of fashion towards the end of the century. Kimonos, fans, screens, blue and white porcelains and 'Aesthetic' furniture decorated even ordinary English households. Observing the Japanese fashion at the time, Oscar Wilde, declared 'In fact, the whole of Japan is a pure invention ... The Japanese people are ... simply a mode of style, an exquisite fancy of art.' 20 Perhaps this was not so far from the truth: while Britain's rather fanciful view of Japan was supported by the art brought back by British painters, the real Japan was changing rapidly towards what it saw as a Western way of life.

NOTES
1 *Cassell's Guide to the International Exhibition 1873*, London 1873, p.20
2 Halén 1991, p.38
3 *Alexandra Palace Guide*, London 1875, p.7, quoted Halén, ibid., p.40
4 E. W. Godwin, 'A Japanese Warehouse', *The Architect* Dec. 23, 1876, p.363
5 Ibid.
6 Menpes 1888, p.192
7 Ibid.
8 Ibid., p.193
9 Ibid.
10 Ibid., p.192
11 Together with a large collection of souvenir photographs, George Henry's letters to Hornel, surviving in the collection of Hornel Trust, Kirkcudbright, indicate that both Henry and Hornel relied largely on photographic sources for their Japanese painting. Also, it is worth noting that Henry and Hornel were members of the Photographic Society of Japan, which was originally founded in 1889.
12 A. L. Liberty, 'The Industrial Arts and Manufacturers of Japan', *Journal of the Society of Arts*, London 1890, p.674
13 Ibid., p.682
14 Ibid
15 Ibid., p.633
16 Ibid., p.634
17 Burne-Jones, letter to A.L. Liberty, Dec.17, 1897 (MSS, Westminster City Archives)
18 Ibid.
19 Ibid.
20 O. Wilde, 'The Decay of Lying', originally published in *The Nineteenth Century*, January 1889, taken from *De Profundis and Other Writings*, Penguin Books, 1986, p.82

Cat.217 *The Geisha*, 1896

THE BRITISH INFLUENCE ON JAPANESE PAINTING

Within the history of Japanese Western-style painting Britain has played a special part. 1 The availability of British art books and art material in Japan must first be examined. If we consider how the Japan trade was dominated by Britain, one must assume that through these established trade routes a certain amount of art - related goods must also have been imported into Japan. Art books were particularly important as learning material. A characteristic example is the drawing of an oak tree that was copied by Nakamaru Seijuro (1840-1895), an early Meiji art teacher and portrait painter, from a drawing by J. Needham reproduced in Vere Fosters' *Drawing Books* published by Blackie & Son, Publishers. 2 We also know that Mori Miyoshi, the teacher of Aoki Shigeru and Sakamoto Hanjiro, used at least two English art books. 3 The documentation of artists' materials during the Meiji period has still a long way to go, but it seems that British colours, canvases and papers were widely used in Japan. 4

Japanese Western-style oil painting was dominated by the Wirgman circle for about ten years before the arrival of Fontanesi in 1876, as discussed by Takashina elsewhere in this catalogue. Charles Wirgman, a reporter for *The Illustrated London News*, is credited with being the first Western teacher of oil painting, but the precise nature and extent of his teaching is still not clear. He knew so many Japanese artists, not all of whom can be categorised as his pupils, but many painters may have been influenced by simply observing him paint. It is less well known that he gave painting lessons to Westerners also. It is said that Wirgman taught Nicholas Phillipps Kingdon, a Yokohama businessman and an amateur artist who married Utagawa Mura from the family of Ukiyo-e printmakers. 5

While a number of Japanese painters studied oil painting in Britain during the Meiji period, their achievement in their home country was less than it might have been because many of them died only a few years after their return to Japan and so were not able to develop their full potential. Kunisawa Shinkuro (1848-1877) died three years after his return, Hyakutake Kaneyuki after two years and Hara Busho after five. Kunisawa, an important teacher but perhaps a less important painter, managed to set up

Cat.248
HYAKUTAKE KANEYUKI
(1842-1884)
Barnard Castle, c.1878

Cat.259
HARA BUSHO (1866-1912)
Lady Montague, 1907

a painting school that was influential during the early Meiji period, but Hyakutake and Hara made little impact on the artistic scene in Japan. The early death of Hara, one of the greatest Japanese oil painters of the Meiji period, was particularly tragic. His high calibre has only recently emerged, because his major works were for long inaccessible.

Britain had a special role to play in the development of watercolour painting in Japan. Within the hierarchy of the fine art media, watercolour naturally came second to oils, whether in London or Tokyo. Nevertheless, the Japanese had a special affinity with watercolour because their traditional painting also used water-soluble pigments, though they saw watercolour as a specifically Western medium. Britain had the richest watercolour tradition and an important stimulus to the rise of watercolour in Japan was given by the exhibitions of visiting British painters, such as John Varley, Jr (1891) or Alfred Parsons (1894). One of the ardent advocates of watercolour, Miyake Kokki, wrote how these two exhibitions converted him to the medium. When Oshita Tojiro published his *Guide to Watercolour Painting* (Suisaiga no Shiori) in 1901, as many as 20,000 copies were sold. 6 The first decade of the twentieth century saw an unprecedented flourishing of watercolour painting and a number of artists chose to go to Britain, simply because of its renown in this medium.

Victorian painting also contributed to the development of the Romantic and Symbolist movement in Japanese painting and literature. The leading art magazine of the day, *Myojo* (Morning Star), contained many articles on British painters and hardly anything on

Cat.371
MAKINO YOSHIO (1869-1956)
Buckingham Palace from Green Park, 1929

French art. The emphasis was on Rossetti and Burne-Jones, 7 and artists such as Albert Moore or G.F. Watts were well known among those Japanese painters.

Least discussed of all are those Japanese artists who not only went to Britain but stayed there for a considerable length of time and were active there. Ishibashi Kazunori stayed in Britain from 1903 to 1918 and again from 1921 to 1924, and he was a member of the Royal Society of Portrait Painters. Kurihara Chuji was active in Britain from 1912 to 1924 and again from 1926 to 1927. He was a member of the Royal Society of British Artists. Urushibara Mokuchu (Yoshijiro) was active mostly in Britain but also in Paris for nearly thirty years until his return to Japan in 1934. Makino (Markino) Yoshio, the most successful Japanese painter in Britain, first went to America in 1893, moved to London in 1897 and stayed there until 1942, when he was repatriated. More research is needed, however, to round out the picture of the achievements of these artists.

NOTES

1 See essay by Takashina Shuji for the role played by the West in the development of Meiji period oil painting. The detailed analysis provided by Nakamura Giichi in *Kindai Nihon Bijutsu no Sokumen - Meiji Yoga to Igirisu Bijutsu* (A Byway of Modern Japanese Art - Western Style Painting of the Meiji Period and British Art), published in 1976, laid the groundwork. Pioneering exhibitions concentrated on specific aspects: *Shigeru Aoki and the [sic] Late Victorian Art* in 1983; *1908/09 Rondon no Seishun: Zengo* 1990 (Youth in London: around 1908/09) in 1990.

2 Reproduced in Nakamaru Seijuro 1988, p.22

3 *The Nation's Pictures*. A selection from the finest modern paintings in the public picture galleries of Great Britain reproduced in colour, Cassell, London 1902; A. F. Grace, *A Course of Lessons in Landscape Painting in Oils*, Cassell, London 1885, 2nd ed. Grateful thanks are due to Mr Hashitomi Hiroki of the Ishibashi Museum of Art, Kurume, for this information and for the help provided in examining these books. The colour plates of the latter are particularly poor.

4 Grateful thanks are due to Mr Kanba Nobuyuki for making this point regarding the canvases. Important recent research results in this area are published in Sakamoto et al. 1991.

5 Kingdon apparently assumed the artist's name of Utagawa Kindon, but no work of his has survived. Grateful thanks are due to Mr Utagawa Toyokuni, Mr Utagawa Takashi, Ms Hisako Ito and Dr Narazaki Muneshige for information regarding Kingdon.

6 Fukuda 1988, p.529. This book includes the reprint of Oshita's Guide.

7 Nakamura 1976, pp.22-38 provides a good analysis of these issues.

Cat.289
JAMES GUTHRIE (1859-1930)
Miss Helen Sowerby, 1882

Cat.293
PHILIP WILSON STEER (1860-1942)
The Kimono, c.1894

LATE VICTORIAN AND EDWARDIAN PAINTING AND JAPAN

The Royal Academy's near-monopolistic dominance of the fine art scene in the Victorian period began to crumble during the second half of the nineteenth century. The first decisive move towards diversification came with the foundation of the Grosvenor Gallery in 1877 by Sir Coutts Lindsay. The Gallery's first exhibition was particularly remembered because of Whistler's libel case against Ruskin, who described one of Whistler's exhibits, *Nocturne in Black and Gold: The Falling Rocket* (c.1874: Detroit Institute of Art), as 'flinging a pot of paint in the public's face.' 1 Although the trial ended in Whistler's nominal victory, it was at the cost of his own bankruptcy. However, his opinion on art received much public attention. During the trials, he discussed the idea of art for art's sake and said that the Nocturnes were painted purely out of his artistic interest, 'an arrangement of line, form and colour.' 2

An elaborated version of Whistler's theory was delivered at his 'Ten O'Clock' lecture in 1885, in which he preached the autonomy and superiority of Art over Nature and concluded with a memorable comment: 'the story of the beautiful is already complete - hewn in the marbles of the Parthenon - and broided, with the birds, upon the fan of Hokusai - at the foot of Fusi-yama [sic].' 3 Thus the philosophy of art for art's sake was consolidated. With this theory, Whistler became a major influential force among the artistic circle of the following generation.

The Grosvenor Gallery did not have an openly antagonistic attitude towards the Royal Academy. Indeed there were a number of Academicians among the painters invited to exhibit. Nevertheless, it was regarded as a breath of fresh air in its early years and was the main showcase for the painters of Japonisme and the Aesthetic Movement, such as Albert Moore and Whistler. However, by the mid-1880s it was no longer at the forefront of the British art scene, that role having been assumed by a new association of young artists signalling the second important shift away from the monopoly of the Royal Academy. The New English Art Club formed in 1886 with the clear intention of counteracting the pervasive power of the Academy. More democratic than the Grosvenor Gallery, the club was under the strong influence of French art. Many of its members had actually trained in France, and the naturalism of the French painter Jules Bastien-Lepage had a great impact on them. However, the New English Art Club was a rather volatile association and its ideology changed considerably during its history.

Whistler was a powerful catalyst for the Glasgow Boys, who, attracted by Japanese art, made important contributions to the New English Art Club from 1887 to about 1890. Another group of artists, which centred on the strong personality of Walter Sickert, Whistler's pupil, also came into prominence during the same period and organised the *London Impressionists* exhibition in December 1889. Sickert wrote the introduction to the exhibition catalogue, in which he defined Impressionism: 'essentially and firstly, it [Impressionism] is not realism. It has no wish to record anything merely because it exists. It is not occupied in a struggle to make intensely real and solid the sordid or superficial details of the subject it selects. It accepts, as the aim of the picture, what Edgar Allan Poe asserts to be the sole legitimate province of the poem, beauty.' 4 It was, however, the ethos of the Aesthetic Movement, reflecting strongly a Whistlerian view, rather than that of French Impressionism.

The pervasive influence of Whistler was particularly felt in portraiture of women which were often entitled *Woman in Kimono* or *Japanese Fan*, where Japanese objects were used to enhance the beauty of the work. The key image here was Whistler's *Symphony in White No.2: The Little White Girl* (Cat.64), where this formula was adopted for the first time in 1864. In this painting, Japanese objects are used sparsely but prominently, giving a strong accent of colour within the composition. Painters of the New English Art Club eagerly took up this formula, as seen in Théodore Roussel's *The Girl Reading* of 1886-87 (Cat.96), or Philip Wilson Steer's *The Kimono* of 1894 (Cat.293).

During the last years of the nineteenth century it is difficult to distinguish whether a painting's Japonisme is directly inspired by Japanese art or is filtered through that of other Japonist painters, such as Whistler. Similarly there are many works produced in the early years of this century in which the artists use Japanese objects not to evoke exoticism but to increase the aesthetic value of the painting and to associate the sitter with the beauty represented by the objects, for instance Duncan Grant's *James Strachey* of 1910 (Cat.363).

Cat.363 DUNCAN GRANT (1885-1978)
James Strachey, 1910

By this year, 1910, the fashion of Japan had become so fully integrated into the cultural life of Britain that a major popular exhibition at the White City, combining industrial, commercial and artistic displays of both countries, was staged. The Anglo-Japanese Exhibition was the third in a series of huge events designed to celebrate the political and cultural ties between Britain and its international friends, and was the culmination of interest in Japanese culture. It was no accident that in Bernard Shaw's *Pygmalion* written in 1912, the heroine Eliza appeared in kimono after having been scrubbed and cleaned of Covent Garden grime. There the kimono, commonly associated with the notion of beauty, was used to symbolise the heroine's transformation.

NOTES
1 J. Ruskin, *Fors Clavigera*, 2 July 1877, quoted by Farr 1984, p.13
2 J. Pennell 1908, vol.I, p.234, Ibid.
3 D. Sutton 1963, p.116
4 Sickert's introduction to the catalogue of the *London Impressionists* exhibition, reprinted in D.S. MacColl, *Life, Work and Setting of Philip Wilson Steer*, London 1945, pp.175-6

BEYOND EAST AND WEST

With the death of the Meiji Emperor and the accession of the Taisho Emperor in 1912, we enter a period when new artistic relationships developed between Britain and Japan. Japan's international prestige was high after winning the wars against China and Russia and the diplomatic relationship between Britain and Japan had been cemented with the Anglo-Japanese alliances of 1902 and 1905. The crowning expression of the friendship felt between the two countries was the 1910 Anglo-Japanese Exhibition. 1

A certain unease was felt by the British as to how to treat a non-Western nation as an equal partner. Paul Greenhalgh has pointed out that on this occasion the British had to adjust previous anthropological and phrenological calculations that normally emphasised the degeneracy of non-white races: 'One curious similarity runs through the whole, that is, the striking similitude between Japs and our own people. This resemblance manifests itself in manner, physical stamp and shape of head ... distinctive indications of considerable mental power...'. 2 Such an attitude is reflected in the more equal relationship between the British and Japanese artists of a new generation.

The career of Bernard Leach epitomises this new attitude. The friendship of Leach and Hamada Shoji is so well known that it is often not realised that Leach also functioned as a catalyst in areas other than pottery within a larger circle of Japanese artists and intellectuals, especially that of the Shirakaba (Silver Birch) Group. The role played by Leach within the history of the artistic relationship between Britain and Japan represents a new beginning rather than the crowning glory of the Victorian and Edwardian periods. The accolade for this should go to the 1910 Exhibition.

First of all, Leach's relationship with the Japanese was that of a colleague rather than a teacher. He went to Japan to teach etching, but quickly realised that it was he who wanted to learn from the Japanese. He then learnt the art of pottery from Ogata Kenzan VI, but with most of the other Japanese artists his relationship was that of a friend on equal terms with no subservience on either side. This is very different from Josiah Conder's relationship with the Japanese. As an architect he was the revered teacher, but as a painter he was a pupil of Kawanabe Kyosai and probably would never have regarded himself as Kyosai's equal. For Leach and also for the Japanese artists it was more of a relationship of give and take.

Secondly, in his pottery Leach took up a Japanese art form and made it his own. This is very different from incorporating Japanese motifs or compositional devices into established Western art forms such as oil painting or furniture design. Even within pottery-making there is a clear break with Victorian Japonisme in that he showed little interest in Japanese motifs and ornaments, but was concerned with the total form of a pot or the finish of the glaze. It is most instructive to examine the pots upside-down. When presented this way many Victorian pieces show lack of care in the handling of glaze and form, whereas Leach pays equal attention to all parts of the pot, a characteristic attention to detail symptomatic of the whole approach to the tea ceremony. 3

Thirdly, Leach contributed articles on British art to Japanese magazines aimed at Japanese readers. This was not common. Most Western Japanese specialists, even those resident in Japan, wrote in foreign language newspapers and journals aimed at Westerners, and most Western articles on Western art appearing in Japanese magazines were not originally aimed at the Japanese and had appeared in the first instance in the West.

One might feel Leach to be a special case. He was certainly a special case in the sense that Whistler was in the early 1860s when he initiated a new relationship between the two cultures. One of Leach's later books is called *Beyond East and West*, 4 an apposite title. At the end of Leach's first visit to Japan (1909-1920), Yanagi Soetsu, Leach's friend and a driving force of the Shirakaba Group, wrote that: 'He [Leach] is trying to knit the East and West together by art, and ... he will be remembered as the first to accomplish as an artist what for so long mankind has been dreaming of bringing about.' 5 During the 1930s dark clouds were thickening on the political horizon and a dreadful interlude in the history of the Anglo-Japanese relationship was looming, but the foundation had been laid for a new aesthetic dialogue between Japan and Britain.

NOTES
1 For the 1910 Exhibition see essay by Conant
2 Greenhalgh 1988, p.96-97
3 We are grateful to Dr Oliver Watson of the Victoria and Albert Museum who drew our attention to this point.
4 First published in 1978.
5 Quoted from Leach 1985, p.134

Cat.394 BERNARD LEACH (1887-1979)
Self-portrait

Cat.395 BERNARD LEACH (1887-1979)
Portrait of Yanagi Soetsu

Cat.401
HAMADA SHOJI
(1894-1978)
*Dish with Floral
Decoration cut thorough
the Slip*, 1923

Cat.405
TOMIMOTO KENKICHI (1886-1963)
Old Tree, 1924

The British in Japan in the Nineteenth Century

Sir Hugh Cortazzi

Japan was closed to the rest of the world for over two centuries (from about 1634 until 1853). Her only window to the outside world was through Nagasaki where there was a small Chinese colony and a Dutch merchant base on the artificial island of Dejima in the bay. Here the Dutch factors were carefully guarded and contacts with the Japanese were strictly limited and controlled.

By the middle of the nineteenth century, Japan's isolation was an anachronism. American and Western ships were busily trading with China. The first 'Opium War' (1839-42) had been fought, treaty ports had been established in China and Hong Kong had been ceded to the British. American whaling ships were cruising in northern pacific waters. Foreign shipping wanted safe harbours and supplies. Western merchants sought new markets and there was a growing demand for Oriental products.

The instrument which forced the reluctant opening up of Japan was the American expedition of Commodore Perry of the US Navy and his so-called 'Black Ships' in 1853. An initial treaty was concluded by the Americans in 1854. The British, Dutch, Russians and French quickly followed suit but the first treaties were very limited in scope. Only Nagasaki, Hakodate and Shimoda were available for foreign shipping. All were remote from Edo, the modern Tokyo, which was the capital of the Tokugawa Shogun, the 'military' rulers of Japan. There was no provisions for trade.

The first American consul, Townsend Harris, worked hard to gain better facilities. New treaties were signed in 1858 which led to the opening of more treaty ports, provided for extra-territorial rights for foreigners in the ports and permitted the development of trade. In addition to Nagasaki and Hakodate, Kanagawa was to be opened for trade from 1859. Hyogo (Kobe) and Niigata were to open later and foreigners were also to be allowed to reside in Edo and Osaka. Special permission was required by foreigners travelling outside the vicinity of the treaty ports.

The first British residents arrived in 1859. A small number went to Nagasaki and Hakodate but the main settlement was at Yokohama. The treaty specified Kanagawa. However Kanagawa was on the main highway, Tokaido, between Edo and the Imperial Capital of Kyoto. The Japanese authorities feared trouble between the 'Western barbarians' and factions of radically anti-foreign samurai. Accordingly, they decided unilaterally to move the treaty port to Yokohama across the bay from Kanagawa. Yokohama was a small fishing village surrounded by marshland and could be cut off by a series of canals thus enabling the Japanese to keep the foreigners under control and observation. The Western diplomats protested at this breach of the provisions of the treaties but the merchants found Yokohama convenient and Western diplomatic protests led by the British went unheeded.

The British soon took over the leading role in diplomacy and commerce. In retaliation for the murder of a British merchant on the Tokaido in 1862 the British fleet bombarded in 1863 Kagoshima in southern Kyushu, the capital of the Satsuma clan who were held responsible for the murder. They also took the lead in the bombardment of Shimonoseki in 1864 when the Choshu clan closed the straits between Honshu (main island) and Kyushu to foreign shipping.

Cat.29 UTAGAWA HIROSHIGE III (1842-1894)
The Prosperity of Merchant Houses in Yokohama, 1871

The Bakufu, as the Tokugawa Shogun's government was called, was no longer in full control of events. The feudal magnates who had lost out when the Tokugawa won power in the seventeenth century were constantly looking for an opportunity of reasserting their position. For centuries the foreigners had been denounced. Now the Tokugawa had been humiliated by the 'barbarians' and forced to make concessions to them. Anti-foreign feelings were fermented by a current of nationalism which was promoted by scholars who regarded the Tokugawa as usurpers of imperial power.

The so-called 'Meiji Restoration' in 1868 when the Tokugawa rule was ended and the young Emperor Meiji became the nominal source of power in the land marked the beginning of a new era. The leadership was assumed by samurai from the outer fiefs, in particular from Choshu and Satsuma. The French had actively supported the Tokugawa in the run up to the 'Restoration', while the British had moved closer to the Satsuma and Choshu fiefs which they had earlier attacked.

The objective of the young oligarchs was the modernisation of Japan so that the 'unequal treaties' with the Western powers could be revised and Japan assumed the prominent role in Asia and the world which the leaders thought appropriate. Their task was a formidable one. Japan had little modern industry or infrastructure although commerce was well developed and in some of the fiefs factories and foundries had been established. Before Perry's 'Black Ships' appeared, some iron ore was being smelted and coal-mining had developed in Kyushu. The first reverbatory furnace was built in Hizen (now Saga prefecture and Mito (Ibaragi prefecture) in 1853. But these and other factories and shipyards were totally inadequate as a basis for the industrial revolution which Japan needed. Communications were bad. None of Japan's 'main' highways was, for instance, suitable for wheeled traffic.

There was a real danger that the fiefs jealous of one another would be drawn into destructive strife. Unity was the first requirement and the young Emperor was the symbol around which the country was to unite. The slogan was 'fukoku kyohei' which may be freely translated as 'enrich the country and strengthen the military power of Japan'. To this end Japan had to learn from the West. The old feudal customs had to be discarded. Industry and commerce had to be developed and the infrastructure built up.

These objectives were not achieved without many difficulties. Opposition to modernisation was a major factor in the civil war of 1877, the so-called 'Seinan War' or the 'Satsuma rebellion'. Thanks to the determination and dedication of the new leaders and the help which Japan received from the many foreign experts employed by the Meiji government Japan changed almost beyond recognition in the final decades of the nineteenth century.

The Japanese victory over China in 1895 surprised most Westerners. The Japanese began to be respected. The first treaties with their extra-territorial provisions finally ended in 1899 and Japan could begin to claim equality with the West. The Anglo-Japanese Alliance of 1902 and the Japanese victory in the Russo-Japanese War of 1904-5 earned widespread respect for the Japanese achievements.

The first foreign residents found the natives hostile. Murders and assassinations were frequent and violence common. The Tokugawa officials were seen as (and perhaps were indeed) bureaucratic, incompetent, shilly-shallying and deceitful. The Japanese merchants with whom the foreigners came in contact were regarded at best as dishonest, at worst as dissembling rogues. The merchants in the rigid class system prevailing under the Tokugawa were at the bottom of the pile and had had no experience of doing business with foreigners.

Many of the foreign merchants were little better. They wanted to make a quick fortune. They too were not always honest. They tended to be arrogant and were inclined to despise the natives. They were hard-living and quarrelsome. There were, of course, exceptions. One of these was Thomas Glover in Nagasaki who helped some of the leaders of the 'Meiji Restoration' of 1868 to study abroad and who was instrumental in supplying ships and arms to the fiefs who were in the vanguard of the forces ranged against the Tokugawa shogunate.

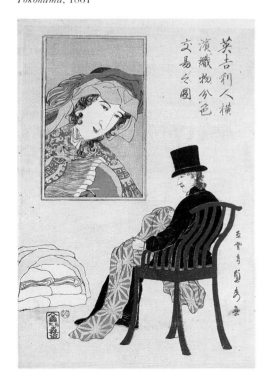

Cat.24 GOUNTEI SADAHIDE (1807-?)
An Englishman Sorting Fabrics for Trade at Yokohama, 1861

Yokohama in the early years of the settlement was like a Wild West frontier town. Built of wood the town was subject to frequent fires. There was no proper drainage or water supply and cholera was rife. So was venereal disease. The Japanese in accordance with their normal custom provided pleasure quarters, the so-called 'Gankiro', where the foreigners could enjoy sex, dancing and other entertainments. In 1864 a British garrison had to be stationed at Yokohama to ensure the safety of the settlement.

But in a few years after the Restoration the merchants began to feel safe and the tone changed as more foreign women came to join their menfolk. The settlements became respectable if not always sedate. The clubs and hotels flourished. Foreign shops, theatres, breweries and market gardens were developed and the communities enjoyed their traditional pastimes of horse racing, gambling and billiards.

Yokohama remained the most flourishing foreign settlement during the nineteenth century. Its only near rival was Kobe which the Kobe residents declared to be a cut above Yokohama in its society and facilities although this was disputed by the foreign residents of Yokohama. Nagasaki declined and Hakodate never really took off as a foreign settlement. Niigata attracted only a handful of foreigners as the port failed to develop.

Most of the residents of Yokohama were content with expeditions to places in the vicinity such as Tokyo and Kamakura or to the mountains around Mt Fuji, especially to Miyanoshita and Hakone. As the railways developed Nikko also attracted many visitors.

The colony in Kobe was well placed for visits to Kyoto which became much more accessible after 1876 when the railway line was opened between Kobe and Kyoto. The favourite area for the foreign colony in Kobe was however the hot spring resort of Arima in the hills behind the town.

Some of the more adventurous of the foreigners wanted to travel more widely and as passports became more freely available British travellers went to other parts of the country. Until the railway was completed in 1889 many did the journey from Kobe to Yokohama by sea. Others who were prepared to endure the discomforts and who after 1868 could obtain the necessary permission followed the old Tokaido route from Kyoto to Tokyo. In the early days this had to be done in a rickshaw or sedan-chair 'kago'. There was no wheeled traffic before the 'Restoration' and it took some years before the road was passable for carriages. But some of the more adventurous regarded this route as rather tame and commonplace. They opted instead for the tougher but more scenic way from Kyoto to Edo via the Nakasendo (literally the route through the mountains). On this route which took some ten days to traverse in those days many of the passes were best crossed on foot. From Hakodate a few foreigners attempted to travel into Hokkaido, the northern island where they were intrigued by the Ainu inhabitants and their primitive ways. But there were few passable pathways and good horses were difficult to obtain.

Few of the British residents learned much Japanese. Many got by through gestures and shouting. Some, however, learned a kind of pidgin Japanese which went by the name of the Yokohama dialect. Surprisingly their Japanese servants and the local shopkeepers managed to fathom the wants of their foreigners as expressed in the limited vocabulary of the dialect. For their part the foreigners had fun in reading the peculiar English learned and used by the Japanese in the early days. Basil Hall Chamberlain 'a renowned British scholar' termed this 'English as she is Japped'. Henry Luce, a British Member of Parliament who visited Japan in the recess in 1884, was amused by the following letter written by a clerk in a European trading house to his master (East by West, Vol.1, p.281, London 1885):

November 7 1883

My dear Talbot,

Dear Sir - Will you please give me a only one day Holddy - becouse I am very sorry my house set in fire at this early morning therefore I must look after my family and Co. [sic]

YOUR UPSTAIR BOY

Sir Alfred East visited Japan in 1889 , and he was amused to find on a Western menu such strange dishes as 'mouton with red currant dam' and 'sluffle' (soufflé!). (The Japan Diary of Sir Alfred East R.A.MS.)

The foreign residents generally found it difficult to adapt to Japanese customs and food. The traveller was urged to take with him most of his supplies, including Liebig's meat extract, and to provide himself with lots of Keetings powder to deal with the bed bugs he was likely to encounter in Japanese inns. Few could cope with Japanese arrangements for their ablutions, especially the lack of privacy, or with the excessive heat of the Japanese bath water. Some pretended to be shocked by Japanese obliviousness to nudity. Others found the smells due to the inadequate or non-existent sanitary facilities particularly obnoxious. Even if they found Japanese cuisine not to their taste many got to like Japanese *sake* although some visitors such as Luce did not. He wrote (Vol. I, p.238) that 'it tasted as if it had been procured by washing out a decanter that had held sherry, leaving the liquid to acquire a fine stale flavour'.

Christopher Dresser, despite his enthusiasm for many aspects of Japanese culture, found Japanese food hard to swallow (*Japan, its Architecture, Art and Art Manufacturers*, London 1882, p.25): 'I try to eat the putty-like compound with green exterior, but in attempting to bite a piece from the mass I encounter a serious difficulty, for instead of being wholly successful in my attempt I find that in removing my saucer from my mouth I am drawing out an attenuated string of the ductile dainty, and that the portion in my mouth is still connected with the larger mass now resting on the floor ...'

As communications with Japan developed, an increasing number of globe-trotters visited Japan in the course of their world tours. Their impressions and prejudices tended to reflect those of the merchant communities in the treaty ports. They were more likely to see the picturesque characteristics of Japanese life. Many fell for the simpering serving girls in the tea houses. They one and all adored the happy Japanese children they encountered - none more perhaps than Rudyard Kipling who went to Japan in 1889 and again in 1892. An exceptional globe-trotter was Isabella Bird who

Cat.49
KUSAKABE KIMBEI (1841-1934)
Postman, late 19th century

came to Japan in 1877 and made an unforgettable journey through Northern Japan and into Hokkaido. The record of this journey in *Unbeaten Tracks in Japan* (London 1880) is a classic of Victorian travel.

The globe-trotters found much that was beautiful in Japan. They were mostly romantics who deplored the modernisation which they felt was destroying the fine purity of Japanese traditions and aesthetics. Few were ready to accept willingly that Japan could not stand still.

But not all the British who came to Japan were merchants or globe-trotters the majority of whom were unwilling or unable to adapt to nineteenth-century Japan. Among the diplomats and consuls were men who were able to behave with dignity. Some worked hard to master the Japanese language and began to travel widely in the 'Interior' as the area outside the treaty ports was called and to appreciate Japanese culture.

The first British Consul-General and Minister was Rutherford Alcock who arrived in 1859. He came at a particularly difficult and insecure time, but he managed to see a good deal of Japan and to appreciate aspects of Japanese art. He prepared the Japanese section of the International Exhibition of 1862 and wrote and published in London in 1878 one of the first books in English about Japanese art under the title *Art and Art Industries of Japan*. He was a friend of the designer Christopher Dresser whom he encouraged to visit Japan.

Alcock's successor who arrived in 1865 and stayed as the British Minister in Japan until 1881 was Harry Parkes, irascible, arrogant and intolerant, but a man of great courage and ability. He was fortunate to have on his staff some outstanding young men. One of these was Ernest Satow who played an important role in shaping British policy towards Japan in the crucial years before the Restoration. An able scholar of Japanese he returned to Japan as British Minister in the final decade of the nineteenth century. Another of Parkes' assistants was A. B. Mitford, later Lord Redesdale, whose *Tales of Old Japan* was a classic of its day and who shared with Satow many of the more adventurous diplomatic moments at the time of the Restoration. The Japan Consular Service was established and the young British entrants to the service were required to acquire a good working knowledge of Japanese - spoken and written. Many in addition to Satow, such as W. G. Aston and J. H. Gubbins became outstanding Western scholars of Japan.

The Meiji government sent many young men to study abroad. They were enthusiastic and painstaking students who absorbed every aspect of Western knowledge, especially in the areas of science and technology. Many of them also achieved high standards of proficiency in the English language. In parallel the Japanese government employed many Western advisers and teachers (the so-called o-yatoi-gaijin) who were tempted to Japan by relatively high salaries. They made a significant contribution to Japan's modernisation but their services were dispensed with as soon as suitable Japanese replacements could be found and trained. The British were predominant in the field of engineering. Richard Brunton was employed in 1868 to establish a lighthouse system. He also advised on telegraphs, port facilities and other engineering projects, including the first railway from Yokohama to Tokyo. This was built by British engineers and after its completion in 1872 was initially run by British railway-men. Henry Dyer who came to Japan from Glasgow in 1873 at the age of twenty-four was appointed Principal of the Engineering College established in Tokyo. This later became the engineering department of Tokyo Imperial University. Josiah Conder (1852-1920) was from 1877 to 1888 employed by the Japanese government as professor of architecture at the College of Engineering in Tokyo. After this employment ended he stayed on in Japan and ran his own firm of architects. He taught many Japanese the basic principles of European architecture and designed over fifty major Western buildings in Tokyo. He also wrote pioneering works about Japanese landscape gardening and about Japanese flower

arrangement. John Milne came to Japan in 1876 to teach geology at the College of Engineering. In 1880 he and other scientists founded the Seismological Society of Japan. Captain Francis Brinkley of the British army first came to Japan in 1867. In 1871 he became a military instructor to the new Japanese army and later taught mathematics at the College of Engineering. He married a Japanese lady, edited a foreign- language paper and wrote much about Japanese history, language and culture. Henry Palmer was a British army engineer who, on his fourth visit to Japan in 1882, was asked by the authorities to prepare plans for the first modern waterworks built at Yokohama.

Japanese flowers and plants generally were hardly known in the West when Japan re-opened. The country soon attracted many plant collectors. One of the most famous was Robert Fortune who came before the Restoration and returned with many specimens hitherto unknown in Britain (*Yedo and Peking: A Narrative of a Journey to the Capitals of Japan and China*, London 1863). The debt horticulturalists owe to Japan is clear from the list of plants in common use in Britain today.

Among the British visitors to Japan were a number with a serious purpose. They wanted to learn more about this 'mysterious' country. One such visitor was Sir E. J. Reed who visited Japan in 1879. The two volumes which he wrote about his visit and about Japan and its history were read by many later visitors including Rudyard Kipling. But perhaps from the artistic point of view the most important visitor in the nineteenth century was Christopher Dresser who arrived in Japan in 1876. His book *Japan, its Architecture, Art and Art Manufacturers* (1882) had a seminal influence on artistic developments in Britain in the final decades of the nineteenth century.

Every visitor to Japan was attracted by the curio shops which sprang up in the treaty ports and holiday resorts. The globe-trotters found these shops ubiquitous and irresistible. Henry Lucy who was in Japan in 1884 describes (*East by West*, Vol. I, p. 267) how they were visited by 'curio men' in their hotel in Nikko. He went on: 'The curio men are one of the institutions of foreign travel in Japan. They live in places principally resorted to by Europeans, and take note of every fresh arrival. On the afternoon of the Mikado's birthday, when we lunched at the British Embassy at Tokyo (actually it was in those days only a Legation), the drawing room was crowded with curio men who had heard that there were guests, and scented business from afar. They entered the house uninvited, but not unwelcome, for there are worse ways of spending an hour in the afternoon than in examining the varied stores of a Japanese pedlar.'

Kipling described a visit to a curio shop in Kobe in 1898: 'Through room after room he [the dealer] led us, the light fading as we went, till we reached a tiny garden and a woodwork cloister that ran round it. Suits of old-time armour made faces at us in the gloom, ancient swords clicked at our feet, quaint tobacco pouches as old as the swords swayed to and fro from some invisible support, and the eyes of a score of battered Buddhas, red dragons .... glared at us from over the fence of tattered gold brocade robes of state. The joy of possession lives in the eye [Kipling was then a young journalist with a very limited purse]. The old man showed us his treasures, from crystal spheres mounted in sea-worn wood to cabinet on cabinet full of ivory and wood carvings, and we were as rich as though we owned all that lay before us.' Kipling in fact managed to buy a few things. The average globe-trotter bought much more. Perhaps it was this same shop the British artist Alfred East visited that spring. He had his pick of 'a quantity of old prints' through which he 'waded' selecting what he required. He vowed that he would not be tempted away from his sketching again, but found the temptations of curio buying frequently irresistible.

The visitors generally admired what they saw of the decorative side of Japanese art. The globe-trotter tended to buy indiscriminately and to choose colourful and pretty-pretty examples rather than the more restrained objects which had appealed to Japanese men of taste. Foreign demand and industrialisation of the process of production inevitably led to the production of items to meet foreign tastes and to a repetitiveness in production which inhibited inspiration. The authorities wanted to ensure that standards were maintained and designs improved. They accordingly imported Western teachers of painting and sculpture and promoted Westernisation. Many Japanese copied Western dress and manners not always successfully or elegantly. The craze for Westernisation inevitably led for a time to a decline in traditional arts and crafts. However fortunately, thanks in particular to the American Ernest Fenollosa, interest in and support for Japanese traditional arts was revived and this in due course led to a reaction against Westernisation.

Sir Rutherford Alcock's *Art and Art Industries in Japan* (London 1878) set the mould for the majority and British opinions about Japanese art in the final decades of the nineteenth century. He explained (p.14) that his purpose 'was to indicate what the Japanese seem to have done for Art, in creating a new and, to a great degree, an original school of decorative design'. He argued that 'all branches of Japanese Art, apart from their popular picture-books, are decorative in their main purpose'. He declared (p.15) that 'Of high Art, such as has been cultivated in Europe since the dark ages, the Japanese know nothing. But the range of true artistic work in its application to industrial purposes in Japan is very wide, and more varied than anywhere in Europe. There are a peculiar grace and delicacy, both of design and execution, in all their work, even in utensils for the common purposes of daily life...' Christopher Dresser, who became the main exponent of Japanese design in Britain in the final decades of the nineteenth century, following his visit to Japan in 1876, was more broad-minded than Alcock. Alcock had failed to see the merits of Japanese architecture. Dresser recognised the greatness of some of the ancient buildings in Japan and appreciated the importance of religious influences but he too concentrated on the decorative characteristics of Japanese art. He drew attention to 'that simplicity of treatment, that angularity of drawing, that quaintness of rendering, that exquisite grace and that life-like character which makes all their better works so charming for those who can appreciate high art qualities' (*Japan. Its Architecture, Art and Art Manufactures*, London 1882, p. 320).

Other visitors such as Sir Edward Reed (*Japan: Its History, Traditions, and Religions with the Narrative of a Visit in 1879*, London 1880, Vol. I, p. 98) noted the limitations of Japanese art: 'It is melancholy to consider what limits their arts even now have, and we cannot help hoping that Art like Woman will in Japan speedily lay aside its conventional aspect and movements, and proudly and joyously display its nobler aspects.' He and many other British visitors at that time were fascinated by the quaintness and novelty of Japanese art and particularly struck by the grotesque elements which they found especially in Japanese prints.

In 1889 Alfred East visited in Kyoto 'a school for all the arts'. He was received 'with the greatest politeness, but I must confess to a sense of disappointment when I saw the method employed in the manufacture of their so-called bronze work (which was very popular with the tourists). It is original no doubt, to begin with, but it is repeated over and over again. The same peculiar smirk of the bird, the same sort of branch, the same peculiar twist of the stork's neck, the same bent twig, the same arrangement of the blossoming tree. These things are not actually copied but the same motif is observed all through their designs. They employ the same boy till he can be trained to be so dextrous in modelling a certain bird, foot, or branch that he can do it excellently well, but set him to do anything original and he is perfectly helpless.' (The Japan Diary of Sir Alfred East R.A. MS)

Later he went to an exhibition in Ueno in Tokyo. He commented in his diary: 'We saw many beautiful things at the Exhibition in old and new lacquer. The latter proves they have not lost the art. Rather I should say they have improved upon it, certainly as far as

Cat.280
ALFRED EAST (1849-1913)
Kioto Scene with a Shrine, c.1889-90

Cat.274
MORTIMER MENPES (1860-1938)
Japanese Children, c.1887-88

design goes. We saw ivory carving, good in artisanship, bad in result, enamels and enamel without cloisonné, the brass divisions which edge or draw the design were a sad perversion of another of the purely national art expressions. We also saw the fine art if it can be called such, as painted Kakemono, which are for purely decorative purposes. The painter always has this purpose in view before him in his work. This causes him to conform to the necessities of its intended surroundings. There is too the feeling of the dearth of originality again here; either they are in the old Chinese conventional lines, or they are more or less copies of some emancipated Japanese artist (emancipated I mean from the Classic school) their unconventionality becoming a conventionality. Here we notice the same theme worked upon over and over again, the same idea plagiarised into hundred poor expressions.' He thought that 'Their only national art pure and simple' was lacquer. He doubted whether the Japanese possessed 'a fine art, an art which is self contained and self interesting, an art whose only motive is the expression of human emotions and passions ... nature was made for all men, let every bird sing his *own* song and every picture be the painter's *own* expression ... how does the art of Japan bear this test of individuality? It simply breaks down ... but is not quite fair to compare a purely decorative art to a fine art.' Hardly surprisingly Alfred East found that he could not agree with the great American art critic Ernest Fenollosa who did so much to encourage the Japanese to revitalise their traditions in painting and the arts. East recorded in his diary that he disapproved of Fenollosa's 'assertion that the only art of the world which was vital was that of Japan'.

When Mortimer Menpes went to Japan at the turn of the century he was readier to appreciate Japanese art in more than just its decorative aspects. Dorothy Menpes recording her father's views in *Japan: A Record in Colour* (London 1901) declared: 'It would be utterly impossible for the Japanese to keep art out of their lives. It creeps into everything, and is as the very air they breathe. Art with them is not only a conscious effort to achieve the beautiful, but also an instinctive expression of inherited taste.'

British visitors to Japan in the nineteenth century hardly surprisingly tended to reflect the interests and prejudices of their class and milieu. Japan was seen as exotic and quaint and until the end of the century the British were inclined to treat the Japanese with both contempt and arrogance mixed with an element of admiration. Some, such as Lafcadio Hearn and Sir Edwin Arnold, became enamoured with Japan. Few saw much below the surface, but there were exceptions such as the scholar Basil Hall Chamberlain and diplomats like Ernest Satow. Among the artists who visited Japan Christopher Dresser was outstanding and Alfred East interesting in their observations, but there was no British visitor or resident who had the intuitive eye and the insight of the Americans Edward Morse and Ernest Fenollosa.

LIT: Barr 1967; Barr 1968; Cortazzi 1987; Cortazzi and Webb (ed.) 1988; Halén 1990.

East Meets West

WESTERN - STYLE PAINTING IN MODERN JAPANESE ART

Shuji Takashina

The introduction of Western painting techniques into modern Japan occurred in roughly four stages, from the end of the eighteenth century to the beginning of the twentieth.

The first stage occupied the period from the end of the eighteenth century until the opening up of Japan in the mid-nineteenth century, that is, the period when the country was closed under the policies of the Tokugawa shogunate. During this period, the Japanese were forbidden to visit the West or to associate with Westerners, so almost the only knowledge they were able to gain about Western painting was through imported books and the illustrations in them. Nonetheless, pioneering artists burning with curiosity and intellectual fervour familiarised themselves with the methods of expression in Western painting through these illustrations and engravings, building up the foundations for the introduction of Western art after the Meiji Restoration.

The second stage lasted for about twenty years, from 1854, when the country was opened up, until 1876, when the Technical Art School in Tokyo was founded. This was the turbulent period following the end of the Shogunate during the early period of the Meiji Restoration, when it became possible for Japanese to associate with Westerners, although within certain well-defined limits. Very few Japanese artists actually went to study painting techniques in Europe. Almost no paints, canvas or other materials suitable for Western-style painting were available in Japan, and artists had to go to a great deal of trouble just to obtain a single paint-brush. However, out of these early and difficult encounters there finally emerged artists who specialised in Western-style painting.

The third stage also lasted for about twenty years, from 1876, when the first government-run institution for art education was established in Japan, until 1896. In this period, for the first time, systematic art education was carried out by Antonio Fontanesi, who was invited from Italy. His stay in Japan was only a brief two years, and the Technical Art School was closed in 1883, but his influence was felt in the development of Western-style painting for a long time thereafter.

The fourth stage began in 1896, when Kuroda Seiki, who had studied in France for nine years, was appointed Senior Professor in the Department of Western Art, newly established in the extremely traditionalist Tokyo School of Fine Arts, which had been opened in 1887 to replace the Technical Art School. The new style propounded by Kuroda Seiki differed considerably from that of Fontanesi's students, but eventually this 'new school' became the mainstream of Japanese Western-style painting.

In this way the artistic distance separating the West and Japan gradually shrank over a period of more than a century, beginning at the end of the eighteenth century. It is interesting that at each stage Japanese artists took a different Western nation as their model, reflecting the historical situation of the period concerned. In the first stage, when the country was closed, the most important country was Holland, Japan's only trading partner. Artists and intellectuals devoted themselves to Dutch studies, learning about the history and culture of the West through Holland. In the second stage, the English-speaking countries - the United States and Great Britain - who were instrumental in the opening up of Japan, played the most important role. Fukuzawa Yukichi, who had learned Dutch at the Ogata Juku in Osaka, was shocked at not being

Cat.247
YAMAMOTO HOSUI (1850-1906)
Portrait of Mrs Sonoda Kei, 1885

Cat.226
CHARLES WIRGMAN (1832-1891)
Portrait of a Young Woman

able to understand the English language on signs when he visited Yokohama, and started out anew to study English. This episode shows plainly that the shift from Dutch studies to English studies was a major feature of Japan's reception of Western culture in this period, and the same was true for art. Takahashi Yuichi, the most outstanding painter of this period, learned oil painting from Charles Wirgman, a reporter on *The Illustrated London News*, and Kunisawa Shinkuro, a peer of Takahashi Yuichi and the first to open a private school of Western painting, called Shogido, studied in London between 1870 and 1874. After Kunisawa's death (1877), Shogido was carried on by his student Honda Kinkichiro. Here lectures were given using translations of works on technique that Kunisawa had brought back from England. Later, these works on technique were gradually translated and published in Japanese and widely used. They included the theory of landscape painting and portrait painting and lectures on anatomy, along with *Discourses on Painting by Mr. R.* (published in 1890). This was probably the first time Sir Joshua Reynolds was introduced into Japan.

Cat.228
CHARLES WIRGMAN (1832-1891)
A Post Town, 1872

In the third stage, which began with the establishment of the Technical Art School, not unexpectedly Fontanesi's homeland, Italy, was considered the centre of art. In his lectures Fontanesi dealt mainly with Italian artists, such as Titian, Tintoretto and Guido Reni. It was only in the fourth stage, when Kuroda Seiki appeared, that the realisation took hold among Japanese Western-style painters, as was the case with contemporary European painters, that France, particularly Paris, was the centre of art.

For Japanese intellectuals during the era when the country was closed, for those who came in contact with Western culture through written works and engravings, the essence of Western painting was above all the reproduction of the true form of nature. In his work *Discussions on Western Painting*, written in 1799, Shiba Kokan, artist, art critic and natural scientist, argued as follows:

'If a painting does not reproduce reality, it cannot be called outstanding. Because Chinese and Japanese paintings are principally composed of outlines, even if the artist attempts to draw a sphere, he can only draw a circle, and it is impossible for him to represent the bulge in its centre. And because the Western art of drawing and painting allows one to reproduce the distinction between a circle and a sphere, it is infinitely superior to what is found in Japan.'

According to Kokan, the value of painting consists primarily in its capacity to reproduce the various forms of the external world exactly as they appear to the eye, and he refers specifically to perspective, modelling, shading and other means of three-dimensional expression. Thus his philosophy had characteristics in common with zoology, botany, astronomy, geography and other disciplines which were also grounded in the observation of nature. Kokan's engraving *The Artist's Studio* (1794), which bears the signature 'Shiba Kokan, Inventor of Engraving in Japan', has at its centre the figure of an artist working at his easel, surrounded by piles of books, a globe, a compass, an engraving printing press and various other equipment for experiments, indicating that the artist's activities are at the same time highly intellectual ones. In fact, Kokan also drew maps of the heavens and earth and has left works in which he made minute drawings of such things as insects observed through a magnifying glass. That is, he believed that the role of painting was to reproduce the forms of nature, and the closer the world depicted came to the real world, the more outstanding the picture.

In this respect, it is highly symbolic that Shiba Kokan painted a work entitled *Zeuxis Painting a Picture of Grapes*. Unfortunately, the location of this work is unknown today and the only references that remain are some old pre-war photographs, but its theme is the well-known story in which the ancient Greek artist Zeuxis painted a picture of a bunch of grapes that was so close to reality that birds came to try to pick them. The scene is Zeuxis' studio with a picture of a bunch of grapes on a stand and two spectators in the room, looking on in wonder. Kokan, who was an admirer of Western culture, signed the work in Roman letters and gave the date according to the Western calender: 'Kookan Schildert, AD 1789'. This signature is incorporated into the picture on the lower edge of the Zeuxis' painting. From this we get a glimpse of Kokan's determination and pride, likening himself to Zeuxis.

Cat.246
TAKAHASHI YUICHI (1828-1894)
Books and Objects, c.1875-76

This attitude of reproducing visible reality as accurately as possible was continued in the same way by Takahashi Yuichi. That Takahashi Yuichi deeply respected Shiba Kokan is clear not only from his having left a portrait of Kokan, whom he himself had never met, but also in his other works, in which he tried to depict very ordinary objects - kitchen implements and other articles used in daily life - just as they were. For example, in *Tofu and Aburaage* he endeavoured to depict the different qualities of a variety of bean curd. In *Salmon*, which has been designated an important cultural property, the thoroughgoing realism of the feeling of the wetness of fish and the painstaking reproduction of each fish scale, go directly back in spirit to the 'truth' Shiba Kokan aimed for, even though the style of expression differs. In his later years, Takahashi Yuichi held an Exhibition of the History of Oil Painting in front of which he deliberately hung portraits of Shiba Kokan, Kawakami Togai and Fontanesi and paid them homage. This, too, probably acknowledges his strong awareness of being Kokan's successor. That he displayed a portrait of Fontanesi (who was no longer in Japan at the time) alongside those of Kokan and Kawakami Togai, his own immediate teacher, demonstrates his admiration of this Italian painter who had come from Europe, the home of art. However, although Takahashi himself was probably aware of it, Fontanesi's view of painting differed greatly from those of Kokan and Takahashi Yuichi in one respect. Not only Takahashi, but Fontanesi's Japanese students as well, were almost completely unaware of this.

This dedicated painter from Turin made scrupulous preparations when he came to Japan, bringing with him an enormous quantity of models and materials necessary for art education. Among them were photographs and print reproductions of famous European paintings, plaster figures, mannequins with joints that moved, pigments for oil painting and watercolour, charcoal and conté crayons, drawing paper, anatomical charts and books. Through these materials and Fontanesi's outstanding teaching ability, the Japanese first received education in orthodox Western European painting. The curriculum of the Technical Art School shows that Fontanesi's teaching methods were highly systematic. He had the students learn in stages, first by having them copy his own sketches, then sketching plaster models, going on to draw mannequins and finally sketching live human models. In the case of landscapes, too, he proceeded in sequence, first having them reproduce prints and sketches, then making sketches from life with pencil and finally painting from life in oils. This method of teaching in stages was normal in the art schools of Europe at the time, but in Japan, of course, this was the first time it had been used.

But Fontanesi did not teach only the techniques of drawing. He also tried to transmit traditional European art philosophy to the Japanese. Fuji Masazo, one of his students, has left his notes of Fontanesi's lectures, which contain paragraphs like the following:

'There is one very important thing which must not be forgotten when one sketches natural landscapes. It is very rare to find a superb painting which reproduces a particular setting exactly as it is, even if one thinks that the landscape itself *is* stunningly beautiful. For this reason, in cases where the entire landscape, for example, its trees and bushes, appear as something hard to look at or even unsightly, we must think about eliminating a number of its particular features, a tree here or a bush there, in order to arrive at the appropriate composition for a work of art. However, one must never add trees or bushes that do not actually exist in the scene itself that the artist is representing. So if you are thinking about painting a beautiful landscape, first you must eliminate in advance its unsightly features, then arrange each one of its elements, and *only then begin* to reproduce it.'

In other words, in addition to 'nature as it is', Fontanesi believed in a philosophy of art transcending this. If Shiba Kokan and Takahashi Yuichi had been asked what beauty was in painting, they would probably have replied without hesitation, 'beauty is reproducing the truth in nature'. But Fontanesi believed that nature is imperfect, that in its unaltered state it is not beauty. Of course depicting 'the truth in nature' was very important, but for him this was nothing more than a means, not the ultimate purpose of painting. To Fontanesi, the purpose of painting was to express a philosophy of art different from the form of the actual external world as it was, and to achieve this, painting was not 'nature as it is,' but must reproduce 'nature as it should be', corrected and perfected in line with the philosophy of beauty.

This line of thought was not particularly unusual in Western Europe. Or rather, it was the philosophy of the most orthodox Western European classicism. Fontanesi was not a classicist in the seventeenth-century sense, but he was heir to the philosophy of academicism, spawned by classicism, and therefore tried to transmit this philosophy to his Japanese students. However, his philosophy was not necessarily adequately understood by Japanese painters. One reason is that his lectures, given through an imperfect interpreter, were difficult to understand, but more than this, it was because the view held since the eighteenth century, that Western painting is a technique to depict the forms of nature accurately, was much too strong. Japanese artists learned the techniques of painting from Fontanesi, but they did not learn his aesthetics.

A similar situation can be seen twenty years later when the Department of Western Art was established at the Tokyo School of Fine Arts. Because Kuroda Seiki had learned the academicism of Raphael Collin, who was influenced by the Impressionists, this style, as the 'new school', was considered to oppose the 'old school' of Fontanesi's students, but although the styles differed, the ideal that Kuroda sought to implant in Japan was, in fact, traditional European academicism. In fact, the four-year curriculum that Kuroda initially created for the Department of Western Art was as follows: first year, sketching plaster figures (charcoal sketching); second year, sketching human models including nudes/charcoal sketching; third year, techniques of oil painting; fourth year, graduation work (first semester devoted to conceptualising, second to actual production). That is, as in Fontanesi's case, he employed a graduated educational method proceeding from sketching to oils, from drawing from real life to conceptual painting having a theme.

Moreover, as with Fontanesi, he also considered drawing from life to be nothing more than a means and believed that painting must express an ultimate philosophy or idea, and he argued that in addition to actual technique, 'education of the mind' was also necessary. As he explained:

'For education of the mind in painting, that is, distribution of people, handling of light, mixing colours, to teach painting while nurturing the painters' powers of imagination, a theme is absolutely necessary. In particular, historical painting is highly appropriate to expand powers of imagination as much as possible. Therefore, beginning in the third year, students will be given a historical painting as a theme once a week to educate their minds.

Of course this does not mean stressing historical painting alone. Taking up abstract themes like "knowledge" or "love" is, of course, a lofty means of fully displaying the powers of imagination, but this cannot be accomplished easily in only two or three years study. Rather, it is appropriate to the students to have them first study using the themes of historical painting....'

However, Kuroda Seiki's attempt was not necessarily completely successful either, because Kuroda himself considered drawing from life his forte, rather than historical painting, and felt even more strongly that drawing from life was the purpose of painting. Moreover, the academic philosophy that history painting having a clear philosophy was 'lofty' was itself being discredited in Europe, too, just at this time. As a result, the introduction of academic philosophy that Kuroda intended was never fully accomplished in Japan.

In 1900, on the occasion of the Paris Exposition, Kuroda entered two paintings. The first, *Wisdom, Feeling and Passion*, portrayed allegorical nudes against a decorative background of gold in the academic style. The second, *By the Lake*, conveyed the feelings of everyday life using his own wife as his model. The first work was very well received in the French milieu of the time and received second prize. However in Japan it was given a very modest reception. Perhaps this was because for the Japanese observers of that period the realism of *By the Lake* was much easier to relate to and understand.

Alongside Kuroda Seiki, Fujishima Takeji and Aoki Shigeru are regarded widely as the other outstanding representatives of Western-style painting in Japan during the last third of the Meiji period. From the mid-1890s onwards they came under the strong influence of European oil painting and gave rise to a lively boom in the Japanese art scene of the time. Aoki, who died at the early age of twenty-eight, and Fujishima, before he left in 1905 to study in France and Italy, were both able to have contact with Western art in Japan since, at the turn of the century, many books of paintings and fine arts magazines had been introduced into Japan. By means of reproductions they were able to become conversant with the latest European developments. These two artists were particularly captivated by the Symbolist movement in art which emerged in England, France and Germany, and the works of the artists who were painting in this fashion. Fujishima had a deep respect and admiration for the works of Puvis de Chavannes, and he enthusiastically set himself to duplicate copies of works by Odilon Redon. Aoki, when asked by a journalist which painters he was particularly fond of, gave the names of Burne-Jones, Watts, Rossetti, Moreau, Fantin-Latour and Böcklin. As can be inferred from these names, he had already become dissatisfied with the ideal of simply reproducing the real world and, based on a deep affection for the world of history and mythology, was attempting to translate into painting the worlds of music and poetry as well.

Fujishima Takeji, for example, was friendly with a number of young poets of the time. He painted the cover and illustrations for *Dishevelled Hair*, the collected poems of the popular female poet Yosano Akiko, and was responsible for the covers for the poetry journal *Morning Star*. If we look at the cover of *Dishevelled Hair* or the illustrations in *Morning Star*, in which a woman's face is depicted within undulating curved lines, it becomes clear that he had fallen under the influence of the Art Nouveau style. In his notebooks there are many sketches that can be thought of as Art Nouveau or Jugendstil.

Cat.327
FUJISHIMA TAKEJI (1867-1943)
Designs for the magazine 'Myojo'
(Morning Star)

Cat.323
AOKI SHIGERU (1882-1911)
Paradise under the Sea
1907

Cat.326
FUJISHIMA TAKEJI (1867-1943)
Reminiscence of the Tempyo Era
1902

His oil paintings include a work showing a standing figure of a woman, wearing an ancient Japanese costume, and holding a stringed instrument from the Nara period known as *kugo*. This is called the *Reminiscence of Tempyo Era*, the period from A.D. 710 to 794. His composition, incorporating a horizon represented by a low stone wall and a vertical feature consisting of a paulownia tree, reminds one of Puvis de Chavannes' *St Geneviève Watching over the City of Paris*: the background beyond the wall is painted out in gold. The composition, in which there is scarcely any feeling of depth, captures and reflects the traditional Japanese ornamental sensitivity. It goes without saying that these lively decorative motifs were those favoured by the Art Nouveau painters. The nostalgia felt for the far-off Tempyo era, hinted at by means of the musical instrument, as well as his use of other motifs in various paintings, gives vivid proof of Fujishima's characteristic symbolism.

Fujishima's 'Butterfly' paintings, another of his representative themes, amply demonstrate his characteristic approach to his compositions through lively decorative motifs and intense feelings. In his *Butterfly Sketch Book*, there are more than two thousand assorted drawings of butterflies and flowers, motifs especially beloved of Fujishima. Among these there are butterflies actually seen and studied by Fujishima himself, as well as a significant number copied from the works of Redon. All in all, this provides proof of his profound relationship with the *fin de siècle* artists in Europe.

Compared to the symbolic and sensual qualities of Fujishima's works, those of Aoki are quite literary. He selected his themes from favourite Japanese myths such as 'Yamato Takeru' and from stories from the Old Testament such as the story of King David. Aoki also came under the influence of Fujishima and drew from historical sources rooted in the Tempyo era. However, the style in those works was closer to that of such painters as Hodler and Albert Moore. The pose of the nude in *The Hot Springs* is borrowed from Burne-Jones' *Pygmalion*, and the style of *The Transmigration of the Soul* is taken directly from Fantin-Latour.

In the manner briefly outlined above, Japanese painters from the end of the Edo period to the end of the Meiji period proceeded to incorporate into their works Western techniques of realism, and struggled in their encounters with Western painting to the point where they began to become conversant with the styles of Symbolism, styles which made possible a representation of the non-visible world. Oil painting in Europe from the middle to the end of the nineteenth century prospered under the influences received from Japan and underwent a development from realism to symbolism. In Meiji Japan, under the overwhelming influence of Western painting, a similar historical development is also visible. In spite of Kipling's well-known saying, it certainly seems that East and West met each other, and combined with one another with true eloquence.

1907 Fer
du Bolton Studio
London

Hara Busho working on
Nude Woman (cat.257)
Bolton Studio, London

Cat.356
KAMISAKA SEKKA (1866-1943)
Hyakka (hundreds of flowers),
early 20th century

Refractions of the Rising Sun
JAPAN'S PARTICIPATION IN INTERNATIONAL EXHIBITIONS 1862-1910

Ellen P. Conant

I

The centuries-old custom of holding fairs and local exhibitions was transformed by the British in 1851 when they invited all the nations of the world to compete. Its prime patron, Prince Albert, regarded the exposition as 'a true text and a living picture of the point of development at which the whole of mankind has arrived'. 1 Originally conceived as a means of bolstering trade and improving national industries, these exhibitions paradoxically revealed the 'unfathomable multiplicity of the world' while reaffirming 'their collective national identity in an updated synthesis of progress' that stimulated 'the energy, enterprise, and intellect of the people and quicken human genius'. 2 Over the course of time economic viability became incidental to their function as gigantic vehicles for international public relations that enhanced the status of the host country.

Although newly arrived on the international scene, the Japanese were quick to perceive the importance of these exhibitions and to exploit the opportunities they afforded. Between 1862, when Japanese handicrafts were first displayed at the International Exhibition held in London, and 1910 when the Japan-British Exhibition was held there towards the close of the Meiji era, Japan underwent a more rapid and far-reaching transformation than any other country. Despite the enormous strain that this imposed upon the nation, the Japanese participated in thirty-six of the eighty-eight exhibitions held worldwide during that period. 3 These exhibitions offered them a convenient means of acquiring the most diverse and up-to-date information needed to further their industrial, technological and military development, while at the same time affording them the opportunity to display their artistic and technical attainments and to foster their trade. It served to heighten their sense of national identity and to garner international prestige. Their primary goal was to redress the unequal treaties foisted upon them by the foreign powers and to achieve a position of parity with the Western nations. Their success is reflected in the concerted efforts of British authorities in 1910 'to draw still closer the bonds of friendship so happily existing between the two Island Empires of the East and West.' 4

II

The Far East was only indirectly represented at the Crystal Palace Exhibition of 1851 by a collection of Oriental artefacts that included some Japanese objects which had been organised by the British East India Company. These and other Japanese wares were shown in 1853 at exhibitions held in Dublin, Ireland and New York City. 5 Some eighty Japanese objects belonging to Dutch collectors were to be seen at the next international exhibition held in Paris in 1855, and the exceedingly large pseudo-Oriental vases that figure so prominently in Prosper Lafaye's painting of *Napoleon III and Eugénie visiting the Christofle display at the Universal Exposition, Paris, 1855*, reveal that Western firms were already adept at producing their own version of Orientalism for the European market. 6 Although special attention was given to the industrial arts in an effort to develop new forms and decorative styles adapted to contemporary techniques of production, critics were troubled by their 'universal likeness' and pervasive revivalism, prompting Henry Cole to suggest that people look to the East for 'a fresh well of art'. 7 Increasingly aware of the mediocrity of everyday objects produced by machine and many architects, designers and craftsmen looked at the art of the Middle

Ages for a means of reviving the handicrafts. This search for an idealised past extended also to distant, exotic realms such as the Orient, particularly Egypt and the Near East. Accounts of Perry's expedition, Lord Elgin's mission, and numerous books by other early travellers aroused a keen interest in Japan which had been virtually unknown at the time of the Crystal Palace exhibition.

fig.2
The International
Exhibition of 1862
the Japanese Court

The Tokyo government (*bakufu*) was too beset by foreign demands and domestic dissension to accede to the invitation tendered in 1859 to participate in the International Exhibition that was to be held in London in 1862 and the committee therefore turned to the newly appointed British Minister to Japan, Rutherford Alcock, who while serving as Consul in China had helped select material for the 1851 exhibit. 8 Alcock took advantage of carefully guided outings near his residence in Edo and later Yokohama, as well as three more extended trips to Hakodate, Mt Fuji and nearby Atami, and overland from Nagasaki to Edo, to collect a 'fair sample of the industrial arts of the Japanese, and their capabilities of production in rivalry with the nations of the West', which was tastefully installed in the Japanese Court of the International Exhibition of 1862, along with additional material contributed by other Yokohama residents. 9 The exhibit assumed official status when members of the Japanese embassy then touring Europe appeared prominently in the opening ceremonies. Few of the items listed in Alcock's catalogue as old predated the Edo period and most were of recent manufacture. Some of the finer pieces with crests may have been gifts from *bakufu* officials. Other items appear to anticipate Meiji motifs and decor. It is apparent from illustrations that Alcock was unaware that much of what he had acquired was already influenced by Western models and produced for Western markets, a distinction often overlooked in discussions of their influence on Whistler, Godwin, Burges and other enthusiasts.

The Japanese Exhibition held at the Old Society of Painters in Water Colours in Pall Mall East in February 1854 provides graphic evidence that, by the time Perry arrived at Uraga, the Japanese were already skilled at producing a wide variety of export wares that Western critics and connoisseurs, then and later, were wont to attribute to Japan's benighted attempts at Westernisation during the *bakumatsu* (last years of the Edo

Period) and early Meiji. 10 Recent studies document the rapid development of porcelain in the early seventeenth century and the Japanese skill in adapting Chinese prototypes to suit native needs and taste, while at the same time maintaining, despite the Tokugawa policy of seclusion imposed in 1639, a thriving export trade with China and the West throughout the seventeenth and eighteenth centuries. 11 Scholars have yet to tackle the voluminous official records that document this trade after the government took control of the Dutch East India Company in 1798, and the difficulty in determining which wares pre- and post-date the 'opening up' of Japan is further complicated by the increased importation of Western artefacts during the first half of the nineteenth century. 12 Only after Westerners were once again able to visit Japan could they gradually come to distinguish what was Japanese from other Oriental objects and native wares from those produced for export. Their fascination with the exoticism of Japanese form and decor remained tempered, nevertheless, by an instinctive preference for export wares designed to appeal to Victorian artistic sensibility.

The sharp distinction that Victorian society drew between 'the reforming and ennobling influences of Art, by which was meant pictures and statues' and the decorative arts led Alcock to maintain that:

'In all the mechanical arts the Japanese have unquestionably achieved great excellence. In their porcelain, their bronzes, their silk fabrics, their lacquer, and their metallurgy generally, including works of exquisite art in design and execution, I have no hesitation in saying they not only rival the best products of Europe, but can produce in each of these departments works we can imitate, or perhaps equal.'

while at the same time asserting that:

'There is much, especially in the province of art properly so called, to which the Japanese can not make the slightest pretensions ... No Japanese can produce any thing to be named in the same day with a work from the pencil of a Landseer, a Roberts, or a Stanfield, a Lewis, or Rosa Bonheur, whether in oil or water-colours; indeed, they do not know the art of painting in oils at all, and are not great in landscape in any material ... As to the size and value of private or of public buildings, it would go hard with the Japanese if their civilisation, either mental or moral, were to be judged by such a test. They have no architecture ... the special conditions of the soil exercising an absolute controlling power over all architectural development.' 13

Alcock also acknowledged that many of these objects had been purchased for a pittance and, given the exchange rate he enjoyed, even the expensive ones could not have been costly. Their sale soon thereafter probably netted him a tidy sum and confirmed his reputation as an expert. Such monetary and status considerations may have prompted other visitors and residents to collect Japanese art.

The Japanese envoys repeatedly toured the fair and noted in their diaries the importance of such exhibitions and the necessity for Japan to participate. The accolades invariably bestowed on excessively large and prodigiously elaborate feats of technical virtuosity, such as the Gobelin tapestry reproducing Titian's *Assumption of the Virgin*, and the St George Fountain executed in majolica by Messrs Minton at Stoke-on-Trent, 14 may have encouraged them and their successors to foster for foreign display the most elaborate strains in Edo and early Meiji art at the very time when Whistler, Godwin and other discerning admirers were attracted by the simplicity, economy and expressiveness of traditional Japanese art.

Other ideas stemming from the exhibition influenced the bright young men from Choshu who came to study in England in 1863. The premise that architecture is 'the shrine in which Arts and manufactures are held. From architecture in succession are developed sculpture and painting' 15 seems to underlie Ito Hirobumi's decision to add architecture to the curriculum of the Imperial College of Engineering in Tokyo established by the Ministry of Public Works and to found an auxiliary Technical Art

School. 16 So too the notion 'that beauty is cheaper than ugliness, that a knowledge of Art is essential to successful industry, and that, so applied, it not only bears a high commercial value, but diffuses a reforming and elevating influence throughout the masses of the population' 17 may account for this statesman's persistent efforts to improve the production and design of Japanese artefacts and to promote exhibitions, museums and art schools so as to raise the level of public taste and professional competence. Inoue Kaoru, also from Choshu, returned from his curtailed period of study in England as zealous an art collector as he was a government official. Machida Hisanari, who led a contingent of students sent by Satsuma in 1865, organised on his return in 1868 an exhibit of the foreign products purchased abroad. He laid the foundations for the Ueno Imperial Museum (today's Tokyo National Museum) and also initiated the programme to preserve and protect national treasures. The Satsuma students evidently advised their *han* (feudal clan) and nearby Hizen (present-day Saga prefecture) to participate, along with the *bakufu*, in the Paris exhibition of 1867, to which some were sent as delegates.

Cat.120
CHARLES ALFRED CHASTEL DE BOINVILLE
(1849-?)
*Lecture Hall at the Imperial College
of Engineering*, 1877

Anglo-French political and economic rivalry in the Far East led the French Minister, Léon Roches, to cultivate close ties with the *bakufu* which thereby felt obligated to take part in the Paris Exposition of 1867. 18 China, Siam and Japan were sandwiched in between Persia and Egypt. The entry to the Japanese exhibit was flanked by two elaborate suits of armour sent by the Daimyo of Satsuma that attracted crowds. Once again the decorative arts predominated, along with a limited number of hanging-scrolls, screen, albums, possibly prints, as well as some ethnological, pedagogical and scientific material. Although most of the artefacts had been specially produced for the occasion, the French were lavish in their praise. Eugene Rimmel asserts that 'Japanese porcelain and bronzes have been long known and celebrated in Europe, but never had we seen such fine specimens as those sent by [sic] Bizen'. Indeed his admiration extends to 'those wonderful paper stuffs out of which they make ... even pocket handkerchiefs' from which he could only conclude that 'in that happy country, people are never afflicted with a cold in the head'. 19

The Japanese delegation, headed by Tokugawa Akitake, the younger brother of the Shogun, did not allow these encomiums and rampant exoticism to cloud their pragmatic assessment of Japan's competitive position, current requirements and future aims. Notwithstanding the praise, their reports stressed the need to improve their materials and methods of producing even the highly vaunted pottery and other crafts. They purchased a wide variety of objects that were later exhibited by Machida to educate the public and promote industrial development. Two of the Japanese delegates, Yamataka Nobuakira and Sano Tsunetami, became influential members of other exposition committees and art organisations. The interpreter, Alexander von Siebolt, the eldest son of the noted Japanologist, Philipp Franz Voigiebolt and his brother Heinrich were later involved in negotiations concerning the Vienna exhibition where both served as interpreters. 20 Accompanying the delegation was Léon Dury, a French national on leave from his teaching position in Nagasaki, who on his return assisted the Vice-Governor of Kyoto, Makimura Masanao, to hold the first Kyoto Exhibition in 1871 and to introduce new material and techniques for improving the manufacture of Kyoto's famed craft industries. 21 Meiji officials were eager to foster the export of these crafts which were so admired abroad as a means of obtaining the foreign currency needed to purchase Western technology. They therefore assisted noted craftsmen to establish factories in the Tokyo-Yokohama area and train other craftsmen made redundant by the 'Restoration' to produce artefacts suitable for export.

In December 1871, the Meiji government agreed to take part in the Vienna Exhibition of 1873. A special bureau was set up to formulate plans, headed by Okuma Shigenobu, and the officials appointed to supervise the project included Inoue Kaoru, Machida Hisanari and another Satsuma student, Terajima Munenori, who had attended the Paris

Exhibition, as had Sano Tsunetami, Yamataka Nobuakira and Tanaka Yoshio. Determined to make an impressive appearance at their first international event, the fledgingly Meji government allotted from their meagre budget the large sum of 600,000 yen to finance what proved to be an intensive three-year scientific, industrial and artistic seminar involving craftsmen, technicians and merchants that had far-reaching consequences. Key officials spent a year selecting suitable products, had many made to order under government subsidy and included, possibly at the suggestion of a German chemist engaged to improve the production of crafts, Gottfried Wagner, wares of a more traditional nature that were widely admired in Vienna, thereby stimulating the propensity for eclecticism latent in early Meiji. Domestic production was further influenced by the extended exhibition in Tokyo both the material shipped to Vienna and the astonishing array of new material purchased there. After the exhibition was over, Sano and Wagner toured Europe seeking the advice of museum and art school directors as to what manner of institutions and training might best serve Japan's needs. 22

These exhibitions occurred in such rapid succession that the key officials came to form a permanent bureaucracy that spanned most of the Meiji era, but their continuity of service and experience was offset by the need to conform to the differing aims and policies of the various ministries to which they were successively transferred. 23 For example, the Philadelphia exhibition of 1876 at which Americans gleaned their first extensive view of Japanese culture was held under the auspices of the Home Ministry, and was the focus of special attention because the Minister, Okubo Toshimichi, needed to increase Japan's export trade in order to pay off a politically dangerous English loan. Since America was a major market, he allocated the largest sum of any of the third participating nations and succeeded in taking 'the Centennial by storm'. Americans were captivated both by the elaborately wrought, exceedingly large and ornate bronzes and pottery that had been made for the fair and the technical virtuosity of delicate, finely wrought lacquers, textiles and paintings. At the same time they could not fail to be impressed by the evidence of Japan's rapid mastery of Western technology. The inexpensive trinkets purchased in the bazaar sparked a taste for Japonisme that spread throughout the country. 24 A quasi-official company, the Kiritsu Kosho Kaisha, Industry and Commerce Company, that had been created following the Vienna Exhibition to handle the shipment of exhibition materials and the trade they generated established a shop in New York in 1877 to exploit this new market for Japanese wares. 25 Some of the objects displayed at the exhibition were sold to museums that had recently been founded in Boston, New York, Baltimore and Washington, with the commendable aim of developing the taste and artistic appreciation of the public.

In 1877 the ministry sponsored the first National Industrial Exposition to improve the quality and design of export products and to stimulate industrialisation and the expansion of domestic markets. Two additional ones were held in Tokyo in 1881 and 1890, one in Kyoto in 1895 and a final one in Osaka in 1903. They facilitated the acceptance of new materials and processes brought back from abroad and the carnival-like atmosphere helped to make the Japanese public more receptive to new ideas and merchandise. The many foreign residents and tourists who flocked to these fairs enabled Japanese entrepreneurs personally to gauge Western interests and taste and thereby enhance their chances of success abroad. More specialised exhibits and a wide variety of local fairs enabled the government to reach a nation-wide audience.

Although Japonisme was at its peak of popularity when the Paris Exhibition was held in 1878, the shop that the Kiritsu Kosho Kaisha opened in Paris that year operated at a loss and the entire operation was abandoned in 1891. Japanese officials gradually came to realise that exoticism was not a readily marketable commodity, and that while Japanese craftsmen were willing to adopt new materials and techniques of manufacture, they were not willing nor able to cater objectively to foreign taste nor to convert to mass production in order to be economically competitive abroad, particularly at a time when

念紀會覽博業勸國内四五第

DAI. GOKWAI. NAIKOKU. KWANGIYO. HAKURANKUYAI. KINEN

Cat.149
*Postcard of the fifth National
Industrial Exhibition, Osaka* 1903

the domestic economy was expanding. Moreover, the success of Western Japonisme and the widening appeal of Art Nouveau stiffened the competition. Meanwhile the appreciation of Japanese art of earlier periods was steadily increasing. The South Kensington Museum purchased a collection of Japanese pottery in 1878 and commissioned Shioda Makoto to write the catalogue. 26 The British Museum paid a handsome sum in 1881 for the paintings and prints collected by Dr William Anderson during his six years residence in Japan and engaged him to catalogue and publish the collection. 27 Henri Cernuschi and Emile Guimet established museums in the 1870s in Paris and Lyons respectively. A growing number of American collectors such as Ernest F. Fenollosa, William Sturgis Bigelow and Edward S. Morse were becoming more discriminating and willing to buy a wider range and finer quality of Japanese art. Ukiyo-e gained an increasingly enthusiastic and knowledgeable patronage although circumspect Japanese officials quailed at the esteem that cultivated Europeans bestowed on prints of their demi-mondaines.

The Vice-Minister of Education, Kuki Ryuichi, sent by them to observe developments in education and art at the Paris Exposition of 1878 and he also attended the Provincial Congress of Orientalists that was held at Lyons. 28 He was impressed by the depth of knowledge of and interest in Japanese art and civilisation, and also by the importance that the French attached to artistic achievement and their own cultural heritage. He returned from Paris convinced that his government was foolish to promote Western art, apart from its technical applications, when Japan possessed an artistic tradition that could serve as a source of national pride and international prestige. The following year he helped to establish Ryuchi Kai (reorganised and renamed Nihon bijustu kyokai, Japan Art Association, in 1886) which sought to capitalise on foreign esteem of Japanese art, and to stimulate a greater interest among the Japanese in their artistic heritage as a basis for the production of Arts and Crafts and the modern renovation of Japanese painting and sculpture.

After serving as Minister to the United States, Kuki was appointed director of the Tokyo National Museum in 1888 and thereby served as vice-director of national and international expositions and chief juror, as well as a member of other important art organisations. His influence helped to counteract the Western orientation of the Minister of Education, Mori Arinori, and assured the exclusion of Western art from the curriculum of the Tokyo Art School when it was founded in 1889. The *yoga* (Western-style painting) artists, who had been increasingly discriminated against during the 1880s, reacted to Kuki's divisive policies by partly abstaining from the third National Industrial Exhibition and boycotting en masse the World's Columbian Exhibition held in Chicago in 1893.

Kuki, his cohort Okakura Kakuzo, and their circle had a major voice in determining the nature and contents of the art exhibits. Crafts by then were a minor component of Japan's burgeoning export trade and pride pressured them to petition at last for permission to exhibit in the Palace of Fine Arts without having to conform to Western classifications. 29 This necessitated their drawing distinctions between 'Arts and Crafts' and other works in the same media and even by the same artists who were exhibited in other buildings. Both the government and private entrepreneurs laboured to present an art exhibit that attested to the academic accomplishment, technical refinement and artistic idealism that had come to characterise Meiji official art, with its accompanying emphasis on eclecticism, historicism, the archaeologically accurate reproduction of ancient works and the rediscovery of lost skills, particularly pottery glazes. 30 Entrepreneurs such as Kawashima Jimbei, Iida Shinshichi and Hayashi Tadamasa funded the production of elaborate and time-consuming artefacts that were widely acclaimed. Japanese women artists, unlike their Western counterparts, were relegated solely to the Women's Building. 31 Japan's national pavilion was a modified copy of the Hoo-do, Phoenix Hall, in Uji with each of its three sections reproducing the architectural style of the Fujiwara, Ashikaga and Tokugawa periods and their interiors decorated in that style by teachers and students of the Tokyo Art School. 32 A reading of the diverse publications that addressed all segments of society suggest that these impressive efforts were admired but not well understood or even liked.

Nationalism and cultural chauvinism were the luxuries afforded to members of a politically, economically and military strong Japan that had been achieved by dint of the unswerving determination of those Meiji modernisers who pragmatically adapted those elements of Western civilisation necessary to secure Japan a position of parity with the Occidental nations. Western art was an integral part of modern Japanese culture, especially architecture, and *yoga*, was bound to flourish. The return to Japan, after close to a decade of extensive artistic training in Paris, of the socially prominent Kuroda Seiki who, along with his many colleagues and pupils, secured *yoga* a new prestige. He used his political influence to introduce a course on Western art at the Tokyo Art School, and took advantage of the preparations for the Paris Exposition of 1900 to secure the resignation of Kuki and Okakura as directors of both the museum and the art school.

With Francophile circles led by Kuroda Seiki and Hayashi Tadamasa firmly in control, the *yoga* artists were for the first time well represented at the Paris Exposition in 1900. 33 Although Kuroda and many other artists were as accomplished as their Western counterparts and had won awards in European salons, latent exoticism and cultural ethnocentricity led the public to dismiss their efforts as demeaning and deleterious to a nation possessing so remarkable an artistic heritage. Nor were the merits of *nihonga* (traditional-style painting) more readily perceived for even in this most artistically advanced capital, the Gold Medal was awarded to a meticulously rendered painting of a tiger by a comparatively minor painter, Ohashi Suiseki, which was no match for *Tiger* by Kishi Chikudo that was acclaimed in Chicago in 1893. To complement the two major exhibitions fielded by the French, one from its origins to 1800 and another from 1800-1899, the Japanese organised their first retrospective exhibition of Japanese art for which they issued an official history of the art written specially for a Western audience. 34 Art Nouveau, which had been influenced by Japanese art, was triumphant and thereafter made its way to Japan where it, in turn, influenced Japanese art. 35 The many *nihonga* and *yoga* artists who attended the exhibition travelled widely and on their return petitioned the government to establish in 1907 an official salon, the Bunten, that, in keeping with the Japanese spirit of compromise, assured all the dissident factions in the Japanese art world their access to official recognition.

It is not possible within the confines of this brief essay text to discuss the many other major and minor expositions, or any of the lesser exhibitions in which Japan participated or to chart with equal care the shifting policies, diversity of artistic styles and altered perceptions observable over half a century. This abbreviated survey fittingly concludes where it began, in London, with the Japan-British Exhibition held at Shepherd's Bush in 1910. Unlike the other exhibitions, it was a bi-national event, as had been the Franco-British Exhibition of 1908. Britain hoped thereby to strengthen its political, strategic and economic ties with Japan, the major emergent power in East Asia, that had been formalised by the Anglo-Japanese Alliance of 1902 and, more specifically, to safeguard its control of one-quarter of all Japanese imports. While the treaty had undoubtedly facilitated Japan's incursions in the Kwantung area of Southern Manchuria

fig 3
Japanese Shops at the Japan-British Exhibition, London 1910

and impending annexation of Korea, the country was recovering from a severe depression and hoped to redress the trade imbalance by providing England 'with a clearer impression of the great gifts and qualities which lie at the root of Japanese progress'. 36

The exhibition lacked a distinctive Japanese character which was mitigated by the many Japanese gardens scattered about the grounds, including some miniature ones that sought, with the aid of painted backdrops, to reproduce noted Japanese scenic sights. Another prominent feature were the twelve large tableaux with wax figures clad in traditional robes representing major epochs in Japanese history, from Emperor Jimmu to present-day Japan replete with its heroes, Admiral Togo and General Nogi. The war department showed elaborate dioramas of major battles and recent victories. Virtually an entire building was devoted to Japan's 'beneficent' activities in Formosa, Kwantung and Korea. There were native villages where visitors could see carvers, metal workers, lantern makers, potters, fan makers, embroiderers and other artistic craftsmen actually at work, and then go on to savour different brews at the Japanese and Formosan teahouse. Europeans inured to the cheap Japanese goods that had flooded the continent in recent years were all the more impressed by the fine artistic workmanship, the tasteful display and dignity of the Japanese section.

The Palace of Fine Arts offered the critical observer an unparalleled opportunity of comparing the art of both nations. 37 The British retrospective of painting and sculpture apparently was not on a par with what had been shown at the Franco-British Exhibition but the modern school, featuring over 1,000 works by living artists, many of whom have since been consigned to oblivion, was highly praised. The other half of the building revealed to the British public a wider range of Japanese art than hitherto seen. Lawrence Binyon stressed the signal honour accorded the English public by Japan's willingness to send a retrospective exhibition of 'treasures quite beyond price, the finest examples of their greatest masters of all periods, from the eighth to the nineteenth century', which could not be seen even by travellers to Japan. 38 Collectors had reluctantly acquiesced, related Mutsu Hirokichi, 'on the distinct understanding that we shall never again commit such a sacrilege'. 39

Lawrence Binyon praised the excellent copy of the Tamamushi Shrine, the skilfully wrought models of the Kondo of Koryuji and seven other famous temple structures, as well as copies of five lacquer objects belonging to the Imperial Household that were permanently on view. Among the authentic works, which were changed fortnightly, he cited rare examples previously known in the West only through copies and forgeries, or the excellent reproductions in the periodical *Kokka*. 40 An increasing knowledge of early Italian painting was thought to have made the British more receptive to the beauty of Oriental art and such an early painting as the *Juichimen Kannon*, belonging to Inoue Kaoru, was believed to possess the sublimity of a Piero della Francesca. 41 The first 'authentic' landscapes by Shubun to be seen in Europe were admired for their precision and delicacy while the several Sesshus were found disappointing. Binyon thought the Ukiyo-e paintings less attractive than the prints but praised the works of Matabei and Korin. Many of the most admired early paintings, ironically, have since been reattributed and certainly the list of noted collectors should dispell the myth that the nobility were so impoverished after the Restoration that they disposed of all their art treasures. The twenty-two works lent by Kuki Ryuichi bear witness to the considerable benefits that accrued to Meiji bureaucrats! 42

While the Japanese were praised for 'working in the great Chinese tradition and having made it their own', the modern works were criticised for betraying the struggle between Eastern and Western ideals, both old and new. The forty-one *nihonga* paintings, selected on the basis of their popularity in the Bunten, were judged inferior to the old masters but easier to understand and the eighteen *yoga* paintings, although admittedly

In Japanese Section,
Japan-British Exhibition, London, 1910.

Cat.352
Postcard of the
Japan-British Exhibition, London 1910

somewhat tame, were considered better than those exhibited in St Louis in 1904 and hopefully would continue to improve. 43 A comparison of the applied arts confirmed the undiminished skill of modern Japanese craftsmen but some lessening of their sense of colour and design. The textiles, including those in Building 13, were highly praised and found moreover to be reasonably priced. If some supernatural means of communication could be found, the envoys who attended the exhibition of 1862 would have been gladdened to learn that among the Japanese works that impressed visitors to the Japan-British Exhibition of 1910 was an embroidered wall-hanging that reproduced the *Hibo Kannon* of Kano Hogai executed by Sugawara Naosuke who had laboured for three years, at the behest of the president of the Japan Mail Steamship Company, to render by means of 12,100 different shades of silk and twelve shades of gold thread the most delicate effects of drapery, clouds and atmosphere. 44 As at the outset, so at the conclusion of the Meiji era, it was still the technical virtuosity and exotic subject-matter of Japanese art that elicited the greatest Western admiration.

III

There was more than a modicum of truth in the wry quip of a Japanese diplomat 'that his people had been sending artistic treasures to Europe for some time, and had been regarded as barbarians, but that, as soon as they showed themselves able to shoot down Russians with quick-firing guns, they were acclaimed as a highly civilised race', and if 'a juster impression of the capacity and achievements of the Japanese people prevails today', it was precisely because of Japan's waxing political and military rights! 45 The trade imbalance persisted and was not easily or rapidly redressed. Culturally the exposition afforded the British an opportunity to view 'the range and excellence of the artistic genius and achievement of the Japanese race' but, half a century after Alcock, the views expressed in the popular press were still strangely far of the mark.

It was said that since Whistler had first extolled Japanese prints and 'praised the daintiness and the exquisite frivolity of Oriental art', the British had come to realise that the Japanese had little regard for Ukiyo-e prints or its antecedent school of painting, as compared with 'their more serious religious and landscape art, which was mainly an imitation of a still greater Japanese art' and it was this aptitude for imitation that accounted for their successful 'imitation of European nations in the art of war'. Although their painting expressed profound religious emotion and delight in the beauties of nature, and possessed qualities comparable to those of Fra Angelico, Piero

Cat.358
TAKEUCHI SEIHO (1864-1942)
Moon in Venice, 1904

della Francesca and Michelangelo, it lacked the expressive power of Michelangelo's *Creation of Adam* or Titian's last *Pieta* or Rembrandt's *Supper at Emmaus*. Later Japanese painting was considered 'incessantly witty, which makes its brilliant decorative schemes more interesting than modern European decorative painting'. 46 Variations on these themes were sounded by the authors of the many books on Japanese art that appeared in the course of the next decade or two.

As half a century earlier, it was the influx of Western ideas that evoked the gravest misgivings. *Nihonga* was thought to 'cleave too religiously to their traditions,' and *yoga* to be 'but a weak reflection of the teaching of Dusseldorf, of Munich, of Paris, London even'. Japan was still being admonished, as by Ernest F. Fenollosa almost three decades earlier, to 'realise that, in the practice of her own methods, she holds a great and enviable treasure, by the loss of which the world will be poorer' and that Western ideas should merely 'strengthen and inspire adherents of old tradition rather than weaken them'. 47 The demise of traditional architecture for other than domestic dwellings was also deemed imminent by a writer who portentously declared that 'if she can only secure scientific, political, and commercial progress at the price of the loss of her traditional arts, her loss may be almost greater than her gain'. 48

Such apprehensions concerning the survival of Japanese art, its aesthetic integrity and the deleterious effects of Western influence was a persistent refrain of commentators on these exhibitions throughout the Meiji era. A retrospective reading of their views reveals how woefully unaware they were of the realities that confronted Japanese authorities and artists alike and how ill-equipped are many current authors to evaluate such comments in the context of the period and in relation to the artistic quandaries confronting both Japan and the West. Seeking first to study the influence of Japan on Occidental art of the nineteenth and early twentieth centuries, scholars then investigated Western Japonisme and, in their search for prototypes, made valiant effort to identify, by means of fragmentary records bearing vague entries and garbled spelling that survive in European institutions and the scant reproductions, the actual objects displayed in these exhibitions. They have belatedly come to realise that, apart from retrospective art exhibitions, the bulk of what was displayed was not only of recent manufacture, but conceived and designed for that purpose. Many of these objects were acquired by the new museums and collections established at that time but as the individuals involved became acquainted with a wider range of Japanese art, these early acquisitions were deemed decadent and debased; many were deaccessioned and others relegated to basement storerooms where they languished and deteriorated. Some of the more traditional pieces were ascribed to early periods. This deprecatory attitude has only recently abated and rising market values have bought to public view a wide variety of wares that are still difficult to identify for want of comprehensive studies of the various Japanese crafts of the Meiji era. Much that was thought lost is being resurrected and collections long ignored are finally being inventoried and catalogued. Through such pioneering attempts at 'dialogue' as this exhibition, it should eventually be possible to gain a better understanding of the contents of these early exhibits, a more just evaluation of their merits and a more informed consideration of the forces at work.

NOTES
1 John Allwood, *The Great Exhibitions* (London *c.* 1977), p.8
2 Robert W. Rydell, *All the World's a Fair: Visions of the Empire at American International Expositions, 1876-1916* (Chicago and London 1984), p.4
3 Yamamoto Mitsuo, *Nihon hakurankai shi* (Tokyo 1970), pp.199-205. He does not include the two exhibitions in which Japan participated prior to the Meiji Exhibition of 1867; his overall count is subdivided into world exhibitions, special exhibitions focusing on specific technologies or media, and mutual Exhibition which involve two countries. Allwood, op. cit., pp.180-5, considers only forty-nine of these expositions to be international and thereby excludes the Japan-British exhibitions of 1910
4 *Official Report of the Japan-British Exhibition, 1910* at the Great White City, Shepherd's Bush, London (London 1911), pp.310, 313

5 Allwood, op cit., p.25; Elizabeth Gilmore Holt ed., *The Art of All Nations 1850-1873: The Emerging Role of Exhibitions and Critics* (Princeton, 1982), p.361, fn.10; Yoshida Mitsukuni, *Zusetsu bankoku hakurankai shi* (Tokyo 1985), pp.138, 174

6 Geneviève Lacambre, 'Chronologie', Galeries nationales du Grand Palais, *Le Japonisme* (Paris 1988), p.68; for reproduction of painting, see Yvonne Bruhammer, 'National, International and Universal Expositions and the French Decorative Arts', Cooper-Hewitt Museum, *L'Art de Vivre, Decorative Arts and Design in France 1789-1989* (New York 1989), p.57

7 Holt, op. cit., p.357

8 Rutherford Alcock, *The Capital of the Tycoon: A Narrative of Three Years' Residence in Japan*, 2nd ed. (New York, 1877) vol. II, p.247

9 London, International Exhibition 1862, *Catalogue of Works of Industry and Art, Sent from Japan by Rutherford Alcock* (London 1862)

10 Toshio Watanabe, 'The Western Image of Japanese Art in the Late Edo Period', *Modern Asian Studies*, 18, 4 (1984), p.669; Tanita Kiryoki?, 'Eikoku ni okeru Jyapanizumu no keisei ni kansuru joron', *Hikaku bangaku nenso*, 22 (1986), pp.90-2.

11 John Ayers et al., *Porcelain for Palaces: The Fashion for Japan in Europe 1650-1750* (London 1990)

12 The author is indebted to Dr C.J.A. Jorg of Groninger Museum, Groningen, The Netherlands, for this valuable information concerning his ongoing study of these records

13 Alcock, op. cit., vol. II, pp.241-3

14 J. B. Waring, *Masterpieces of Industrial Art and Sculpture at the International Exhibition 1862* (London 1863) vol. III, pp.209, 300

15 'The International Exhibition 1862', *The Art Journal Catalogue of the International Exhibition* 24 (London 1862), p.11

16 Ellen P. Conant, 'Principles and Pragmatism: The *Yatoi* in the Field of Art, Edward R. Beauchamp and Akira Irie ed., *Foreign Employees in Nineteenth Century Japan* (Boulder 1990), pp.140-1, 144

17 J. Beavington Atkinson, 'Art in its influence on Art-Manufacture', *The Art Journal Catalogue of the International Exhibition* 24 (London, 1862), p.298

18 Ellen P. Conant, 'The French Connection: Emile Guimet's Mission to Japan, A Cultural Context for Japonisme', Hilary Conroy, Sandra T. W. Davis and Wayne Patterson, *Japan in Transition: Thought and Action in the Meiji Era, 1868-1912* (Rutherford, 1984), pp.114-17

19 Eugene Rimmel, *Recollections of the Paris Exhibition of 1867* (Philadelphia 1868), p.252

20 Josef Kreiner, 'Heinrich Freiherr von Siebold: ein Beitrag zur Geschichte der Japanischen Völkerkunde und Urgeschichte', *Beiträge zur Japanischen Ethnogense: 100 Jahre nach Heinrich von Siebold* (Bonn 1980), furnishes valuable material about the careers of both brothers

21 Conant, *A French Connection*, pp.128-31

22 Wagner's report, translated into Japanese by Asami Tadamasa, appears in 'Okoku Hakurankai Jimukyoku', *Okoku hakurankai hokokusho: hakubutsukan bu ni* (Tokyo 1875) n.p.

23 Ellen P. Conant, 'Meiji shoki Nihon ni okeru bijutsu to seiji, Fenorosa no eikyo o megutte', Haga Toru et al., *Kindai Nihon no shiso to geijutsu* (Tokyo 1974), pp.61-85. Japanese exhibition studies have eschewed discussion of broader political issues such as racism, dealt with by Rydell, op. cit.

24 William Hosley, *The Japan Idea: Art and Life in Victorian America* (Hartford 1990)

25 Hida Toyohiro, *Kiritsu Kosho Kaisha, The First Japanese Manufacturing and Trading Co.* (Kyoto 1987); see also Hasegawa Sakae, 'The Kiritsu Kosho Kaisha', *Andon*, 9,4 (1989) No.36 pp.121-31

26 Makoto Shioda, *Japanese pottery, being a native report*, translated from the Japanese into English by T. Asami and edited by A. W. Franks, with an introduction and catalogue by A. W. Franks, (London 1880). Although involved in these expositions through to 1910, there is as yet no adequate study of Shioda

27 William Anderson, *Descriptive and Historical Catalogue of a Collection of Japanese and Chinese Painting in the British Museum* (London, 1886)

28 For background see Takahashi Shinji, 'Kuki Ryuichi', Fukuzawa Yukichi nenkan, 3 parts, 1982-83. It is interesting that an individual who, according to the author of an ongoing study, Hiroko McDermott, had no secure political base could wield such influence in the field of art

29 In as much as Japanese art was not exhibited in the art building at the Paris Exposition of 1889, it is worth comparing the American classifications contained in the Office of the Director General, World's Columbian Exposition, *General Regulations for Foreign Exhibitors at the World's Columbian Exposition in Chicago* (Chicago, 1891) and the correspondence concerning these rules contained in the Rinji hakurankai jimukyoku, *Shikago rinji hakurankai jimukyoku hokoku* (Tokyo 1985)

30 World's Columbian Exposition, 1893, *Official Catalogue*, Part X, Department K: *Fine Arts* (Chicago 1893) and World's Columbian Exposition, *Revised Catalogue, Department of Fine Arts* (Chicago 1893) which lists what was actually exhibited and where it was installed

31 World's Columbian Exposition, 1893, *Official Catalogue*, Part XIV, *Women's Building* (Chicago 1893), pp.111-12. At the Paris Exposition of 1900, the women artists exhibited alongside the men

32 Okakura Kakuzo, *The Ho-o-den*, An illustrated description of the buildings erected by the Japanese government at the World's Columbian Exposition, Jackson Park, Chicago (Tokyo, 1893)

33 Paris, Exposition internationale universelle de 1990, *Catalogue Général Officiel*, II. Group II. *Oeuvres d'art*, Classes 7 and 10 (Paris 1900), pp.465-80. It is worth noting that *nihonga* and *yoga* are not subdivided in the catalogue, although they are invariably discussed that way in Japanese texts. In order to conform to French categories, however, the exhibition was limited to painting, sculpture and three architectural projects

34 Japan, The Imperial Japanese Commission to the Paris Universal Exposition, 1900, *Histoire de l'Art du Japon* (Paris 1900). This text was later published by Japan, Teishitsu hakubutsukan, Tokyo, *A history of Japanese arts*. Translated by Takenobu and K. Kawakami from the Japanese original compiled by the Imperial Museum under the control of Baron R. Kuki, rev. ed. (Tokyo 1908). The copy in Avery Library, Columbia University, bears the note that 'The present compilation was undertaken at the instance of the French Exhibition Affairs Office of the Imperial Government for the Paris World's Fair held in 1900'. the contretemps over the preparation of this volume merits a study in and of itself

35 Philippe Jullian, The Triumph of Art Nouveau: Paris Exhibition 1900 (New York 1974)

36 'Japanese Pictures at the Japan-British Exhibition', *Morning Post*, 14 May, 1910, *The British Press and the Japan-British Exhibition*, privately printed by Count Hirokichi Mutsu (London *c.* 1911), Part I, p.61

37 London, Japan-British Exhibition, 1910. *Fine Arts Catalogue* (London 1910); see also A. L. Baldry, 'The Japan-British Exhibition', *Art Journal*, 72 (London, 1910), p.257-64

38 Lawrence Binyon, 'Japanese Masterpieces in London', *Saturday Review*, 28 May, 1910, *The British Press*, Part I, p.77

39 Hirokichi Mutsu, *Japan at the White City*, a paper read before The Royal Society of Arts, London, January 19, 1910 (London 1910), p.9

40 *Kokka*, Essence of Japan, was founded in 1889 by Takahashi Kenzo and Okakura Kakuzo soon after they were appointed respectively director of publications for the Cabinet and Chief Curator of the Tokyo Imperial Museum. It was noted for its excellent articles and fine reproductions of major works of art in the possession of temples, shrines, nobility and private collectors. Originally printed solely in Japanese, English summaries of articles and illustrations were included from April 1902 to June 1905 and from July 1918 to the present; from July 1905 to June 1918 the text was printed entirely in English and was a major source for Binyon and others interested in the traditional arts of Japan

41 London, Japan-British Exhibition, 1901, *An Illustrated Catalogue of Japanese Old Fine Arts* (Tokyo 1910), No. 2, where it is attributed to Kose no Kanaoka, but the article, 'Japanese Pictures at the Japan-British Exhibition II', *The Times*, 6 June, 1910, *The British Press*, Part II, p.8, points out that, 'according to Mr Binyon, experts ... will not allow him a single authentic work'. Journalists were clearly relying on two recently published works by Binyon, *Painting in the Far East. An introduction to the history of pictorial art in Asia, especially China and Japan* (London 1908) and *Japanese Art* (London 1909)

41 The only other single individual to exhibit a larger number of works was Fukuba Toru, who issued a separate catalogue, see London, Japan-British Exhibition, 1910, *Catalogue of Fukuba's Collection of Ukiyo-ye Paintings* to be shown at the Japan-British Exhibition (London 1910). The owner, whose real name is Kuwabara Yojiro, had a French edition published the following year when the paintings were exhibited at the Musée des Arts Décoratifs of the Louvre

42 London, Japan-British Exhibition, 1910, *An Illustrated Catalogue of the Japanese Modern Fine Arts* (Tokyo 1910). Shimbi Shoin also published that same year Japanese versions of both the Old Fine Arts and Modern Arts catalogues

43 Mutsu, op. cit., p.10

44 'The Anglo-Japanese Exhibition', *Morning Post*, 14 May, 1910, *The British Press*, Part I, pp.60-1

45 'Japanese Painting', *The Times*, 10 September, 1910, *The British Press*, Part IV, p.3

46 'Japanese Art, Old and New', *Westminster Gazette*, 26 November, 1910, *The British Press*, Part IV, p.31

47 'Japanese Architecture', *Illustrated Carpenter and Builder*, 1 July, 1910, *The British Press*, Part II, pp.25-7

48 Phylis Floyd, *Japonisme in Context: documentation, criticism, aesthetic reactions*, Ph.D. Thesis, University of Michigan (Ann Arbor 1983)

Cat.361
ISHIBASHI KAZUNORI (1876-1928)
A Woman reading Poetry, 1906

CATALOGUE

CONTENTS

The authors of the catalogue entries are noted by the following initials:
TS - Tomoko Sato; TW - Toshio Watanabe

NOTES TO USERS

Within each section entries for individual works are arranged chronologically, grouped under the same artist, manufacturer or topic. Except for the editors and contributors, Japanese names are given, following convention, surname before given name(s), unless otherwise stated. Accents are omitted in the transliteration of Japanese names and terms. Measurements are in centimetres. For two-dimensional works image sizes are given height before width. For three-dimensional works, including pottery, height (H) before width (W) or diameter (D), followed by depth (D). Widest dimensions are given for the measurements of the objects of irregular shapes.

The literature (LIT) cited at the end of the bibliographies and the entries only indicates major or latest publications, and is in no way comprehensive. The sources directly related to the subject of the exhibition are indicated by authors' names followed by publication dates, and reference should be made to the Selected Bibliography at the back (pp.169-172) where full information can be found. Other sources are given in full, but are excluded from the bibliography.

The placing of signatures and inscriptions on the work is indicated by the following abbreviations: t.r. - top right; b.r. - bottom right; r.c. - right centre; t.c. - top centre; b.c. - bottom centre; l.c. - left centre; t.l. - top left; b.l. - bottom left

Certain schools and exhibition bodies are abbreviated in places as follows:
RA - Royal Academy of Arts; NEAC - New English Art Club; RSA - Royal Scottish Academy

Cat.1
ARNOLDUS MONTANUS
(c.1625-1683)
Atlas Japannensis, 1670
(Title page)

THE EMBASSAYS TO
THE
EMPEROURS
OF
JAPAN

Cum.
prevelegien

I. PROLOGUE

ARNOLDUS MONTANUS (c.1625-1683)

Montanus's *Gesantschappen aen de Kaisaren van Japan cum prevelegien* was published in Amsterdam in 1669. It was one of the most celebrated travel books of the seventeenth century in Europe and contained a description of the geographical, cultural and natural features of Japan. The English edition, *Atlas Japannensis* (Cat.1), was published in the following year in London, translated by John Ogilby (1600-1676), the writer and geographical printer, illustrated with over a hundred engravings. Cats 2 and 3 are plates taken from the English edition.

1
Atlas Japannensis
Translated by John Ogilby, published in London 1670, 39.6 x 26 cm
The Japan Society, London

2
Iedo, 1670
Coloured engraving, 28 x 77 cm
Sir Hugh and Lady Cortazzi

This panoramic view of Edo (today's Tokyo) is taken from a traditional viewpoint on imaginary high ground, and depicts groups of Japanese engaged in various activities. In this print, the mountain with a waterfall seen on the far right is 'Tacajama' (Takayama), and Edo Castle, described as the 'Emperor's banqueting house', is seen in the centre on the horizon.

3
The City Osacco, 1670
Coloured engraving, 26 x 69 cm
Sir Hugh and Lady Cortazzi

Osaka is seen from Osaka Bay, and is depicted as a prosperous commercial city, busy with trading ships and fishing boats. Impressive rows of storehouses are seen above the pier in the centre. Although the key does not give the names of buildings, it includes 'Water Castle', 'Temple with 263 images', and 'Temple with an image of 50 foot high [sic]' as interesting features of the city.

ENGELBERT KÄMPFER (1651-1716)

Born in Lemgo, in northern Germany, Kämpfer was a physician and traveller. He arrived at Nagasaki in 1690 as the physician to the Dutch East India Company's station there. He stayed in Japan for two years, and twice accompanied the Dutch station director to Edo, where he had an opportunity to meet the Fifth Tokugawa Shogun Tsunayoshi (1646-1709). *The History of Japan* was written on his return to Germany and was based on his observations and research in Japan, but he could not find a publisher before his death in 1716. Then Sir Hans Sloane (1660-1753) bought

the manuscript and it was in London where his writings were published for the first time in the English language, edited and translated by Sloane's Swiss secretary, Johann Caspar Scheuchzer (Cat.4). This book was illustrated with many copper plates based on Kämpfer's sketches but, as Beatrice M. Bodart-Bailey has shown, modified and Westernised by Scheuchzer.

LIT : Kreiner 1990

4
The History of Japan (two vols)
Translated by Johann Caspar Scheuchzer, published in London 1727, 35.3 x 24 cm
The Japan Society, London

EMANUEL BOWEN (dates unknown)

5
A New and Accurate Map of the Empire of Japan
Published in London 1747
Coloured engraving, 35 x 43 cm
Signed and inscribed t.l.: Laid down from the Memoirs of the/ Portuguese and Dutch;/and particularly from the Jesuit Missionaries,/as publish'd by the St Bellin at Paris,/Being adjusted by/Astronomical Observations/By Eman. Bowen
Sir Hugh and Lady Cortazzi

The way in which the area to the north of Honshu (main island) is depicted is noteworthy, as is the inclusion of the Land of Dwarfs, seen in so many Japanese maps of the period. 'Kubiteshima', the north-western island of 'Ooshima', in the Straights of 'Kamtshatka [sic]', is described thus: 'Japanese say "Tis [sic] inhabited by the Pigmyes"'. The map also gives other information regarding 'Tsussima [sic]' (Tsushima), north-west of Kyushu: 'Small Desart [sic] Islands on some of which the Japanese are said to keep Garrisons.'

JAPANESE

6
Tankard with Silver-gilt Rim, 1660-80
Porcelain painted in Kakiemon colours, H.15 cm
Burghley House, Stamford

LIT : Lang 1983 (83); *The Burghley Porcelains* 1986 (98 pair); Ayers et al. 1990 (87)

A tankard of European form, decorated with Japanese motifs in the Kakiemon colours red, blue and turquoise. The siver-gilt mouthrim is a European addition. The term 'Kakiemon' derived from Sakaida Kakiemon in Arita, south-west of Kyushu, who was the legendary inventor of a red enamelling technique after a Chinese example. A large number of hybrid porcelain wares of this kind were produced for the European market.

JAPANESE

7
Two Goblets, 1670-90
Porcelain painted in Kakiemon colours, H. 13.5 cm each
Burghley House, Stamford

LIT : Lang 1983 (85); *The Burghley Porcelains* 1986 (107); Ayers et al. 1990 (89)

These export-ware goblets also show European shapes and are enamelled in delicate colours developed in the mid-seventeenth century in Japan.

JAPANESE

8
Pair of Ingot-shaped Dishes, c.1680
Blue and white porcelain, D. 16 cm each
Burghley House, Stamford

WORCESTER PORCELAIN COMPANY

The firm was founded in 1752 in Worcester, following a union of the two factories, one based in Bristol and the other, the 'Worcester Tonquin Manufacture'. Its London shop was opened in the following year for the sale of its products. Following the examples of Bow in Sheffield and Chelsea in London, the Worcester Company began to adopt Kakiemon motifs in the 1760s.

9
Cup and Saucer, 1765
Porcelain, painted in Kakiemon colours and gilt
Cup: H.3.2 cm, D. 8.3 cm, Saucer: D. 14 cm
Trustees of the Victoria and Albert Museum, London

The design shows a skilful mixture of Kakiemon motifs and colours, especially red, and the Rococo rocaille and colours, especially turquoise and gold.

10
Pair of Vases with Cover, 1765
Porcelain, painted in Kakiemon colours and gilt
H. 28 cm and 28.9 cm
Trustees of the Victoria and Albert Museum, London

This type is called a 'Hampton Court' jar, because of a famous pair of Japanese jars in Hampton Court Palace, which must have been produced as export ware, as matching a pair of such jars is regarded as a Western taste.

11

Plate, 1765-70
Porcelain painted in Imari-style, D.24.8 cm
Mark: a simulated Chinese character in blue
Trustees of the Victoria and Albert Museum,
London

LIT : Ayers et al. 1990 (350), (238)

The term 'Imari' is derived from the port of this
name, from which the porcelain ware from the
Arita area was exported. Imari ware was often
characterised with the combination of underglaze
blue and overglaze enamel. Cat.11 shows rich
decorations of geometrical and floral motifs,
executed in this style. There is a Japanese Imari
plate in the Victoria and Albert Museum which
may be the original model for this Worcester
plate.

JAPANESE AND ENGLISH

12

Lacquer Cabinet with Carved Wood Stand, c.1680
Japanese lacquer cabinet inlaid with mother-of-
pearl and carved gilt stand
Cabinet: 43 x 69 x 61 cm; stand: H. 74 cm
Burghley House, Stamford

Throughout the seventeenth and eighteenth
centuries, Japanese lacquer cabinets were
fashionable as exotic and useful furniture. This
cabinet, mounted on the Baroque-style gilt stand

made by the English manufacturers, entered the
inventory of Burghley House, the home of the
Earls of Exeter, in 1688. It has two doors hinged
to reveal eight small drawers, with carrying
handles at the sides. The panels are decorated
with inlays of mother-of-pearl, a Japanese
technique, which was particularly admired
at the time.

MARTIN CARLIN (?-1785)

13

Lady's Writing Desk, c.1780
Oak carcass veneered in ebony with panels of
black and gold Japanese lacquer and mounted in
ormolu, H. 78.8 cm, W. 45.7 cm, D. 34.3 cm
Trustees of the Victoria and Albert Museum,
London

Martin Carlin, who produced some of the most
elegant Louis XVI furniture, was a German but
moved to Paris, and in 1766 became a maître-
ébéniste. This piece with an adjustable reading-
stand incorporates many Japanese lacquer plates.
The front panel shows circular motifs arranged
in an asymmetrical manner with one pair
overlapping and the others cut off at the edge
of the panel. This desk belonged to John Jones,
a famous Victorian collector, who also owned a
bookcase which contains painted roundels by
Dante Gabriel Rossetti (see Section IV) to whom
and possibly to W.E. Nesfield (see Section V),
this table may have been known.

Cat.14

JAPANESE

14

Plaque of the Portrait of John Locke,
last quarter 18th century
Metal, covered in black lacquer with gold
hiramaki-e lacquer decoration and gold details,
12.2 x 9.3 cm
Inscribed top: Jean Locke; and back: Philosophe:
né en 1632, mort en 1704
Trustees of the Victoria and Albert Museum,
London

LIT : *The Silk Road on the Sea* 1982, pp.220-6; Earle
1986, p.158

The large-scale export of Japanese lacquer ended
by the late seventeenth century, but around the
end of the eighteenth century a number of
lacquer plaques with portraits of famous
personalities from European history since
Roman times were produced for export. These
were copied from European books and even
imitate the fine stippling of the engraving.
Cat.14 was based on a portrait by Sir Godfrey
Kneller (1646-1723) reproduced in Dreux du
Radier's *L'Europe illustré*, published in Paris in
1777. There is another plaque of John Milton's
portrait in the Rijksmuseum in Amsterdam.

Cat.18

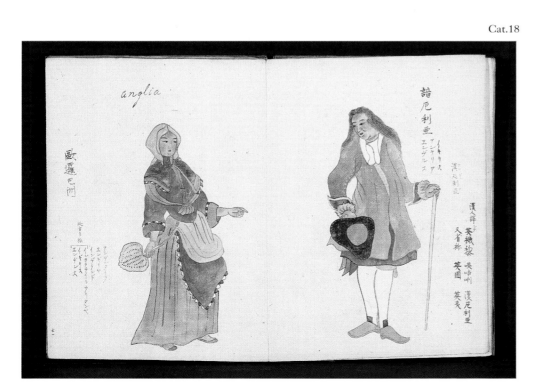

Cat.15   Cat.16

ISHIKAWA MOKO (dates unknown)

Despite being the younger brother of Ishikawa Tairo (c.1765-1817), the Edo-born painter and scholar of Dutch painting, very little is known about his life and work except for Cat.15 and *Flowers and Birds*, which he painted with his brother in 1796 after the Dutch painter, Willem van Roijen. Van Roijen's painting was commissioned by the Shogun's Household, painted in oil in 1725 and shipped to Nagasaki in 1726. The painting was later donated to the Gohyakurakanji Temple in Honjo, but badly damaged and lost by the end of the Edo period.

15
A Girl and Her Cat, c.1796
Ink on silk (hanging scroll), 115 x 50 cm
Signed and sealed b.c.: Miss Trimmer/door
Leeuw Berg
Yamato Bunkakan Museum, Nara

LIT : Sakamoto 1972, pp.26-8; *Development of Western Realism in Japan* 1985 - 6 (89)

This ink painting is based on an English print (Cat. 16), which reached Japan probably through the Dutch trade. It is signed in Dutch 'door Leeuw Berg' but the English inscription 'Miss Trimmer' is a faithful copy from the print. To the 'progressive' Japanese scholars and artists, European prints were rare and important sources of information from which they could learn new ideas of perspective and light and shade - the way to represent the world realistically - based on scientific observations. Copying was traditionally regarded as the best means of learning in every field of science and arts, and scholars and artists copied European examples to understand their techniques.

16
AFTER CATHERINE READ 1723-1778
Miss Trimmer, mid-17th century
Mezzotint, engraved by James Watson
Yamato Bunkakan Museum, Nara

LIT : Sakamoto 1972, July, pp.26-8; *Development of Western Realism in Japan* 1985 - 6 (89)

The print is a reproduction of the painting by Catherine Read. She was born in Scotland and trained in Paris. Read was active in London from 1745 onwards and known as a portrait painter of celebrated ladies. Mezzotint was a popular means of reproducing of paintings in the eighteenth century, particularly in England. The print bears the price '2" [shillings]' and the shop's name 'Ryland & Bryer at the Kings Arms, Cornhill'. A version in glass-coloured print also exists.

ISAAC TITSINGH (?-1812)

Titsingh, formerly chief agent to the Dutch East India Company at Nagasaki, lived in Japan for fourteen years. While in Japan, he collected a large number of Japanese artefacts, including books, paintings, maps and coins. On his return, he published his writings on Japanese history and culture through the French publisher, Nepveu. In 1818, six years after his death, Titsingh's manuscripts and Japanese collection were bought by Nepveu. Translated into English by Frederic Shoberl, Cat.17 was compiled from Titsingh's manuscripts and consisted of his private memoirs, observation of Japanese manners and customs, and remarks on Japanese literature and art.

17
Illustrations of Japan
Translated by Frederic Shoberl, published in London, 1822.
Illustrated with 13 colour plates, engraved by R. Ackermann, London
32.2 x 26 cm
The Japan Society, London

The book includes thirteen coloured prints reproducing Japanese originals, including illustrations of marriage and funeral ceremonies. In the translator's address, Shoberl welcomed the access to such comprehensive information, and, referring to a relaxation of Japan's isolation policy since the beginning of the nineteenth century, he urged Britain's serious consideration 'for attempting with some chance of success to establish a connexion with this populous insular empire'.

TEIBIEN JOSHUN (dates unknown)

18
Illustrations of Foreign Peoples and a Russian Embassy to Japan, 1840
Coloured manuscript, ink and watercolour on Japanese paper, folding album, 28 x 20.2 cm
Signed and sealed: Teibien Joshun
The Japan Society, London

Reflecting growing Japanese interest in foreign countries, many illustrations of foreigners were produced from the late eighteenth century onwards. This manuscript, entitled in Japanese *Jisshoku Ichiran (Catalogue of True Colours)*, is a copy of illustrations produced in the early 1820s. On one side it shows pictures of foreigners from more than twenty countries, ranging from Asians to Europeans. The English man and woman are depicted in eighteenth-century costumes, under the title 'anglia'. Note that great attention is paid to the details of costumes.

On the other side is an account of a Russian delegation who sailed from St Petersburg on 11 August 1803 and reached Japan in September 1804. It records that there were eighty-five people on board including four Japanese who had been picked up after being shipwrecked, and gives detailed accounts of the Russian crew, their uniforms, religion and customs, accompanied by coloured illustrations and a world map.

Little is known about the artist, Joshun, whose studio name was Teibien from Edo, but the British Library has a book illustrated by the artist, also called 'Joshun'. The book, *Hyoryu-ki (An Account of a Castaway)* (1863), is on a similar subject, which is Hamada Hikozo's account of his American experience after being shipwrecked, and the signature in this book might be by the same hand as the illustrator of Cat.18.

NOTE
We are grateful to Yu-Ying Brown at the British Library for assisting in reading the manuscript and for information about the *Hyoryu-ki*.

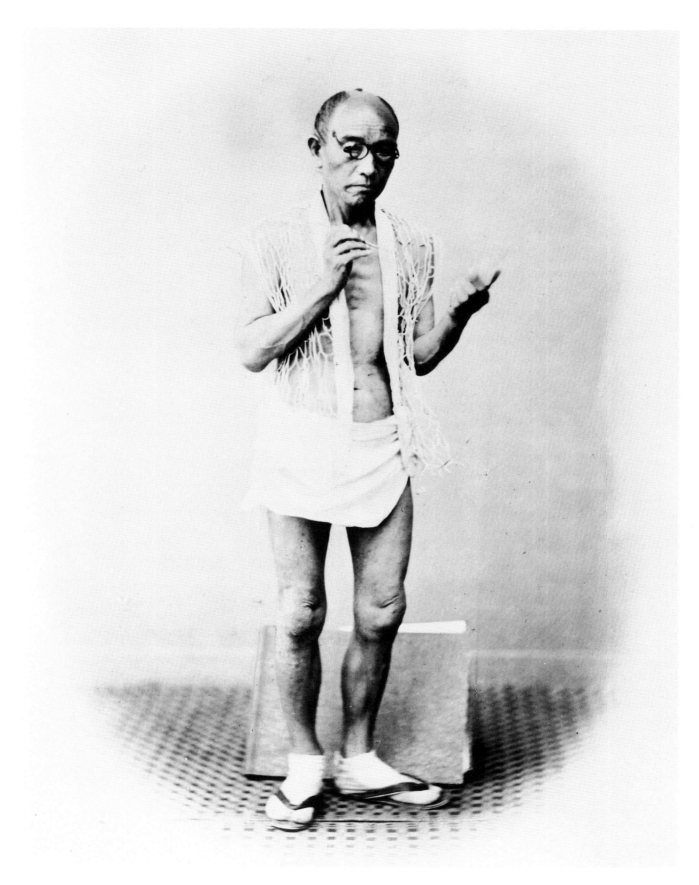

Cat.33 FELIX BEATO (1825-?) *Our Artist*, c.1867-68

II. THE OPENING UP OF JAPAN

19

The Ambassador's 'Full Powers' document signed by Queen Victoria with Sealed Silver Box
Lord Elgin

James Bruce, the 8th Earl of Elgin (1811-1863), was appointed British High Commissioner and Plenipotentiary in the spring of 1857 to open up relations with China and Japan. At the time, the British-Chinese relationship had been strained due to the 'Opium War' followed by the Treaty of Nanking of 1842, which resulted in the handing over of Hong Kong to Britain. While China was hoping to abandon the treaty, Britain wished to revise it to expand the British market further. Anti-British feeling spread among the Chinese, culminating in 1856 in the 'Arrow' incident, in which the Union Jack was taken down from the British ship of that name. This gave the British a pretext to send Lord Elgin's mission to China.

LAURENCE OLIPHANT (1829-1888)

When Oliphant became Lord Elgin's private secretary in 1854, he was an established writer and had travelled widely in Asia and the Crimea. Oliphant accompanied Lord Elgin, then Governor-General of Canada, to Washington in order to conclude the Reciprocity Treaty with Canada. For Lord Elgin's expedition to the Far East, Oliphant was again appointed as his secretary and was later to provide a two-volume account of the voyage (Cat.20). Oliphant returned to Japan in 1861 when he became the first Secretary of the British Legation. Within a week, on the night of 5 July, the Legation was attacked by a band of assassins, who were hostile to the policy of opening up Japan. Together with Charles Wirgman, the correspondent of *The Illustrated London News* (see Section IX), Oliphant survived though he was seriously injured.

20

Narrative of the Earl of Elgin's Mission to China and Japan in the Years 1857, '58 and '59,
Edinburgh and London 1859, Vol.II,
22 x 14.7 x 4 cm
Lord Elgin

Accompanied by his brother Frederick Bruce and Oliphant, Lord Elgin set off for the Far East in April 1857 and reached Hong Kong in early July. The task in China was not easy: eventually Lord Elgin secured the Treaty of Tientsin in June 1858, which provided for the posting of a British minister to Peking, but, to his great regret, only after the bombardment and occupation of Canton. By the time Lord Elgin reached the Bay of Nagasaki on 3 August of that year, the Japanese authorities had heard the news of what had taken place in China.

Japan features in the second volume of Oliphant's report, illustrated with colour engravings based on Captain Bedwell's watercolours (Cat. 21). The volume contains colour reproductions of Japanese woodcuts by Kunisada and Hiroshige.

Cat.28

CAPTAIN F. B. BEDWELL, RN
(dates unknown)

21

Sketches in China and Japan, 1858-59
Album of watercolours bound in red morocco leather, 32.5 x 46.8 cm
Lord Elgin

This album includes sixteen Japanese scenes, recording Lord Elgin's visit to Japan. They cover the period from the time of arrival at Nagasaki to the climax of his stay: the delivery of the steam yacht *Emperor*, Queen Victoria's present to the Shogun, following the conclusion of the Treaty of Edo. The four watercolours below are taken from this album.

A. *Residence of the Earl of Elgin, YEDDO*, 1858
Watercolour on paper, 23 x 32.4 cm
Signed b.l.: F. le. B. Bedwell
The British party were accommodated in the Tozenji Temple near Shinagawa on the edge of Edo Bay. 1 European-style furniture and beds were specially provided. Tozenji was to house the British Legation in 1859 when the first British Consul-General, Rutherford Alcock was posted to Japan.

B. *Interview between the British Ambassador and the Prime Ministers [sic] of Japan, at the Imperial Palace, Yeddo*, 1858
Watercolour on paper, 23.5 x 32 cm
Signed b.l.: F. le. B. Bedwell

The 'Imperial Palace' in the caption meant Edo Castle, the residence of the Shogun. Lord Elgin found its moats 'spectacular' and 'really very grand' 2 To most of the Westerners at that time, the distinction between the 'Shogun', the head of the Tokugawa government, and the 'Mikado' (Emperor), the spiritual head of the nation who resided in Kyoto, was not clear. In this watercolour, the British party are seen on the right and the Japanese Commissioners on the left. The man crouching in the middle is probably the chief Japanese interpreter, Moriyama Einosuke.

C. *Exchange of Full Powers between the British Ambassador and the Japanese Commissioners, Yeddo*, 1858
Watercolour on paper, 24 x 36 cm
Signed b.l. vertically on the pillar:
F. le. B. Bedwell

Negotiations were carried out in English, Japanese and Dutch assisted by the Dutch interpreter, Hendrick Heusken, who had been borrowed from the American Legation 3 Dutch was the only European language understood by the Japanese with any precision. The Treaty of Edo, officially called 'Treaty of Peace, Friendship and Commerce, between Her Majesty and the Tycoon of Japan' was signed on 26 August 1858 in English, Japanese and Dutch.

D. *The Kanôn Temple, Yeddo [sic]*, 1858
Watercolour on paper, 23.7 x 31.8 cm
Signed b.l.: F. le. B. Bedwell

The British party were follwed by curious Japanese crowds wherever they went. On their visit to a temple in the most crowded part of Edo, Lord Elgin commented in his letter home 4 : 'We were followed by large multitudes, but nothing disagreeable took place. At the temple, we found a scene somewhat resembling Greenwich Fair. Immense number [sic] of people amusing themselves...Stalls covered with toys and other wares; kiosques [sic] for tea; show places.'

NOTES
1 S. Checkland, *The Elgins*, 1988, p.157
2 Lord Elgin, MSS 18 Aug. 1858
3 Osborn 1859, p.119; Checkland, op.cit., pp.155-6
4 Lord Elgin MSS 27 Aug. 1858

22
Lord Elgin's Souvenirs from Japan
Lord Elgin

On 27 August 1858, on the ship back to China, Lord Elgin wrote: 'My trip to Japan has been a green spot in the desert of my mission to the East'. He found the Japanese had a 'joyous, though polite and respectful demeanour' and 'the social and moral condition of Japan has astonished me quite as much as its material beauty'. 1 His letters from Japan recorded visits to souvenir shops on several occasions and purchases of silk, lacquer work and ceramics. The following exhibits are some of the surviving objects brought back by Lord Elgin.

A. *Pair of Storks on Rock*, c.1858
H. 48cm, D. 28cm

This pair is part of the presents Lord Elgin received from the Japanese. Sherard Osborn recorded: 'Lord Elgin received a very handsome ornament for a table in the shape of a brace of birds beautifully cast in white metal' alongside with other gifts such as silk, lacquer, porcelain and ivory. 2

B. *Lacquer Picnic Set*, c.1858
22.5 x 37.5 x 34.5cm

C. *Japanese Tobacco Set*, c.1858
Pipe (kiseru): L. 22.8cm ; wicker pipe case: L. 27.5cm; tobacco pouch: L. 9.7cm

Wickerwork appealed to the British party. Items in wickerwork are illustrated in Oliphant's book (Cat.20).

D. *Three Netsukes*
(a) *Baby with Tengu Mask*, c.1858
Ivory, H. 2.5cm
Signed: Sangetsu
(b) *Long-haired Woman on Sake Cup*, c.1858
Ivory, H. 2cm
Signed: Jugyoku
(c) *Woodcutter and Old Woman*, c.1858
Ivory, H. 6cm

E. *Lacquer Document Box*, c.1858
43 x 33.5 x 15 cm

NOTES
1 Lord Elgin MSS 22 August, 1858
2 Osborn, 1859, pp.194-5

GOUNTEI SADAHIDE (1807-?)

23
Dinner at a Foreign Merchant's House in Yokohama, 1861
Colour print from woodblocks, 34.7 x 23.6 cm
Signed b.r.: Gountei Sadahide ga
Titled t.r.: Yokohama ijin shoka shuen no zu
Sir Hugh and Lady Cortazzi

LIT : Hashiyama, 1983 (124)

An English merchant is at the dinner table, being offered wine by a Chinese man from Nanking. The man wearing a head-dress is a Siamese (Thai) servant. The picture shows the Japanese artist's attempt to depict Western cutlery.

24
An Englishman Sorting Fabrics for Trade at Yokohama, 1861
Colour print from woodblocks, 36.7 x 25.3 cm
Signed b.r.: Gounrei Sadahide ga
Titled t.r.: Igirisujin Yokohama ni orimono irowake koeki no zu
Trustees of the British Museum, London

LIT : Yonemura 1990, p.100 (23)

Here a young English merchant is sorting Japanese fabrics, but a large 'framed' female portrait on the top left indicates his loneliness and thoughts of his absent wife or lover. It was an artistic convention in Japan to frame or box an image to indicate some special association with the subject's thought.

25
View of the Iron Bridge at Yokohama, c.1869-70
Colour print from woodblocks (right-hand half of six sheets)
Signed, all three sheets: b.r. (right) Gountei Sadahide ga; b.l. (central) Sadahide ga; b.l. (left) Gountei Sadahide ga
Titled t.r.(right): Yokohama tekkyo no zu
Bodleian Library, Oxford

LIT : Y. Iwakabe, *Yokohama E-chizu (Picture Maps of Yokohama)* Yokohama 1989, pp.32-3 (57)

Cat.56

The Yoshidabashi bridge, formerly wooden, was rebuilt by the British engineer, Richard Henry Brunton (1841-1901), in 1869, and users were charged a toll until 1874. The foreground shows Western-style carriages, street lamps and foreigners in exotic dress, mixing with local Japanese. Over the bridge, the foreign quarter is seen with various flags including the Union Jack.

UTAGAWA HIROSHIGE II (1826-1869)

26
An English Soldier, c.1860
Colour print from woodblocks, 35.5 x 24.2 cm
Signed b.l.: Hiroshige ga
Titled t.r.: Igirisu zu
Sir Hugh and Lady Cortazzi

27
The British Government Building on the Bluff at Yokohama, 1869
Colour print from woodblocks (triptych), 35.8 x 70.6 cm
Signed b.r. (right): Kisai Rissho hitsu
Titled in English t.r.(right): Plan of English Legation at/ Bluff Land in Yokohama
Trustees of the British Museum, London

After the attack on Tozenji, the British Legation was temporarily moved to Yokohama. The complex on the Bluff was built in 1867. This print shows the Legation on the left and the Secretary's residence on the right. A military band is processing up the street, watched by Western, Chinese and Japanese passers-by.

UTAGAWA YOSHIKAZU (FL. c.1850-70)

28
Two English Men, 1861
Colour print from woodblocks, 36 x 24.3 cm
Signed b.r.: Utagawa Yoshikazu ga
Titled t.r.: Igirisujin
Sir Hugh and Lady Cortazzi

LIT : Hashiyama, 1983 (167); Meech-Pekarik 1986,
pp.12-15, fig.7.

UTAGAWA HIROSHIGE III (1842-1894)

29
*The Prosperity of Merchant Houses
in Yokohama*, 1871
Colour print from woodblocks (triptych),
34.5 x 70.6 cm
Signed b.c. (central): Hiroshige ga
Titled t.c.: Yokohama shôkan han'ei no zu
Sir Hugh and Lady Cortazzi

LIT : Hashiyama, 1983 (22)

30
*The Prosperity of Foreign Merchant Houses in
Yokohama*, 1871
Colour print from woodblocks (triptych),
33 x 70.7 cm
Signed b.c. (central): Hiroshige ga
Titled t.c.(central): Yokohama kakkoku shôkan
han'ei
Sir Hugh and Lady Cortazzi

The great fire of 1866 changed the building style
in Yokohama. Public buildings such as merchant
houses and governmental offices were more
commonly made of stone, bricks and stucco
rather than wood. Cats 29 and 30 display a variety
of styles of foreign houses. The streets are
bustling with carriages, men, women and children
of various nationalities, street musicians and
vendors.

IKKEISAI YOSHIIKU (1833-1904)

31
Picture of Foreigners, c.1861
Colour print from woodblocks, 35.3 x 24.2 cm
Signed b.r.: Ikkeisai Yoshiiku ga
Titled t.r.: Gaikoku jinbutsu zuga
Sir Hugh and Lady Cortazzi

This print shows an English couple, the man
wearing a scarf, holding an umbrella and a
walking-stick, and the woman with an enormous
head-dress and skirt, which are hardly English.
The long text on top reads: 'Igirisu: called Igirisu
[England] or Buritania [Britain]. It is a large
island off the European continent. Its capital is
called London, and the people are clever and
strong, proficient and trained well in artillery.'

32
*The Prosperity of an English Trading Company in
Yokohama*, 1871
Colour print from woodblocks (triptych),
36.2 x 75.3 cm
Signed, all sheets, b.r.(right), b.l. (central) and
b.l.(left): Ikkeisai Yoshiiku
Titled t.r.: Yokohama Igirisu shokan han'ei
no zu
Metropolitan Museum of Art, New York
(Gift of Lincoln Kirstein, 1959)

LIT : Meech-Pekarik, 1986 pp.55-6, pl.10

This print shows a magnificent view of a trade
fair held by Jardine, Matheson and Company,
the foremost British firm in Japan. Great
attention is paid to the architectural details
of the interior such as the roof construction,
incorporating a kingpost rooftruss, and Gothic-
style arches. The dazzling display of 'exotic'
Western goods is conveyed through rich colour.

FELIX BEATO (1825-?)

Beato, the Venetian-born British photographer,
arrived in Japan in about 1863. By that time he
was an established war photographer: in the 1850s
he had worked intensively with James Robertson
in the Crimea, in Greece, Egypt and India, and in
1860 he worked with Charles Wirgman in China
to cover the Anglo-French military expedition
and the fall of the Summer Palace.

Beato's friendship with Wirgman, who settled in
Yokohama after leaving China, continued in
Japan. In an article in *The Illustrated London News*
(26 September 1863) Wirgman referred to his
colleague 'Signor B [Beato]' and reported that
Wirgman's house was crowded with curious
Japanese who had come to see their sketches
and photographs. In 1865 they formed a business
partnership, Beato & Wirgman, Artists &
Photographers, which continued until 1869.

In Japan Beato covered the latest political events
such as the assassination of the British officers
near Yokohama in 1862 and the Shimonoseki
War in 1864, but he also travelled round Japan,
capturing with his camera its landscape and
people, subjects virtually unexplored by
Europeans. The culmination of his Japanese
work is seen in his two-volume album,
Photographic Views of Japan (Yokohama 1868),
the year of the 'Meiji Restoration', when the
Tokugawa government was replaced. Each
volume contains approximately one hundred
albumen prints, accompanied as Beato's caption
says, by: 'historical and descriptive notes.
Compiled from authentic sources and from
personal observation.' While the first volume,
Views of Japan, consists of cities and landscapes
in black and white, the second, *Native Types* is
a compilation of the manners and customs of
people, carefully hand-coloured by a Japanese
painter (Cat.33). It is also worth noting that
Beato's photographs of people have striking
similarities to traditional Japanese prints in

terms of composition and subject-matter. 1
Furthermore, this album and especially its genre
photographs were later to be models for popular
'Yokohama-shashin' (Yokohama-photographs). 2
Beato's work featured in this section has been
taken from this album.

The later part of Beato's Japanese career is
ambiguous, but he is known to have been a
successful commercial photographer in Yokohama
until 1877, when he sold his studio together with
the negatives to the Austrian photographer, Baron
von Stillfried. However, Beato did not leave
Japan until around 1885.

NOTES
1 Worswick 1979, p.133
2 Ozawa et al. 1990, p.165

33
Our Artist, c.1867-68
Hand-coloured albumen print, 21.6 x 29.5 cm
Ken and Jenny Jacobson

The artist photographed here was responsible
for the hand-colouring of Beato's photographs.
Beato was possibly influenced by Wirgman in
employing a Japanese painter. The introduction
of photography contributed to the decline of
traditional woodcuts, and many Japanese artists
found new roles in photographers' studios or as
photographers themselves.

34
Ferry Boat, c.1867-68
Hand-coloured albumen print, 21 x 27.2 cm
Ken and Jenny Jacobson

35
*Three Young Officers (Samurai) with
Tea-house Girl*, c.1867-68
Hand-coloured albumen print, 26.5 x 22.3 cm
Ken and Jenny Jacobson

36
*Two Young Girls with Umbrella accompanied by
Maid and Boy Servant*, c.1867-68
Hand-coloured albumen print, 25.9 x 20.4 cm
Ken and Jenny Jacobson

37
*Portrait of Prince Okudaira
(Young Samurai)*, c.1867-68
Hand-coloured albumen print, 26.1 x 20.4 cm
Ken and Jenny Jacobson

38
Street Vendor carrying Two Large Fish, c.1867-68
Hand-coloured albumen print, 20.3 x 25.4 cm
Ken and Jenny Jacobson

39
Three Standing Men, c.1867-68
Hand-coloured albumen print, 35.7 x 20.3 cm
Ken and Jenny Jacobson

This photograph shows two men wearing
Western-style short hair. After 1871, when
hair-styles were no longer regulated, short hair
became more common, being regarded as a symbol
of 'Bunmei-kaika' (cultural enlightenment).

40

Three Officers (Samurai), c.1867-68
Hand-coloured albumen print, 20.3 x 25.2 cm
Ken and Jenny Jacobson

The man on the right sits in a Western-style
chair. This was probably Beato's studio setting,
but through such a combination of the old and
new a moment of Westernisation was captured
in this picture.

41

Three Maikos
(Young Trainee Geisha Girls), c.1867-68
Hand-coloured albumen print, 22.7 x 19.5 cm
Ken and Jenny Jacobson

Young girls in kimono or courtesans in traditional
settings were well represented in Beato's album.
This type of subject was later to be repeated
frequently by other photographers, Japanese and
Western, and it formed a stereotype in souvenir
photographs.

42

Three Japanese Ladies with Palanquin, c.1867-68
Hand-coloured albumen print, 19.4 x 24.4 cm
Ken and Jenny Jacobson

In the Meiji period 'jinriki-sha' ,or rickshaws,
took over from 'kago' (sedan-chairs), as public
transport. In the transitional period, both types
commonly appeared in photographs as they
were one of the subjects which appealed to
Western tourists.

43

Fishmonger, c.1867-68
Hand-painted albumen print, 20.7 x 29.3 cm
Ken and Jenny Jacobson

44

Masked Man with Sword carrying Large Wrapped
Luggage on his Back, c.1867-68
Hand-coloured albumen print, 26.4 x 20.9 cm
Ken and Jenny Jacobson

45

Standing Fireman showing his Back,
with Lantern, c.1867-68
Hand-coloured albumen print, 26.1 x 20.5 cm
Ken and Jenny Jacobson

Apart from their professional function, fire-
brigades had a theatrical attraction in Japanese
society, because of their acrobatic New Year
shows, boldly designed uniforms, banners and
other accessories. The lantern held by the man
shows the letter 'Y' from 'Y.F.B.' (Yokohama
Fire Brigade) in English.

46

A Shinto Shrine with Torii (shrine gate) and Japanese
figures in the foreground, c.1867-68
Albumen print, 27 x 23.8 cm
Ken and Jenny Jacobson

Cat.42

KUSAKABE KIMBEI (1841-1934)

Born in Kofu, Kusakabe arrived in Yokohama,
the centre of Westernisation, in 1859, and there
he met Felix Beato. In 1863 Kusakabe became
Beato's assistant, at first as a hand-colourist and
apprentice photographer. He accompanied Beato
on his travels in Japan and to Shanghai in 1868.
In 1881 he opened his own photographic studio
in Benten-dori which he moved to Honcho in
Yokohama (Cat.47) in 1890. The shop was
extremely successful and was soon followed by
branches in the city as well as in Tokyo. His
speciality was studio portraiture, and his albums
of hand-coloured photographs, bound in lacquer
covers, called 'Kimbei Albums', were particularly
popular among the Western tourists.

47

Kusakabe Photo Studio at Honcho Dori,
Yokohama, c.1890
Hand-coloured albumen print, 19.5 x 25.5 cm
Ken and Jenny Jacobson

48

Fuji from Hakone's Lake, late 19th century
Hand-coloured albumen print, 20.5 x 26.8 cm
Ken and Jenny Jacobson

The composition and the contrast between light
and shade with delicate hand-colouring make
this photograph resemble a traditional landscape
painting. Kusakabe Kimbei was a competent
painter and in his last years he turned to painting
in the traditional style.

49

Postman, late 19th century
Hand-coloured albumen print, 26.2 x 20.7 cm
Ken and Jenny Jacobson

This photograph shows a traditional postman,
'hikyaku'. With the introduction of the modern
postal system in the early 1870s, this type of
postman had actually disappeared by the time
this work was produced, but the subject, together
with the prominent tattoo on his back, was
popular among the Western tourists as a
'Japanese' scene.

50

Kago, Travelling Chair, late 19th century
Hand-coloured albumen print, 20 x 26.4 cm
Horesh Collection, London

51

Coolies' Wayside Refreshments, late 19th century
Hand-coloured photograph, 20.4 x 26.5 cm
Ken and Jenny Jacobson

52

Kimbei Album, late 19th century
27.5 x 36.1 cm
Horesh Collection, London

The album is bound in black lacquer panels.
The front cover shows a fishing party painted
in lacquer and gold, and contains ivory inlay.

53
Kimbei Album, late 19th century
32 x 40.2 cm
Horesh Collection

The album is bound in black lacquer, the panels decorated with fans and natural motifs in 'kinmaki-e' (gold lacquer picture).

54
Kimbei Album, late 19th century
27.4 x 36.8 cm
Horesh Collection, London

The album is bound in red lacquer panels. The front cover is decorated with an inset picture showing two Japanese ladies at a tea ceremony.

ANONYMOUS

Attribution of the following works (Cats 55 and 56) is not definitive, but the subjects and style show Kusakabe Kimbei's influence.

55
Umbrella Maker, c. late 19th century
Hand-coloured albumen print, 20.6 x 26.9 cm
Ken and Jenny Jacobson

56
Street Mountebanks, c. late 19th century
Hand-coloured albumen print, 20.8 x 26.4 cm
Ken and Jenny Jacobson

TAMAMURA KOZABURO (1856-?)

Tamamura was active in Yokohama in the 1890s and 1900s. Like Kusakabe Kimbei, Tamamura specialised in hand-coloured photographs of traditional Japanese scenes, which were bound between lacquer or cloth covers. Tamamura was a major competitor of Kusakabe in Yokohama, but Tamamura's hand-colouring technique is less elaborate. His photographs were also reproduced by means of the new collotype process to cope with larger commercial demand.

LIT : Worswick 1979, p.124, 148; S. Takenoya, 'Bakumatsu-Meiji no omona shashinka' in Ozawa et al, Tokyo 1990, p.253

57
Famous Scenes in Japan
Published in Yokohama, c.1890s
Album of collotype prints, 30.6 x 38.9 cm
Horesh Collection, London

The album is bound in a silk cover. One of the prints shows the shop-front selling 'geta', traditional wooden sandals. Despite the traditional subject, the composition and striking colours show that this print is rather modern.

OGAWA ISSHIN (1860-1929)

Ogawa was active in Tokyo from the 1880s to the 1910s. His subjects ranged from historical scenes and beauty portraits to natural studies, which were produced as albumen prints or by using the collotype process. His historical subjects include mediaeval settings and show his careful study of the period. His work should be seen against a revival of traditional values in art in the late nineteenth century. Ogawa also contributed to the rise of amateur photography. In 1893 together with the English professor and amateur photographer, William Burton, he organised the first international photography exhibition in Japan, showing about 300 works by members of the Camera Club of London.

58
Illustrations of Japan (3 vols)
Published in Tokyo 1896
Collotype prints on crêpe paper,
24.4 x 17.9 cm each
Horesh Collection, London

These volumes compiled scenes from everyday life in Japan, accompanied by descriptions by S. Takashima, Professor of the Higher Commercial College in Tokyo. The pictures included works by other photographers such as Tamamura, Professor Burton and Kajima Seibi, and were reproduced by the collotype process. This printing process was popular at that time and, in the preface to the book, Ogawa wrote: '[the pictures are] true to nature and free from any retouches by the artists...Unlike ordinary photographs, collotype pictures are permanent, in the sense that they will not fade in any length of time.'

ATTRIBUTED TO OGAWA ISSHIN
(1860-1929)

59
A Semi-nude Japanese Woman, c.1880s
Hand-coloured albumen print, 26.5 x 20.8 cm
Ken and Jenny Jacobson

THE 1862 INTERNATIONAL EXHIBITION IN LONDON

This was an epoch-making event in the history of Japanese art in the West. Though a small amount of Japanese art had been displayed at various large-scale expositions before, here for the first time a substantial amount of Japanese art and artefacts were displayed, in a separate section, to a large number of Westerners. From this time onwards Japan was prominently represented at major international exhibitions held in the West. These large-scale events were open to the public, more accessible than older private collections, and drew vast numbers of visitors.

The 1862 Japan section was largely composed of objects sent in by the British Minister in Japan, Rutherford Alcock, who systematically collected items for this exhibition. By coincidence the first diplomatic mission from Japan to come to Europe since 1613 arrived in London and attended the opening ceremony. The Japan section was widely discussed in the press, especially among design critics and theorists. (See essay by Ellen P. Conant, pp.80)

60
J. B. WARING (ED.)
Masterpieces of Industrial Art & Sculpture at the International Exhibition, 1862 (3 vols),
London 1863
The Corporation of London
(Guildhall Library)

J. B.Waring, who was involved in the organisation of the exhibition, published a three-volume edition of selected items from the show with sumptuous chromolithograph plates. These plates give excellent clues to what type of Japanese objects were shown there. He praises Japanese design very highly at the expense of contemporary British design.

61
SHERARD OSBORN (dates unknown)
Japanese Fragments, London 1861
18.1 x 14.1 cm
London Library

Sherard Osborn was a Captain of the Royal Navy and accompanied Lord Elgin's mission to the Far East. His articles on Japan were published in the arts magazine *Once a Week* in 1860 and then came out as a book in 1861, when Osborn added six new colour facsimiles of Japanese prints, all of them Hiroshige landscapes. He apparently took great care over the faithful reproduction of these prints, which he chose as outstanding examples of Japanese art.

62
JOHN LEIGHTON (1822-1912)
On Japanese Art, London 1863
38.7 x 24.1 cm (cover)
Trustees of the British Museum, London

John Leighton was a prominent designer and design theorist and a friend of Sir Rutherford Alcock. He gave a lecture on Japanese art at the Royal Institution on 1 May 1863, a slightly shortened version of which appeared in the *Journal of the Society of Arts* (24 July 1863). The full text was published privately in only fifty copies. There is one copy in the National Art Library in the Victoria and Albert Museum into which a Kunisada print is pasted and another at the British Museum with an Eisen print. His analysis of Japanese art is on the whole perceptive and positive.

Cat.67
JAMES MCNEILL
WHISTLER (1834-1903)
*Variations in Violet and
Green*, 1871

III. THE INTRODUCTION OF JAPONISME : JAMES McNEILL WHISTLER

JAMES McNEILL WHISTLER (1834-1903)

The American artist Whistler was one of the most influential figures in Japonisme in the West. In 1858 he became an important member of a circle of young Realist artists in Paris. It was within this circle that a strong interest in Japanese art grew and Whistler was one of the most radical exponents of Japonisme. After moving to London in 1859, he acted as an intermediary between the artistic circles of the two cities. He became a friend of the Rossetti circle and also of two important artists of Victorian Japonisme, the Neo-classical painter Albert Moore, and of the architect E.W. Godwin. Whistler made valuable contributions to the Aesthetic Movement and Victorian Japonisme not only with his prints and paintings but also with his interior decoration, such as the Peacock Room, and with his theoretical writings and lectures, such as the 'Ten O'clock Lecture'. Though he won a moral victory at the famous Ruskin-Whistler trial in 1878, he became bankrupt next year and left for Venice for about twelve months. In his later years from about the late 1880s Whistler became an influential figure, especially among younger painters in Britain and America.

LIT : Spencer 1980; Watanabe 1991a; Watanabe 1991b; Young et al. 1980; Spencer 1989

63
Sketch for 'La princesse du pays de la porcelaine', 1863-64
Oil on paper board mounted on wood, 63 x 34 cm
Worcester Art Museum, Worcester, Massachusetts (Theodore T. and Mary G. Ellis Collection)

LIT : Sickert 1908, pp.18; Sawyer 1941, pp.43, 47; Young et al. 1980 (49); Spencer 1989, pp.77-8; Watanabe 1991 B, pp.236-43

The finished version, *La Princesse du pays de la porcelaine* (Freer Gallery of Art, Washington, D.C.), was painted in 1863-64. The 'Princess' was Christine Spartali, whose father later became the Greek Consul-General in London. Her features resembled those of Rossetti's Pre-Raphaelite women, and Whistler was close to his circle at the time. However, the girl in this sketch seems to be a different model, much more Japanese in appearance. The sketch was called 'magnificent' by Sickert and shows Whistler experimenting with the Japanese device of decorative flower branches.

64
Symphony in White, No. 2: The Little White Girl, 1864
Oil on canvas, 76.5 x 51 cm
Signed t.r.: Whistler; originally dated: 1864
Trustees of the Tate Gallery, London

LIT: Swinburne 1866, pp.149-52; Rossetti 1867, pp.274-5; Sutton 1963, pp.39-40; Young et al. 1980 (52); Spencer 1989, pp.76-7

Whistler's mistress Jo Hiffernan posed for this painting, one of the most beautiful of his so-called 'Oriental' phase. Her white dress dominates the painting, but the Japanese fan, the blue and white jar, the red lacquer bowl and the azaleas are used effectively to give colourful accents. His strong interest in the ambiguity of space manifests itself in his use of the mirror, where the reflection of the head is moved so that it can be fully seen. This painting was highly praised by the critic, William Michael Rossetti, and Swinburne, inspired by it, wrote a poem, 'Before the Mirror'.

65
The Artist's Studio, 1865
Oil on millboard, 62.2 x 46.3 cm
The Hugh Lane Municipal Gallery of Modern Art, Dublin

LIT : Young et al. 1980 (62)

For the Salon of 1866 Whistler intended to paint a large picture of his studio with himself, his friends, Albert Moore and Fantin-Latour, and his models. The large version was never painted and both of the two extant preliminary paintings, this and the one at the Art Institute of Chicago, omit the friends. The model sitting down is Jo Hiffernan in the same dress as in Cat. 65 and the other, with a Japanese fan, was referred to as 'La Japonaise' by Whistler. On the left of the picture we can just see his collection of blue and white porcelain shimmering in the dark.

66
Sketch for 'The Balcony', 1867-70
Oil on wood, 61 x 48.2 cm
Hunterian Art Gallery, University of Glasgow (Birnie Philip Bequest)

LIT : Young 1973 (73); Young et al. 1980 (57); Watanabe 1991 B, pp.236-43

The painting *Variation in Flesh Colour and Green: The Balcony* (Freer Gallery of Art, Washington, D.C.) was originally dated 1865 by Whistler and was exhibited at the Royal Academy in 1870. In about January 1867 Whistler apparently had a plan to enlarge this composition. Both the painting and this squared-up sketch show numerous alterations and are difficult to date precisely, but probably most of the sketch is from about 1870. The enlargement never took place.

67
Variations in Violet and Green, 1871
Oil on canvas, 61 x 35.5 cm
Signed with butterfly and dated c.r.: 71; also signed with butterfly and dated on frame t.l.: 1871
Marlborough International, Liechtenstein

LIT : Young 1960, p.48; Young et al. 1980 (104)

The scene depicts the Thames at Battersea and Andrew McLaren Young saw it as presaging Whistler's Thames Nocturnes of the 1870s.

The vertical composition is divided into horizontal bands and together with the high view point shows the strong influence of Japanese prints. These dainty figures in his Thames paintings were referred to as Japanese by his contemporaries.

68
Nocturne: Blue and Gold - Old Battersea Bridge, c.1872-75
Oil on canvas, 66.6 x 50.2 cm
Trustees of the Tate Gallery, London

LIT : Young et al. 1980 (140); Watanabe 1991a

This painting is perhaps the best known of his Nocturnes and also shows the clearest debt to Japanese prints among his landscape paintings. In particular the prints by Hiroshige show elements which are shared by this painting, such as the bridge seen in close-up which creates an abstract rhythm, the monochromatic tonal use of blue, the subtle depiction of the lively riverside cityscape at night, and the capturing of the transient beauty of fireworks.

69 (Barbican only)
Nocturne: Blue and Silver - Cremorne Lights, 1872
Oil on canvas, 50.2 x 74.9 cm
Signed with butterfly and dated: 72
Trustees of the Tate Gallery, London

LIT : Young et al. 1980 (115)

In this atmospheric Nocturne Whistler uses the Japanese device of two bamboo-like branches jutting in from the bottom edge of the picture. The whole painting evokes the mood of a Far Eastern ink painting, where the subject of a solitary boat in a vast river or lake was very popular, as in the painting *Autumn Moon over Lake Tung-ting* attributed to Mu-ch'i in the Tokugawa Reimeikai Foundation, Tokyo. It is unlikely that Whistler had access to this particular painting, but he could have seen similar compositions in printed anthologies of paintings published in Japan.

70 (Barbican only)
Nocturne: Grey and Gold, Westminster Bridge, c.1874
Oil on canvas, 47 x 62.3 cm
The Burrell Collection, Glasgow Museums

LIT : Young et al. 1980 (145)

Whistler stated that this was a view of the Thames from the Houses of Parliament, but the Parliament buildings can only be dimly recognized on the right of the picture. In this painting everything seems to dissolve in this subtle colour scheme of blue with golden accents for the lights.

e, c.1875-77
anvas, 55.5 x 39.4 cm
with a butterfly on frame
an Art Gallery, University of Glasgow
Philip Bequest)

ng et al. 1980 (172)

ne of Whistler's most radical Nocturnes
e depiction of the evening mist through
to... iations is carried to extremes. The
composition of a river bend from a high viewpoint
is a frequent device used in Japanese prints and is
similar to *Nocturne in Blue and Gold: Valparaiso Bay*
of 1866 in the Freer Gallery of Art ,Washington
D.C., one of his earliest Nocturnes.

72
The Little Pool, 1861
Etching and crayon, 10.16 x 12.38 cm
Signed and dated 1861
Inscribed: The Works of James Whistler:
Etchings and Drypoints, are on view at
E. Thomas' Publisher, 39, Old Bond Street
Trustees of the British Museum, London

LIT : Kennedy 1910 (74 Ia); Watanabe 1991a; Watanabe
1991b

This print belongs to Whistler's 'Sixteen
Etchings', the so-called Thames set, and is
dated 1861. It shows the first state, but contains
a crayon addition indicating the mast and rigging
of a barge. Ralph, or 'Serjeant', Thomas, who
published the Thames set, and his son Percy,
sketching, are seen at the top left corner of the
composition, which again shows a river bend
from a high viewpoint in the Japanese manner.
However, arrangements similar to this crayon
addition are frequently seen in Hiroshige, such
as his *Shinagawaoki Shiohigari* (Shell-picking at
Shinagawa) from *Ehon Edo Miyage* (Souvenir
Picture-book from Edo). According to Kennedy
one of the Thomases wrote on this impression
that Whistler added the crayon drawing in
March 1861.

73
The Punt, 1861
Etching, 11.8 x 16.2 cm
Inscribed: Pl.7
Ashmolean Museum, Oxford

LIT : Kennedy 1910 (85 IV); Watanabe 1991b

The first state included Whistler's signature and
the date 1861. This impression is the fourth state
and was published in 'Passages from Modern
English Poets, illustrated by the Junior Etching
Club' (Day & Son, 1862). The striking and
asymmetrical composition of a punt suddenly
protruding into the picture was very unusual at
the time in the West, but was commonplace in
Japan, as can be seen in Hiroshige's 'Shubi no
Matsu' (The Pine- tree of Shubi) from *Ehon Edo
Miyage* (Souvenir Picture-book from Edo).

Cat.73

74
The Storm, 1861
Drypoint, 15.5 x 28.4 cm
Signed and dated 1861
Trustees of the British Museum, London

LIT : Kennedy 1910 (81); Lochnan 1984; Watanabe
1991b

According to Lochnan this print shows the artist
Matthew White Ridley, a friend of Whistler's
from his Paris period, struggling against the storm
during an excursion along the Thames. This
somewhat Rembrandtesque drypoint shows a
starkly asymmetrical composition and the theme
of a man struggling through the driving rain,
unusual in the West, is often found in Hiroshige's
works, such as 'Suhara' from the series *Kisokaido
gojuku tsugi* (Sixty-nine stations on the Kiso road).

75
Old Battersea Bridge, 1879
Etching and drypoint, 19.9 x 29.5 cm
Signed with butterfly and imp in pencil
Hunterian Art Gallery, University of Glasgow

LIT : Kennedy 1910 (177 IV); Lochnan 1984

The Old Battersea Bridge, which was demolished
in 1890, was frequently depicted by Whistler.
He used the bridge to experiment with different
compositional devices which were stimulated by
Japanese prints, as we have seen in Cat.69. This
print shows one of Whistler's most 'Japanese'
compositions with the arching bridge framing
a boat with a white sail.

76
Upright Venice, 1879-80
Etching and drypoint,
Trustees of the British Museum, London

LIT : Kennedy 1910 (205); MacDonald 1976

After his bankruptcy in May 1879, Whistler went
to Venice to produce etchings there which were
commissioned by the Fine Art Society. The

scene in the foreground was added only at the
second state. This delicately executed and
atmospheric print uses a composition with
a high viewpoint and a diagonal shoreline
in the foreground similar to Cat.69 and
to many Japanese prints.

77
Dipping the Flag, 1887
Etching, 8.1 x 17.7 cm
Signed with butterfly on tab
Hunterian Art Gallery, University of Glasgow
(Birnie Philip Bequest)

LIT : Kennedy 1910 (325); Lochnan 1984

Whistler attended the Naval Review off Spithead
in 1887 as the President of the Royal Society of
British Artists and produced a series of etchings
as a contribution to the Jubilee. These etchings
show a wonderful lightness of touch and much of
the surface of the paper is left empty. The device
of a close-up flag-pole contrasted with the horizon
can also be seen in Hiroshige's 'Komagatado
Azumabashi' (Komagata Shrine and Azuma
Bridge) from the series *Edo meisho hyakkei*
(Hundred Famous Places of Edo).

78
Savoy Pigeons, 1896
Lithograph, 19.6 x 13.7 cm
Ashmolean Museum, Oxford

LIT : Way 1896 (118)

Whistler's wife, Beatrix, died in the year 1896.
This sheet belongs to a number of lithographs
Whistler made around this time, which captures
the view from the window of the Savoy Hotel
where they lived. Whistler contrasts the close-up
balcony and the pigeons with the view of the
Thames where the Houses of Parliament can
be seen in the distance. He concentrated the
composition in the middle of the paper leaving
much of the space around blank.

IV. VICTORIAN PAINTERS AND JAPAN

DANTE GABRIEL ROSSETTI (1828-1882)

Born in London, the son of an exiled Italian patriot and scholar. Rossetti grew up in a strongly literary environment, with poetry his greatest passion alongside painting. His younger sister Christina became a poetess and his younger brother William Michael a writer and art critic. Rossetti was a founder of the Pre-Raphaelite Brotherhood in 1848. His mediaevalising doctrine and visionary symbolism appealed strongly to younger artists, and through his followers such as William Morris and Edward Burne-Jones Pre-Raphaelitism became a highly influential aesthetic force in the latter part of the nineteenth century.

Rossetti and his circle were among a small band of Japanese enthusiasts in the early 1860s. How and when he was introduced to Japanese art is not clear and there are contradictory accounts, but by 1863 he must have come across it. In 1863 William Michael Rossetti wrote 'Japanese Woodcuts: An Illustrated Book from Japan' for *The Reader*, and this was probably the first article about Hokusai in Britian. The Rossetti brothers' enthusiasm reached its peak in 1866 when they seem to have met Japanese students from Satsuma (today's Kagoshima) through their artist friend, George Price Boyce. 1 The Satsuma-han group was the leading feudal clan pursuing an open foreign policy, and at that time it was developing close commercial contacts with Britain.

LIT : Surtees 1971; Grieve 1973-78; Tanita 1989; Tanita 1990-91; Watanabe 1991b, pp.159-65, 199-205

NOTE
1 Tanita 1989. This document unearthed by Tanita is not conclusive on whether Dante Gabriel Rossetti actually met these Japanese students.

79 (Barbican only)
The Beloved (The Bride), 1865-66
Oil on canvas, 82.5 x 76.2 cm
Signed with monogram and dated b.l.: 1865-6
Trustees of the Tate Gallery, London

LIT : Surtees1971 (182); *Rosetti Ten*, 1990-91 (35)

Here Rossetti used a green kimono, borrowed from G.P.Boyce, Although the painting was conceived as the bride from the Biblical, 'Song of Solomon', Rossetti's principal interest was in the sensuous effects of colours 'like jewels'. With the effective use of complementary colours such as the greens of silk and the reds of embroideries and hairpins, the kimono is used not to evoke Japan, but to give a rich and luxurious texture to this painting.

Cat.81
EMMA SANDYS (FL. 1868-1874)
Portrait of a Woman in a Green Dress,
c.1870

FREDERICK SANDYS (1829-1904)

Born in Norwich. Studied at R.A. schools under George Richmond. His younger sister, Emma (see Cat.81) was also a painter. From the late 1850s Sandys was associated with Rossetti's Pre-Raphaelite circle and in 1866 he lived in Chelsea with Rossetti. He contributed to the Pre-Raphaelite movement through his woodcuts and illustrations including those for the poems by Swinburne and Christina Rossetti.

LIT : O'Looney 1974

80
Medea, 1868
Oil on panel, 62.2 x 46.3 cm
Birmingham City Museums and Art Gallery

LIT : O'Looney 1974 (72)

Taken from Greek mythology, Medea, the priestess and witch, is here engaged in witchcraft. The composition, dominated by a half-length figure of Medea against the shallow background, has a striking similarity to Rossetti's female portraits of the mid-1860s such as *Regina Cordium (Queen of Hearts)* (1866, Glasgow Museum and Art Galleries). Combined with other exotic ornaments, Japanese motifs including cranes and Far Eastern dragons were used in the background. Japanese and other Oriental motifs are often shown in his paintings from the 1860s and 1870s. One such example is the *Portrait of Colonel Sir William Anderson Rose* (1875, Auckland Art Museum); the sitter, who was Lord Mayor of London in 1862, is portrayed against a Japanese textile decorated with patterns of heron, moon and cloud. A similar idea is also demonstrated in his sister's painting, with the use of a Japanese screen in the background (Cat.81).

NOTE
We are grateful to Betty Elsea for the information about the portrait of Colonel Rose and for the attribution of Cat.81.

EMMA SANDYS (FL. 1868-1874)

81
Portrait of a Woman in a Green Dress, c.1870
Oil on panel, 40.6 x 40.6 cm
Mrs Victoria Scarborough

SIMEON SOLOMON (1840-1905)

Born in London. Studied at R.A. schools, where he formed a sketching club with Albert Moore (see Cats 84 and 85), Marcus Stone and Henry Holiday. His elder brother Abraham and younger sister Rebecca (see Cat.83) were also painters. Around 1858 Solomon met Rossetti and his circle including Burne-Jones, Walter Pater and Swinburne. Solomon illustrated Swinburne's

poems and he was greatly influenced by the poet's Aestheticism in the 1860s. Solomon's career declined sharply after his arrest on homosexual charges in 1873.

LIT : Reynolds 1984; Lambourne et al. 1985-86

82
Lady in Chinese Dress with a Japanese Fan, 1865
Watercolour and gouache on paper, 40 x 35.1 cm
Signed with monogram and dated b.l.: S 1865
Grosvenor Museum, Chester

LIT : Lambourne et al.(49); *Japonisme*, exh. Paris/Tokyo 1988 (72)

The sitter, probably Solomon's sister Rebecca, is depicted here in a rich Chinese dress, holding a Japanese fan, in a domestic setting. Kakiemon-like ceramic plates are seen in the background. The subject and setting show the strong influence of Whistler's *Purple and Rose: Lange Leizen of the Six Marks*, which was exhibited at the Royal Academy in 1864. The same Japanese fan appeared in Solomon's other Oriental painting from this period, *The Japanese Fan* (1865, whereabouts unknown), where Rebecca, this time in an English dress, was portrayed against a pair of Japanese hanging-scrolls of beauty portraits. A similar setting was used by his sister in Cat.83 with a Japanese fan and ceramic plates in the background.

Cat.83

REBECCA SOLOMON (1832-1886)

83
The Wounded Dove, 1866
Watercolour on paper, 45.5 x 35.5 cm
Signed b.l. with monogram
The University College of Wales, Aberystwyth

ALBERT JOSEPH MOORE (1841-1893)

Born in York. Studied at R.A. schools. His father William and elder brother Henry were also painters. At the Royal Academy he was a friend of Simeon Solomon (see Cat.82), Marcus Stone, Henry Holiday and W.B. Richmond, and his detailed and naturalistic style in this period reflected the Pre-Raphaelite influence. In the 1860s Moore undertook wall decorations through the architect, William Eden Nesfield (see Cats 110 and 111), with whom Moore had travelled to the north of France in 1859. This experience, and the interest in classical sculpture, prompted him to adopt a decorative style. Moore met Whistler in 1865, when both artists were preoccupied with 'subjectless' painting. Mutual exchanges began between the two men: while Moore was affected by Whistler's passion for Japanese art, Whistler was inspired by Moore's classical motifs and 'genuine feeling for the juxtaposition and interrelation of colours'. 1 Towards the end of the 1860s their styles became closer: Whistler developed more abstract compositions with colours (see Cat.65), and Moore's paintings began to introduce Japanese motifs, which were to be an important feature of his compositions together with classical female figures. Later in this period they both began to use monograms: Moore the Greek anthemion and Whistler the butterfly derived from his initials 'M' and 'W', and these were incorporated into their compositions. Alongside Whistler, Moore was a leading exponent of the idea of art for art's sake.

NOTE
1 G.Reynolds, *Victorian Painting* 1966, pp.121-2

84
Azaleas, 1868
Oil on canvas, 198.1 x 100.3 cm
Signed b.r. with anthemion
The Hugh Lane Municipal Gallery of Modern Art, Dublin

LIT : Christian et al. 1985 (51)

With this painting Moore introduced a standing female figure draped in a classical robe for the first time in a large-scale composition. The painting was exhibited at the Royal Academy in 1868, and Swinburne called it 'the faultless and secure expression of an exclusive worship of things beautiful'. Japanese elements, such as scattered flower petals, a blossoming tree, and the double crests decorating the vase of azaleas, are harmoniously arranged with classical motifs, and together they represent here the 'things beautiful'.

85 (Barbican only)
A Venus, 1869
Oil on canvas, 160 x 76.2 cm
Signed with anthemion and dated t.l.: 1869
York City Art Gallery

LIT : Baldry 1894, pp.36-8 (103); Staley 1978 (73)

In Cat.85 a standing nude, who is tying her hair with a ribbon, is seen with similarly Oriental

Cat.85

motifs as in Cat.84. Moore's paintings were always based on careful studies; in a preliminary oil study of this painting (Private Collection), the figure is shown partially draped.

JAMES TISSOT (1836-1902)

The Nantes-born French painter Tissot arrived in London in 1871 as a political exile after the fall of the Paris Commune. By that time he had become a well established artist who had exhibited at the Paris Salon regularly and was known as a leading exponent of Japonisme. The highlight of his career in Paris was in 1868, with his appointment as drawing teacher of Prince Akitake, the younger brother of the last Tokugawa Shogun, Yoshinobu. Akitake, then a boy in his mid-teens, represented the Tokugawa government, who participated in the Exposition Universelle of 1867, and he stayed on in Paris for further education until towards the end of 1868.

In London, Tissot was again highly successful: he was a regular exhibitor at the Royal Academy, and his conversation pieces featuring fashionable

ladies were particularly popular among wealthy businessmen. Tissot was a friend of Whistler's, whom he had probably met in Paris by the late 1850s or the early 1860s. Together they exhibited at the Grosvenor Gallery, which was opened in 1877. His life changed radically when he began to live with Kathleen Newton, his mistress, in around 1876: he became withdrawn, almost obsessed with her, and his subject-matter concentrated on her portrait (Cat.87). However, Kathleen Newton died in 1882, which prompted Tissot to return to Paris.

In terms of Japonisme, Tissot's London period was important: while in Paris he featured Japanese 'props' for their fashionable or exotic attraction (see Cat.86), in London he began to assimilate Japanese characteristics into his style of painting. Furthermore, he began to use photographs for his compositions in the late 1870s, and it is conceivable that this also contributed to his new stylistic devices.

LIT : Wentworth 1980, pp.127-46; Ikegami 1980, pp.147-55

86
Jeunes Femmes regardant des objets japonais (Young Girls looking at Japanese objects), c.1869
Signed b.l.: Tissot
Oil on canvas, 61 x 48.3 cm
The Dobra Collection, New York

LIT : Matyjaskiewicz et al. 1988 (16)

Around 1869, Tissot painted three versions of the same subjects: two young girls looking at Japanese objects, all posed in his studio. Cat.86 is from this series; other versions are in the Cincinnati Museum of Art and in a Private Collection in London. From 1867 Tissot lived in the avenue de l'Impératrice, and his studio, called 'l'atelier japonais', was sumptuously decorated with Japanese objects, which probably included purchases from the Exposition Universelle and gifts from Prince Akitake. 1 This painting records an interior with a Japanese screen depicting a mediaeval battle scene, lanterns, and a Japanese doll, together with other Oriental objects.

NOTE
1 Wentworth 1980, p.133

87
La Dame à l'ombrelle, Mme Newton (Woman with a Parasol, Mrs Newton), c.1878
Oil on canvas, 142 x 54 cm
Musée Baron Martin Gray, France

LIT : Matyjaskiewicz 1984-85 (103)

In London, Tissot stopped employing Japanese 'props' in his painting. The only exception reminding us of his Paris period is *The Japanese Scroll* (c.1873-75, Private Collection, San Diego), which shows a girl looking at a long Japanese scroll in his studio in St John's Wood. Although parasols and fans remained his favourite accessories, as used in this portrait of Mrs Newton, in the 1870s he became more interested

Cat.88

in the stylistic principles of Japanese woodcuts. In this painting, such Japanese elements are demonstrated in the use of the narrow vertical format of hashira-e (pillar prints) and Mrs Newton's prominent silhouette against flat colours. During this period he produced numerous portraits of Mrs Newton in paintings and prints, and in style and attitude they shared the spirit of the Japanese tradition of bijin-e (beauty portraits).

88
L'Enfant prodigue; - aux pays lointains (The Prodigal Son; - In Foreign Climes), c.1880-82
Oil on canvas, 100 x 130 cm
Signed b.l.: J J Tissot
Musée des Beaux-Arts, Nantes

LIT : *Japonisme*, exh. Paris/Tokyo 1988 (82)

Cat.88 belongs to the series of four pictures, *The Prodigal Son* (Musée des Beaux-Arts, Nantes), which depicted the Biblical parable in terms of modern life and were exhibited at the Dudley Gallery, London in 1882. The second in the sequence, this painting shows the Prodigal Son in an orgy. Tissot's inscription on the corresponding etching describes the scene: 'the younger son ... took his journey into a far country, and there wasted his substance with riotous living'. Making use of the concept of Geisha girls, Japan was chosen to represent the appropriate decadent image. At that time Japan was the Western tourists' dream: its exotic and indulgent images were created by tourist photographs and writings and, indeed, Tissot was able to refer to such sources for accurate descriptions. Although this painting is reminiscent stylistically of the

'Japanese prop' paintings of the 1860s, Tissot's attitude has changed: Japan is no longer an object of worship but a motif in modern life on which to comment.

FREDERICK LEIGHTON (1830-1896)

Born in Scarborough, Yorkshire. As a child, Leighton travelled widely in Europe with his parents and received an entirely Continental art education, notably under the German Nazarene, Edward von Steinle. By the time he returned to England in 1859, Leighton had become an established artist: his first major work in London, *Cimabue's Madonna* (Royal Collection, on loan to the National Gallery, London), was exhibited at the Royal Academy in 1855, and was then bought by Queen Victoria. He was close to the Pre-Raphaelites including Rossetti, William Holman Hunt and John Everett Millais. In the early 1860s he painted historical and Biblical subjects but from the mid-1860s onwards Leighton's paintings were dominated Greek classical subjects. Through his early contacts with the Continental art scene, he was familiar with the idea of art for art's sake, and with classical motifs he consciously explored the potentials of Aesthetic paintings. Leighton became President of the Royal Academy in 1878.

LIT : Ormond 1975; Newall 1990

89 (Setagaya only)
Mother and Child (Cherries), c.1865
Oil on canvas, 48.2 x 82 cm
Blackburn Museum and Art Gallery

LIT : Newall 1990, pp.52, 62 and pl.32

Leighton was one of the early collectors of Japanese art, and his house, built in the mid-1860s in Holland Park Road (now Leighton House), was known to be furnished with his lavish art collection which included Japanese objects. Nevertheless, unlike his fellow Japanese enthusiasts, Leighton did not compose with Japanese 'props'. Cat.89 is the only known painting incorporating a Japanese element: a gilt screen decorated with cranes in the background. In this painting, the diagonal lines of the cranes' legs and feathers are used effectively to create a harmonious formal arrangement with the woman and child in the foreground.

Cat.89

Cat.90

EDWARD JOHN POYNTER (1836-1919)

Born in Paris. In 1853 in Rome Poynter met the young Frederick Leighton (see Cat.89), who had a great influence on his artistic development. He studied in London at Leigh's Drawing School and the R.A. schools, and from 1856-59 in Paris at Gleyre's Studio, where he met Whistler (see Section III), George Du Maurier, Thomas Armstrong and Thomas Lamont. Poynter was an old friend of the architect, William Burges (see Section V), and Edward Burne-Jones was his brother-in-law. Poynter became the first Slade Professor at University College, London in 1871, and in 1874 Director of the South Kensington Museum in London (forerunner of the Victoria and Albert Museum). As an academic teacher he advocated life drawing. He introduced for the first time in England the French-style art training linked with a studio apprenticeship, which he had experienced in Paris in the 1850s. In 1894 he was appointed Director of the National Gallery, London and from 1896 he also served as President of the Royal Academy.

90
*Mary Constance Wyndham, Lady Elcho
(later Countess of Wemyss)*, 1886
Gouache on paper, 52 x 34.3 cm
Signed with monogram and dated b.c.: 18 EJP 86
Earl of Wemyss and March, K.T.

LIT : G. Jackson-Stops, *The Treasure Houses of Britain*, exh., Washington, D.C., 1985-86 (559)

Mary Constance Wyndham was the eldest daughter of the Hon. Percy Wyndham of Clouds, Wiltshire, Conservative MP for West Cumberland. She married Hugo Charteris, Lord Elcho, heir to the 10th Earl of Wemyss and March, in 1883, and

became an important hostess of the Edwardian social circle, 'Souls'. Poynter was introduced to Lady Elcho through Burne-Jones, and this gouache was exhibited at the Grosvenor Gallery in 1886. Lady Elcho is portrayed here in a typically aesthetic mode: she is wearing a pale-yellow dress, the favourite colour of the aesthetes of the time, and is surrounded by fashionable objects including a Japanese screen, Oriental vases, Japanese woodcut books and a bowl of goldfish.

JOHN ATKINSON GRIMSHAW (1836-1893)

The Leeds-born painter Grimshaw was self-taught and particularly known for atmospheric landscapes and cityscapes at sunset or by moon-light. His activities were based in Leeds, and later in London, where from the mid-1880s he rented a studio in Chelsea near Whistler. His patrons were mainly wealthy Northern businessmen, and by 1870 he had become a successful artist: he lived in a seventeenth-century manor house, Knostrop Old Hall, on the outskirt of Leeds, and in the late 1870s he built a house in Scarborough. In the decade from the mid-1870s, Grimshaw explored figure painting; his subjects included portraits, interiors, fairy-tales and classical subjects. Grimshaw's work during this period shows the stylistic influences of James Tissot and Alma-Tadema. He was interested in photography, and alongside Tissot he was one of the earliest painters who used photographs for his compositions.

LIT : Robertson 1988

91
Dulce Domum, 1876-85
Oil on canvas, 83 x 122 cm
Signed b.l.: Atkinson Grimshaw
Inscribed on back: Dulce Domum - Harmony.
Painted by Atkinson Grimshaw at/his home
Knostrop Hall, Leeds, Yorks. Commenced and
named/1876. Finished January 1885. Painted as

a sequel to a picture/called 'A Question of Colour' by the same painter and mostly/painted under great difficulties, but by God's grace finished/ 1885. LABOR OMNIA VINCIT.
The Manney Collection, New York

LIT : Robertson 1980, pp.39, 46-50 with pls 34, 40 and 110

In the mid-1870s Grimshaw produced a group of paintings featuring the interior of Knostrop Old Hall, with Mrs Grimshaw posing as the fashionable lady à la Tissot. They are *Summer, Spring, In the Pleasaunce* and *Il Penseroso* (all dated 1875, Private Collections), and were characterised by the inclusion of Japanese objects such as Japanese fans, porcelain vases, kimonos and a parasol. Exhibited at the Royal Academy in 1885, Cat.91 was the last and most successful of the series. According to the inscription, the main theme of this painting was 'Harmony' and it was conceived as 'a sequel' to the untraced picture, *A Question of Colour*, and such an idea reflected Whistler's aesthetic doctrine. Furthermore, as a result of a recent saleroom discovery, two more Japonisme pictures by Grimshaw have become known; they were painted in his house in Scarborough in 1878: *The Cradle Song* and *The Chorale* (Christopher Wood).

MAURICE WILLIAM GREIFFENHAGEN (1862-1931)

Greiffenhagen was born in London of Danish descent and studied at RA schools. He began to exhibit at the Royal Academy in 1884. His early work reflects James Tissot and some of his allegorical paintings show strong Pre-Raphaelite and Symbolist influences. From 1906 to 1929 he taught at the Glasgow School of Art.

92
Lady with a Japanese Fan, c.1885
Oil on canvas, 17 x 24.5 cm
Andrew McIntosh Patrick

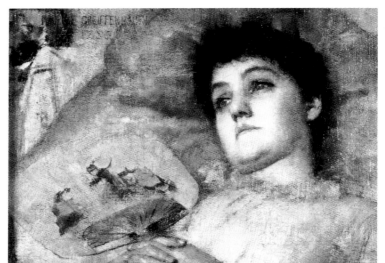

Cat.92

Cat. 93

WILLIAM QUILLER ORCHARDSON
(1832-1910)

Born in Edinburgh. Studied at the Trustees' Academy under Robert Scott Lauder, who was a highly influential Scottish painter of historical scenes, portraits and landscapes. From 1862 onwards Orchardson lived in London, where he was successful as a genre and portrait painter. In addition to his grouping of figures, Orchardson's mature style was characterised by the effective use of empty space to heighten psychological dramas, which was much admired by Whistler, Sickert and Degas. He was involved in the organisation of the Japan-British Exhibition of 1910 in London (see Section XIII) as Chairman of the Fine Arts Committee. 1

NOTE
1. *Official Report: Japan-British Exhibition, London 1910*, p.317

93
Master Baby, 1886
Oil on canvas, 108 x 166 cm
Signed and dated: W.Q.O/86
National Galleries of Scotland

LIT : H.Orchardson Gray, *Life of Orchardson*, n.d., pp.256, 270, 313

A mother is nursing her baby with a Japanese fan. The domestic subject of a mother and child was common in both Victorian genre paintings and Japanese woodcuts. Nevertheless, Orchardson's intimate treatment of motherly love, the simple composition and flat colours indicate his knowledge of Japanese woodcut artists, especially Utamaro.

JAMES CADENHEAD (1858-1927)

Born in Aberdeen. Studied in Edinburgh at RSA schools and in Paris under Carolus Duran. Active in Scotland as landscape painter from 1884 onwards.

94
Lady with Japanese Screen and Goldfish (Portrait of the Artist's Mother), 1886
Oil on canvas, 91.4 x 185.4 cm
Signed and dated b.l.: James Cadenhead 1886
City of Edinburgh Art Centre

LIT : Lasden 1981, fig. 364; Gere 1989, pl.364

The artist's mother is embroidering in front of a large Japanese screen decorated with a Yamato-e-style painting. The detailed rendering of the screen, which shows a mediaeval court scene with aristocratic members on the left watching ceremonial dancing on the right, indicates Cadenhead's careful study of Japanese painting. The screen's rich and flat colours are echoed in the reality of yellow daffodils, goldfish and bunches of thread on the table as well as in the sitter's black silhouette.

KATE HAYLLAR (FL.1883-1898)

Sister of Jessica, Edith and Mary Hayllar, all daughters of the portrait and genre painter, James Hayllar (1829-1920). The sisters studied under their father and all became painters. Specialising in flowers and still-life, Kate Hayllar exhibited twelve works at the Royal Academy between 1885 and 1898. They included the watercolour Cat.95, *The Old Brocaded Gown* and *A Thing of Beauty is a Joy for Ever*, and these subjects reflect the aesthetic mode of that time. Around 1900 she gave up painting to pursue a nursing career.

95
Sunflower and Hollyhocks, 1889
Watercolour, 31.75 x 22.86 cm
Signed and dated: Kate Hayllar/1889
The Corporation of London (Guildhall Art Gallery)

LIT : V. Knight, *The Works of the Corporation of London* 1986, p.136

Sunflowers, hollyhocks, Chinese vases, a Japanese screen, brocade and pale-yellow Oriental silk and carpet. Cataloguing the 'things of beauty' here, this painting exemplifies the current aesthetic taste. In the 1880s, the Aesthetic Movement was in full swing, and English middle-class houses were furnished with suitable objects.

THEODORE ROUSSEL (1847-1926)

Born in Lorient, France, Roussel fought in the Franco-Prussian War. His artistic career began in London, where he settled around 1874. With his English wife, Amelia Bull, he lived in Chelsea from 1879 and became friendly with Whistler in 1885. Although largely self-taught, Roussel was deeply influenced by Whistler, and sometimes in exhibition catalogues he referred to himself as Whistler's disciple. In 1887 he joined the New English Art Club (NEAC), which had been founded in 1886 as a challenging force to the Royal Academy, and its members at the time consisted of Whistler's admirers. In the 1890s the NEAC became the instrument of the Impressionist movement in Britain, and Roussel was to be one of the principal exhibitors.

LIT : F. Rutter, *Théodore Roussel* 1926

96 (Barbican only)
A Girl Reading, 1886-87
Oil on canvas, 152.4 x 161.3 cm
Signed b.l.: Theodore Roussel
Trustees of the Tate Gallery, London

LIT : McConkey 1989, pp.50-1, 57 with pl.43

Shown at the second NEAC exhibition in 1887, Cat. 96 was Roussel's first contribution to the society alongside the portrait of his friend, Mortimer Menpes (see Cats 272-9). Below the diagonal line from the top left, the composition is dominated by the nude girl and the discarded kimono. The kimono, the only decorative element in the picture, is used here effectively to enhance the sitter's stark nakedness set against the dark background. Together with the use of Japanese paraphernalia, Roussel's treatment of the background reflects the influence of Whistler, who painted portraits against undefined expanses of flat colour. Furthermore, the girl's pose and the silhouette of her body contrasting with the surrounding dark colours also recall Manet's *Olympia* (Musée d'Orsay, Paris), painted two decades before.

113

Cat.116 ANONYMOUS BRITISH
Aesthetic Cabinet with Japanese Lacquer Inlay
c. 1870s

V. HIGH VICTORIAN JAPONISME IN ARCHITECTURE AND DESIGN

WILLIAM BURGES (1827-1881)

Burges was a Gothic-Revival architect, designer and antiquarian, who also wrote extensively. Unlike Godwin and Nesfield, he remained true to his Neo-Gothic ideals until his death. He was close to the Pre-Raphaelite circle of Rossetti and was also a close friend of E.W. Godwin. He was inspired by French thirteenth-century Gothic and this is particularly clear in his famous Yatman Cabinet of 1858 in the Victoria and Albert Museum, which was closely based on original French thirteenth-century furniture. This piece with its rich polychromy broke new ground in Gothic-Revival furniture. In architecture his major extant works are the great Cork Cathedral (1863-1904), the restorations of Cardiff Castle (1866-1928) and Castell Coch (1872-91). For the latter two, his patron was the Marquis of Bute and they are examples of highly imaginative fairy-tale Gothic. Burges praised the Japanese section of the 1862 International Exhibition highly, regarded Japanese art as synonymous with mediaeval art and showed in his design how the two can be integrated.

LIT : Crook 1981a; Crook 1981b; Watanabe 1991b, pp.166-74

97
'Wines and Beers' Sideboard, 1859
Painted and gilt wood with a marble top and shelf, 167.6 x 139.7 x 43.1 cm
Trustees of the Victoria and Albert Museum, London

LIT : Crook 1981a, p.295; Crook 1981b, no.B.8, p.77; Watanabe 1991b, 172-3

The central panel of this sideboard depicts 'The Battle between the Wines and Beers' and was painted by Edward J. Poynter (1836-1919). A diaper pattern similar to the one above and below the main picture appears in a Japanese cabinet in Burges's collection. The date of purchase of this Japanese cabinet is not known, but this decoration was a very common one, as can be seen in another example shown at the 1862 International Exhibition and illustrated in Waring's book on this exhibition (pl.288) which is even closer to Burges's design. In the Burges' example, the diaper pattern is contrasted with a checked one. The central portion of the sideboard also gives the effect of a Japanese kakemono with its brocade frame.

98
Diagrammatic Drawing for 'Elephant Inkstand', 1862-63 (From *Orfevrerie Domestique*, p.36)
Ink and watercolour on paper, 48.4 x 30 cm
British Architectural Library Drawings Collection, Royal Institute of British Architects, London

99
Diagrammatic Drawing for 'Elephant Inkstand', 1862-63 (From *Orfevrerie Domestique*, p.37)
Ink and watercolour on paper, 48.3 x 30.9 cm
British Architectural Library Drawings Collection, Royal Institute of British Architects, London

LIT : Crook 1981a, pp.138-9; Crook 1981b, no.C.56, p.115; Watanabe 1991b, pp.169-71

The whereabouts of Cat.99 is unknown, but an early photograph and Burges's own drawings give a good idea of this strange but ingenious object. The piece consists of a Chinese incense-burner in the shape of an elephant, a Chinese cloisonné bowl, a 'green china pot' and a Japanese ivory carving, a netsuke of what looks to be a manzai group - a pair of itinerant comics. The Japanese figures are well integrated into the work and show a new style very much Burges's own.

100
Elephant Candle-stand for Oakwood
Ink and watercolour drawing, 33 x 56 cm
British Architectural Library Drawings Collection, Royal Institute of British Architects, London

LIT : Crook 1981a, note no.98, p.369

This is a drawing of a candle-stand which Burges designed for Thomas Garnet of Oakwood, Bingley.

The candle-stand is also designed to contain lucifer matches and ink. The elephant in this case is likely to be Japanese, as there is a similar original Japanese elephant in the Wallace Collection, London. 1

NOTE
1 We are greatful to Mr Timothy Knox of the RIBA for pointing out the Wallace elephant.

EDWARD WILLIAM GODWIN (1833-1886)

E.W. Godwin was an architect, designer and critic and played a key role in the development of both the Aesthetic Movement and Victorian Japonisme. He was a close friend of both Burges and Whistler. From the Ruskinian Gothic of his Northampton Town Hall, he moved away to a more individualistic style to be seen in buildings such as Dromore Castle for the Earl of Limerick or the White House for Whistler. He was also a versatile designer, of furniture, textiles, wallpaper and for the theatre. Japanese art strongly influenced his work, and his furniture in particular was called 'Anglo-Japanese' which often showed imaginative use of Japanese formal devices and motifs.

LIT : Aslin 1986; Wilkinson 1987 ; Watanabe 1991b, pp.185-97

Cat.97

101

Sideboard, c.1867
Ebonised mahogany and deal with brass fittings
stamped ABERCHROMBIE and four squares cut
from Japanese prints with a seal Sozan (upper
right-hand door and fittings replaced), H. 180.5 x
W. (flaps extended) 251.5 x 51.3 cm, D. 51.3 cm
Bristol City Museums and Art Gallery

LIT : Walton 1976; Aslin 1986, p.27; Wilkinson 1987,
pp.176-7; Watanabe 1991b, pp.191-3

This sideboard was bequeathed to Bristol City
Art Gallery by Edith Craig, daughter of E. W.
Godwin and Ellen Terry, in 1949 and is possibly
the prototype of several other versions. He must
have studied Japanese and Chinese furniture
closely, but the overall effect is very much
Godwin's own. The examples in Bristol, New
York (Museum of Modern Art), and the furniture
maker Watt's catalogue, all show only six legs,
whereas the versions in the Victoria and Albert
Museum and the National Gallery of Victoria,
Melbourne have eight legs for additional stability
and must date from later than 1877, the
publication year of Watt's catalogue.

102

Dromore Castle
Coloured page from *The Architect*, 20 August 1870
Hand-coloured lithograph, 22.5 x 33.5 cm
British Architectural Library Drawings Collection,
Royal Institute of British Architects, London

Godwin was commissioned by Lord Limerick to
build Dromore Castle in 1866 but the building
was only completed in 1873. This illustration in
the architectural periodical, *The Architect* shows
that by this time he had fully developed his
'Anglo-Japanese' style. The furniture designs
show similar characteristics to Cat.101, but
with additional features, and are clearly more
prestigious pieces and designed accordingly.
This illustration cut out of the journal belongs
to the group of working drawings for Dromore
and probably originates in Godwin's office, if it
is not by Godwin himself.

103

Design of a House c.1871 (reproduction)
Sketchbook E 270-1963, p.27
Trustees of the Victoria and Albert Museum,
London

LIT : Girouard 1979, pp.329-35; Wilkinson 1987,
pp.277-9; Watanabe 1991b, pp.194-5

Godwin seems to have begun to show interest
in Japanese architecture at the latest by 1869/70.
Wilkinson pointed out that Godwin studied the
illustrations of *Le Japon illustré* by Aimé Humbert
(Paris 1970). A sketchbook by Godwin in the
Victoria and Albert Museum (E280-1963, p.33)
contains a sketch of a Japanese building which
resembles this design, and shows many Japan-
inspired details. In this half-timbered country
house we can see the converging of the 'Old
English' and the Japanese. Among the extant
buildings by Godwin, Beauvale Lodge in
Nottinghamshire (1871-73) shows similar
tendencies.

104

*Section of a Room containing Furniture in the
Japanese Style*
Ink and watercolour, 18 x 29.5 cm
Inscribed: Anglo-Japanese Designs by E W
Godwin
Trustees of the Victoria and Albert Museum,
London

LIT : *Le Japonisme*, 1988 (230), pp.224-5, col. ill.

105

Figure in an Anglo-Japanese Room Setting, c.1876
Watercolour and pencil, sketchbook, E286-1963
Trustees of the Victoria and Albert Museum,
London

LIT : Aslin 1986, p.25, col. ill.

This highly artificial setting is the epitome of the
Aesthetic Movement with its Oriental overtones.

106 (Barbican only)

Coffee or Occasional Table with Flaps, c.1871
Ebonised wood
Ellen Terry Memorial Museum, Tenterden

LIT : Wilkinson 1987, p.226

This elegant asymmetrical design is evocative
of Japanese furniture with chigaidana (different-
levelled shelves). Another similar piece came to
light recently and is now in the Metropolitan
Museum of Art, New York.

107

Armchair, c.1870
Wood and leather upholstered seat,
83.8 x 53.34 x 53.34 cm
Tom Craig

Cats 108 and 109

108
Chair, c.1880
Wood and upholstered cusion
106.7 x 47 x 47 cm
Tom Craig

109
Wall-hanging, c.1875
Goldcoloured woven silk, patterned with linked
circles and butterfly motif
Woven by Warners, 330.2 x 107.18 cm
Tom Craig

WILLIAM EDEN NESFIELD (1835-1888)

William Eden Nesfield was an artist-architect par
excellence and his collection of Japanese art was
an important part of his artistic environment.
He had befriended most of the Japanophile
artists of the 1860s. He shared offices with
Richard Norman Shaw from 1863 to 1876 and
Nesfield collaborated with Albert Moore. He was
also friendly with, among others, Burges, Simeon
Solomon and Whistler. He used Japanese motifs,
particularly the carved discs which he called
'pies'(!), in the decoration of his buildings, such
as Kinmel Park in Denbighshire, but most subtly
at Cloverly Hall in Shropshire, as can be seen in
his drawings dated 1865 to 1870 in the Victoria
and Albert Museum.

LIT : Aslet 1978; Girouard 1979, pp.318-28; The Friends
of Radwinter Church 1988; Watanabe 1991b, pp.178-84

110
Sketchbook II
22 x 15.2 cm (page size)
British Architectural Library Drawings Collection,
Royal Institute of British Architects, London

This sketchbook contains a number of drawings
by Nesfield which are copies of details taken
from Japanese illustrated books. These are
mainly figures, such as 'the henpecked husband',
who turns up twice, and details of patterns. On
pp.66-7 he copied a 'Japanese landscape'. On pp.
33, 34 and 36 he writes 'From a Japanese novel'.
The sketchbook contains two dates, both of them
1862, and it is likely that Nesfield obtained the
Japanese book at the International Exhibition.

ATTRIBUTED TO WILLIAM EDEN NESFIELD (1835-1888)

111
Folding Screen, 1867
Ebonised wood, in six sections, with fretted and
gilded decorations incorporating twelve paintings
on silk, 207 x 231.8cm
Inscribed: Richard & Agnes. Shaw AD 1867. /
From James Forsyth
Trustees of the Victoria and Albert Museum

LIT : *The Aesthetic Movement and the Cult of Japan* 1972,
p.48; Watanabe 1991b, pp.183-4

This screen was given by James Forsyth to
Richard Norman Shaw and his wife as a wedding

present in 1867. It has been attributed convincingly
to Nesfield in the exhibition catalogue, *The
Aesthetic Movement and the Cult of Japan*, Fine
Art Society, London 1972, on stylistic and
circumstantial grounds. Original Far-Eastern
'flower and bird' pictures are incorporated and it
is covered with a galaxy of Japan-inspired disc
motifs and patterns.

Cat.111

THOMAS JECKYLL (1827-1881)

Jeckyll was a Gothic-Revival architect/designer
who also strove to learn from Japan during the
1860s. He was known to the Whistler circle by
1862, and was one of the most active designers
in the Japanese style. His designs for furniture
(c.1866-70) in Ken Hill in Norfolk for Edward
Green, his interior design for 1 Holland Park,
London, for Alexander Ionides, commissioned
in 1870, and the astonishing cast-iron pavilion for
the 1876 Philadelphia Centennial Exhibition are
remarkable examples of Victorian Japonisme,
whereas the famous Peacock Room for Frederick
Leyland, commissioned in 1876, shows less
Japanese elements than are sometimes ascribed
to it. It was Whistler's wall decorations which
made it an original Japoniste interior.
LIT : *The Aesthetic Movement and the Cult of Japan* 1972,
pp.35, 40-2, 46, 47; Girouard 1979, pp.366-74; Watanabe
1991b, pp.196-7

112
*Fire-Surrounding decorated with the Japanese
Circular Motif 'Mon'*
Executed by Barnard Bishop and Barnard, c.1880
Patinated cast iron, 96.52 x 96.52 cm
Private Collection, England

113
A Pair of Sunflower Firedogs, c.1870
Cast iron, gilt bronze and wrought iron,
83.82 x 26.67 cm
Private Collection, England

114
Set of Fireguard Pieces decorated with Japanese Motif
Brass outer guard: 30 x 122 x 25.8 cm; small
container: 12 x 46 x 8.3 cm; large container with
handles: 17.6 x 54 x 20.6 cm; pair of iron stands:
16.3 x 17.7 cm (with legs L. 10.3 cm)
Andrew McIntosh Patrick

Jeckyll produced many designs for metalwork
in the Japanese taste for the company Barnard,
Bishop and Barnard in Norwich, the culmination
of which was the cast-iron pavilion for the 1876
Philadelphia Centennial Exhibition. Sunflowers
became a favourite motif of his and sometimes
the stylised sunflower is used like a Japanese
mon (family crest). He often covers the surface
of his metal work and furniture with ornaments
of dazzling variety, many of them of Japanese
origin, though by no means all.

ANONYMOUS BRITISH

115
*'Nanban Seigan' Cabinet incorporating Japanese
Lacquer Panels*, c.1870s
34 x 91 x 129 cm
Andrew McIntosh Patrick

LIT : Watanabe 1982; Doi 1988

This unusual cabinet combines Japonisme of the
nineteenth century and Japanese Nanban
(Southern Barbarian) art of c.1600 in one piece.
The drawers of the cabinet are reminiscent of a
desk designed by Thomas Jeckyll for Alexander
Ionides and now in the Victoria and Albert
Museum. However, it is the lacquer panels which
make this work so unusual. All five lacquer
panels probably belonged to one portable
Christian altarpiece (seigan). They show
characteristic geometric patterns, dense flower
and bird motifs and mother-of-pearl inlay. These
lacquer altarpieces were made in Japan and often
incorporated a pediment with the emblem of the
Society of Jesus. The central painting is by the
Dutch painter, Peter Holsteyn the Elder (1580-
1662). It is signed and dated 1627 at bottom right.

ANONYMOUS BRITISH

116
Aesthetic Cabinet with Japanese Lacquer Inlay,
c. 1870s
34.8 x 50 x 121.5 cm
Andrew McIntosh Patrick

VI. EARLY JAPANESE ARCHITECTURE IN THE WESTERN STYLE

THOMAS JAMES WATERS (dates unknown)

A British surveyor who seems to have come to Japan before 1865. Very little is known about his life outside Japan. From 1868 onwards he gained extensive contracts from the Japanese government, including the Takebashi Barracks (1870-74), the Ginza Bricktown and the Osaka Mint (1868-71). Waters dominated the architectural scene until December 1875, when his contract was not renewed and he was dismissed by the government. After the arrival of Josiah Conder from England in 1877, we hear no more of him.

LIT : Stewart 1987, pp.18-22; Fujimori 1982, Chapter I

117
SHOSAI IKKEI (FL. c. 1870)
A View of the Tokyo Ginza Bricktown from Kyobashi, 1873 (reproduction)
Colour print from woodblocks (triptych)

After the downfall of the feudal government, the capital of Japan, Edo, now renamed Tokyo, experienced an unprecedented decline. Many of the feudal residences, which occupied large areas of the city, were in ruins and the population was reduced dramatically. Then in 1872 the city was swept by a big fire, which gave the planners an opportunity to introduce new Western-style town planning, which would also be fireproof. Waters was entrusted with the design of the Ginza Bricktown, where he introduced brick-built terraced houses with Georgian colonnades unifying the street. His plan is often regarded as a failure, but Fujimori Terunobu's re-evaluation of this scheme in a wider context puts the versatility of Waters in a much more positive light, laying the basis for Ginza's future prosperity.

118
Porch of the former Mint in Osaka (Sakurayama Public Hall), 1868-71 (reproduction)

119
Senpukan, Osaka, 1868-71 (reproduction)

One of the urgent tasks of the newly formed Japanese government was the setting up of the National Mint. Waters's design for the Osaka Mint with a large Neo-Classical façade for the factory, though in itself not a particularly elegant one, fits in well with the fledgling government's desire for grandeur. This was also the first large-scale official factory built by them. Senpukan was built as a reception pavilion for visiting VIPs within the factory premises. At one time it became the official resting place for Emperor Meiji whenever he visited Osaka. Around 1893/4 the roof was slightly extended, which provided better protection against the rain, but also gave a stronger Japanese feel to this essentially colonial-style building with the characteristic verandah. 1 The main façade of the Mint was moved to its present site in 1935.

NOTE
1 Stewart (1987, p.20) rightly emphasizes the artisanal refinement of Senpukan compared to the relative awkwardness of the Mint facade, but the lack of a parapet, he mentions, was caused only by this later modification and the original design shows a distinct parapet.

CHARLES ALFRED CHASTEL DE BOINVILLE (1849-?)

Previously he was regarded as a French architect of whom no details were known, but Shishido Minoru's study revealed that he was actually British. Izumida Hideo, who is continuing the research on Chastel de Boinville after Shishido's death, further established that he was of Huguenot origin, and that he was a Fellow of the Royal Institute of British Architects. 1 He stayed in Japan between 1872 and 1881 and did not work as extensively as either Waters or Conder, but the Lecture Hall at the Imperial College of Engineering in Tokyo is generally regarded as his main achievement.

LIT : Shishido Minoru, 'Nihon Seikokai no kenchiku kenkyu. 1. Tokyo Sei Andere kyokai' (The Study of the architecture of the Episcopal Church of Japan. 1. St Andrew's Church Tokyo), *Kaetsu Joshi Tanki Daigaku Kenkyu Ronshu* (Journal of Kaetsu Women's College), vol.28, no.1. pp.13-28

NOTE
1.We are grateful to Professor Fujimori Terunobu for the information on Shishido's and Izumida's research.

120
Lecture Hall at the Imperial College of Engineering, 1877 (reproduction)

LIT : Stewart 1987, pp.33-4

The façade of this building shows a powerful Palladian design, and David B. Stewart sees it as resembling 'a condensed version of William Kent's Horse Guards in London, as executed by Vardy' (p.33). The building no longer exists.

JOSIAH CONDER (1852-1920)

Conder was born in London, trained by Thomas Roger Smith and William Burges, and won the medallion of the Royal Institute of British Architects in 1876. Before Conder had the opportunity to build in England, he took up a post to teach architecture in Tokyo in 1877 at the invitation of the Japanese government. He also designed many important buildings in Japan, both public and private, educated many future leading Japanese architects, such as Tatsuno Kingo, Katayama Tokuma and Sone Tatsuzo and is generally regarded as the father of modern architecture in Japan. In 1888 he resigned from his official post and opened a private practice in Tokyo. From various eclectic Gothic-Revival

Cat.121B

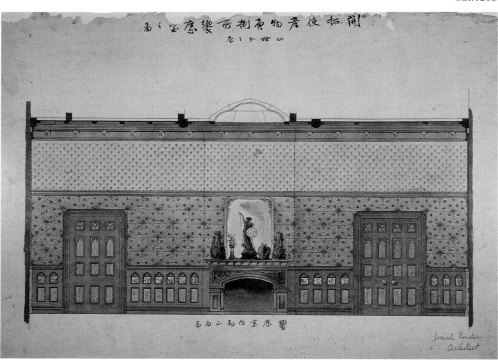

styles, he moved towards a more classical style in his later years. He married a Japanese, built all his works in Japan and died in Japan. He also learnt Japanese painting under Kyosai and was given the artist's name of Kyoei. He wrote extensively on Japanese art; especially his books on Kyosai, on the Japanese garden and on Japanese flower arrangements were very influential and widely read in the West.

LIT : Onogi 1979; Kawahigashi 1980-81 (vol.III contains an extensive bibliography of Conder); Stewart 1987 passim.; *Rokumeikan no yume* 1991

121
Designs for the Hokkaido Colonisation Agency [Kaitakushi]: Sale and Reception Rooms, Tokyo 1878

A. *North and East Elevations*
Drawn by K. Tatsuno
Watercolour, 65 x 100 cm
Signed and dated b.r.: Josiah Conder Architect, b.l.: Drawn by K. Tatsuno 1st May 1878
Bank of Japan, Tokyo

LIT : Kawahigashi 1980-81 (2-5)

B. *Dining Room, Interior, North Side*
Watercolour, 44 x 60.5 cm
Signed: Josiah Conder Architect
Bank of Japan, Tokyo

LIT : Kawahigashi 1980-81 (2-31)

In 1878 the Japanese government commissioned Conder to build the Hokkaido Colonisation Agency's Sale and Reception Rooms. The ground floor was used to display and sell the goods from the northernmost island of Japan, Hokkaido. The first floor served for reception purposes and included a dining room, a drawing room, a billiard room and a bedroom. The exterior is fashioned in a Ruskinian Venetian Gothic, appropriate enough for a building facing a river front, and the interior is pure Aesthetic Movement! In the dining room he uses a pattern which is a variant of the scale motif so beloved of Whistler, and Conder uses other Japanese and Oriental motifs in details. The building was burnt out in the 1923 great Kanto earthquake and was subsequently demolished.

122
Designs for the Ueno Imperial Museum, Tokyo, 1882

A. *Plan of First Floor and Elevation of Internal Wall*
(Setagaya only)
Watercolour, 53 x 110 cm
Inscribed b.c.: Elevation Of Internal Wall A
Tokyo National Museum

LIT : Kawahigashi 1980-81 (3-2)

B. *Front Elevation* (Barbican only)
Watercolour, 35 x 114 cm
Signed b.r.: Josiah Conder Architect
Tokyo National Museum

LIT : Kawahigashi 1980-81 (3-3)

C. *Back Elevation* (Setagaya only)
Watercolour, 29 x 115.5 cm
Tokyo National Museum

LIT : Kawahigashi 1980-81 (3-4)

D. *Two Sections and West Elevation*
(Setagaya only)
Watercolour, 58.2 x 88.4 cm
Titled t.c.: Ueno Hakubutsukan setsumen hyakubun no ichi no zu (the drawing of the Ueno Museum section 1/100)
Inscribed b.l.: sokumen (side section); c.r.: heicho no setsumen (heicho section); b.r.: kootsu no setsumen (kootsu section) and Josiah Conder Architect Aug. 1878
Tokyo National Museum

LIT : Kawahigashi 1980-81 (3-5)

E. *Elevation of Front Entrance* (Barbican only)
Watercolour, 98.5 x 65 cm
Inscribed t.c.: Ueno hakubutsukan chushin no zu (the drawing of the centre of the Ueno Museum), nijubun no ichi (1/20); b.l.: setsumen (section); b.c.: shomen no zu (the drawing of the front)
Tokyo National Museum

LIT : Kawahigashi 1980-81 (3-6)

F. *Side Entrance and Detail of Stairs*
(Setagaya only)
Watercolour, 60.4 x 82.4 cm
Inscribed t.r.: Side Entrance; c.: sokumen kaidan (side staircase); c.: Section; c.l.: Inside, Outside; b.l.: Drawn by Fujimoto Jukichi, 1st Nob.[sic], 1878, Plan; b.r.: Scale Of Shiaku
Tokyo National Museum

LIT : Kawahigashi 1980-81 (3-23)

G. *General View of the Ueno Imperial Museum, Tokyo,* 1882 (Barbican only)
Watercolour on paper, c. 50 x 80 cm
Tokyo National Museum

The first national museum in Japan, the Ueno Imperial Museum in Tokyo is generally regarded as one of Conder's masterpieces. According to Kawahigashi there is a possibility that the ground plan may have been designed by Antonio Fontanesi, the government-appointed Italian painting tutor, though perhaps a more likely candidate is Giovanni V. Cappeletti, an Italian architect also employed by the Japanese government. However, the elevation is clearly Conder's own, where he introduces what he called 'pseudo-Saracenic' elements, which show a strong influence of the architectural theory of his teacher, Thomas Roger Smith. The dated drawings range from August 1878 to October 1879 and show in detail some differences from the executed building, which was officially opened in 1882, but destroyed in the great Kanto earthquake in 1923.

123
Designs for the Unitarian Hall (Yuiitsukan), Tokyo 1893
Watercolour on paper, 46 x 32.5 cm
Inscribed b.c.: Unitarian Hall (now Building) Tokyo, Japan, General View; b.r.: J. Conder delt.
Department of Architecture, Kyoto University

LIT : Kawahigashi 1980-81 (13-5); *Rokumeikan no yume* 1991, p.9

Conder was commissioned to build a new centre for the Unitarian Church in Japan, which was finished in 1894. American Unitarian missionaries arrived in Japan in 1887 and by 1891 they apparently needed larger premises for their activities. The church is a two-storey wooden construction and the interior is in the Western style. The exterior shows an extraordinary mixture of East and West. The weather-boards, a popular technique for Western-style buildings in Japan, give a strongly American impression, whereas much of the roofing relies on the Japanese traditional vocabulary, with even a hint of China. This is Conder's only building in such a strongly hybrid style, and Fujimori Terunobu argues that it was his American patrons who wished this and not Conder, because the Head of the Unitarian Church in Tokyo, Arthur May Knapp, was known to have been an ardent supporter of the blending of East and West. The finished building, which is no longer extant, was slightly different from this drawing.

124
Designs for the Residence of Iwasaki at Hakone - Yumoto, Kanagawa, c. 1906
Watercolour and pencil, 42 x 31 cm
Signed: J.C.
Department of Architecture, Kyoto University

LIT : Kawahigashi 1980-81 (25-2)

This watercolour seems to show Conder's first thoughts for a villa in Hakone-Yumoto for Baron Iwasaki Yanosuke, one of the most powerful industrialists and a very important patron of Conder.

125
Mitsui Club, Tokyo, 1913
(reproduction)

This masterpiece from Conder's late period was built for the Mitsui family to entertain guests and is one of his few extant buildings. It has a reinforced brick structure with white tile cladding outside, one of the earliest examples of this technique in Japan. The dynamic and Baroque elegance of the garden elevation shows the maturity of Conder's classicising style compared to his earlier, perhaps more pedestrian, attempts at Ruskinian Gothic, such as the Hokkaido Colonisation Agency Sale and Reception Rooms.

TATSUNO KINGO (1854-1919)

With Katayama Tokuma, Sone Tatsuzo and Sadachi Shichijiro he belonged to Conder's first graduation class. Tatsuno's student works are fairly pedestrian, but he distinguished himself for his hard work and leadership qualities and managed to graduate top of the class. He was immediately sent to England in 1880 for further architectural studies, and he spent about seven months in William Burges's office until the latter's death in 1881. He came back to Japan in 1883 and when in 1884 Conder's contract ran out, Tatsuno was appointed Professor of Architecture.

From this time until his death in 1919, he reigned supreme in Japanese architecture, providing a strict but solid education for his architectural students and winning an astonishing number of public commissions.

LIT : Fujimori 1979; Onogi 1979; Stewart 1987, passim.; Yoshikawa and Mizuno 1990

126
Bank of Japan, Otemachi, Tokyo, 1890-96 (reproduction)

In July 1988 Tatsuno was appointed as the architect of the Bank of Japan and in August of that year he set out to study Bank buildings in Europe for a year. The result shows that he has closely studied the Banque Nationale at Brussels (1860-74). However, Tatsuno digested the sources, a combination of French Baroque palaces and Palladianism, and created the first purely Western-style building of austere monumentality and complexity built by a Japanese.

127
Former Morioka Bank (Iwate Bank), Morioka, 1908-11 (reproduction)

Like his teacher Conder, Tatsuno was an eclectic architect. However, this type of brick building with stone trimmings developed into his favourite style, often called the Tatsuno style. While he was in London, he noticed the popularity of the 'Queen Anne' style there and in a letter to Sone Tatsuzo he comments that the style has aspects which make it suitable to be adopted in Japan and singles out Richard Norman Shaw. 1 This Japanised 'Queen Anne' style with the colourful contrast of red brick and white stone trimming capped by a dome was extremely influential, and many other architects used it for banks and offices across Japan.

NOTE
1 Quoted in Fujimori 1979, p.140. We are grateful to Professor Fujimori for pointing out this quote to us.

128
Former Residence of Matsumoto Kenjiro, Tobata, Kitakyushu, 1909-11 (reproduction)

LIT : Fujimori Terunobu and Koizumi Kazuko, *Aru Nuvo no Yakata: Kyu Matsumoto Kenjiro tei* (The Art Nouveau Mansion: Former Residence of Matsumoto Kenjiro), Tokyo 1986

For Tatsuno this is an unusual building with its half-timbered exterior and extravagant Art Nouveau interior. It shows uncharacteristic elegance and lightness. The building process was supervised by Kubota Shozaburo, who also supervised the former Konoike Residence, another Art Nouveau building.

KATAYAMA TOKUMA (1853-1917)

Katayama, another first-generation pupil of Conder, became the most important court architect during the Meiji period. He designed important museum buildings, such as the Imperial Nara Museum (1894) or the Imperial

Cat.131

Kyoto Museum (1895). His interiors are on the whole richly decorated by artists and craftsmen.

LIT : Onogi 1979

129
Front Façade, Former Akasaka Detached Palace, Tokyo, 1899-1906 (reproduction)

130
Higashi no Ma (The Eastern Room), Former Akasaka Detached Palace, Tokyo, 1899-1906 (reproduction)

This building has been hailed as the most important monument of the Meiji period. Katayama's task was to represent the Japanese Royal family on at least the same level as those of Europe. For this reason he studied European palace architecture closely and in particular French palaces were important sources of inspiration for him. The exterior is unashamedly Western, but in details he uses Japanese motifs such as Japanese armour, in the way a French architect would use French armour motifs. The structure is reinforced brick with mostly granite cladding outside. The astonishingly extravagant Higashi no Ma, where Orientalism runs riot, is the smoking room and therefore Oriental decoration was regarded as suitable, because of the association of tobacco with the Orient. This building was initially planned as the residence of the Crown Prince, however the Meiji Emperor is said to have objected to the extravagance of the building and in the end the Crown Prince did not use it as his residence at all.

SONE TATSUZO (1852-1937)

Among his first generation of students, Conder regarded Sone most highly as an architectural designer. However, Sone seems to have been more of a scholarly gentleman-architect and worked mostly for private patrons rather than for the government. After Tatsuno's death in 1919, he became the most eminent architect of the pre-Second World War period in Japan.

LIT : Ishida 1979

131
Keio Gijuku University Library, 1908-12 (reproduction)

The founder of Keio Gijuku, Fukuzawa Yukichi (1838-1901), was one of the key intellectuals of the Meiji period who made a great contribution to education and his very influential publications show a strong British influence. Sone had just formed a partnership with Chujo Seiichiro (1868-1936) in 1908, when he received this commission. The floor of this library is reinforced concrete and the walls are a combination of stone and brick. Sone's skilful use of the Gothic vocabulary in creating a harmonious campus building is striking. Though this building suffered fire damage during the Second World War, the front porch has been preserved in its original condition and is a good example of an early Western-style brick building still extant in Tokyo.

VII. THE WESTERN WAY OF LIFE IN JAPAN

THE AGE OF THE DEER CRY PAVILION

The Japanese Government commissioned Conder (see Section VI) to build luxury reception facilities for foreign dignitaries. The immediate purpose of the Rokumeikan, or Deer Cry Pavilion, was to ease the diplomatic struggle for the improvement of the unequal treaties Japan had with the West, by providing a suitable setting for formal and informal negotiations, and to show that Japan had now outgrown its feudal backwardness and had transformed itself into a modern nation worthy of being treated on an equal basis with Western nations. In this building, the upper-class Japanese could mingle freely with foreign guests at various functions, especially balls. The Deer Cry Pavilion became the most potent symbol of unfettered Westernisation during the Meiji period. However, its golden age was short-lived and, with the realisation of the failure to persuade the West to change the unequal treaties, it lost its primary raison d'être. In 1890 its name was changed to Kazoku Kaikan (The Peers' Club) and it was eventually demolished.

LIT : Barr 1968; Tomita 1984

132
JOSIAH CONDER (1852-1920) (see Section VI)
Rokumeikan (Deer Cry Pavilion), 1881-83
(reproduction) c.1892

Conder apparently wished to build it in an overtly 'pseudo-Saracenic' style, but the Foreign Minister Inoue Kaoru, a strong advocate of Westernisation, is said to have rejected his first plan as lacking in stately dignity, presumably wishing for architecture in a full-blown Western style. The executed building nevertheless shows Oriental detailing.

133
YOSHU CHIKANOBU (1838-1912)
Picture of the Ladies' Charity Bazaar at the Deer Cry Pavilion (Rokumeikan ni okeru kifujin jizenkai no zu), 1887 (reproduction)
Colour print from woodblocks (triptych)

LIT: Meech-Pekarik 1986, pp.158-62

One of the events which was introduced at the Rokumeikan in June 1884 was the annual Ladies' Bazaar. The concept of charity work as a leisured ladies' activity was a Western one, quite alien to the traditional role most Japanese women played up to this time. Here we can see that the Westernisation of the role of women was an important part of the intentional effort to modernise Japan, even in the highest quarters. A number of the distinguished members of the all-female committee mentioned in this print had studied in or visited the West. This print also shows how these occasions were seen as

trend-setters for the introduction of Western fashion, and prints of this kind were in themselves part of the process of publicising Western-style dress. In reality, however, bustle dresses such as these were confined mostly to those who were able to attend Rokumeikan balls and were not widespread throughout Japan.

134
JAPANESE
Lady Nabeshima's Dress, c.1881
White rinzu silk satin with fan and flower motifs, habutae silk, silk tassels with wooden beads, whalebone
Nabeshima Hokokai, Saga

This is an original bustle dress from the Rokumeikan period, probably made in Japan. The material is white rinzu silk satin with tassels and wooden beads backed with habutae silk and supported with whalebone. This dress belonged to Nabeshima Naohiro's wife Nagako. Naohiro was the feudal lord of the Saga clan when the 'Meiji Restoration' occurred and he went to England in 1871 to study for about eight years. Naohiro was then appointed Envoy Extraordinary and Minister Plenipotentiary to Italy. The newly married couple arrived in Rome in April 1881 and stayed in Europe until 1882. In the Nabeshima Collection there is another bustle dress belonging to Lady Nabeshima with a label 'E Joyce & Co., Court Dress Maker, 16 Dover St., London'.

135
Portrait of Lady Nabeshima in Rome, c.1881-82
(reproduction)

Pierre Loti, the author of *Madame Chrysanthème* (1887), attended a ball at the Rokumeikan in 1885 and commented very favourably on Lady Nabeshima's appearance.

LIT : Tomita 1984, pp.152, 200-1, 211

JAPANESE

136
Frock Coat, c.1870s
White linen
Katakura Collection, Shiroishi

At the back of this frock coat the sparrows and bamboo crest of the Katakura family is embroidered in exactly the same position as a formal Japanese men's kimono would have such a crest. In this way a Japanese element is elegantly introduced into Western dress. 1

NOTE
1 We are grateful to the staff of Bunka Gakuen Costume Museum and Mrs Obikata Namiko for their help on this item.

JAPANESE

137
Wine Glass with Opaque-White Twisted Stem,
mid-19th century
H. 12.1 cm, D. 5.6 cm
Suntory Museum of Art, Tokyo

LIT : *One Hundred Masterpieces* 1989, pp.50, 115

This wine glass uses the technique of a twisted stem which may have been influenced by imported English examples from the eighteenth or nineteenth century and was made in Japan probably around the mid-nineteenth century.

JAPANESE

138
Ruby-Red Cut-Glass Bowl with Colour Overlay,
mid-19th century
H. 7.2 cm, D. 11.1 cm
Suntory Museum of Art, Tokyo

LIT : *One Hundred Masterpieces* 1989, pp.66, 116

High-quality cut glass was produced in the Satsuma region from 1851 onwards and it often shows the strong influence of Irish and English cut glass, such as the hobnail or the strawberry cut. This bowl is a good example of the use of the strawberry cut in two slightly different sizes.

JAPANESE

139
Blue Cut-Glass Bowl with Circle Design Colour Overlay, mid-19th century
H. 9 cm, D. 10.7 cm
Suntory Museum of Art, Tokyo

LIT : *One Hundred Masterpieces* 1989, pp.67, 116

Each of the blue circle motifs on the side of this Satsuma cut-glass bowl shows a different pattern. This unusual treatment gives a good idea of the variety of cut patterns employed in Satsuma including the hobnail and the strawberry.

JAPANESE

140
Three-Tiered Cut-Glass Boxes
Suntory Museum of Art, Tokyo

The Japanese often used tiered boxes of lacquer or ceramic ware to store sweets or pickled vegetables. Larger lacquer boxes were used for picnic lunches. These glass boxes were probably favoured in summer for their coolness.

OSHIGE CHUZAEMON (1857-1891)

Oshige worked for over ten years at the Shinagawa Glass Company in Tokyo as an apprentice, where over the rather turbulent period of its history a number of British experts were employed until 1888 when the company brought in German experts. Oshige became independent around 1889 and specialised in making high-quality glassware.

LIT : Inoue Akiko, 'Garasu' (Glass), in *Meiji no Soshoku Kogei (Decorative Crafts of the Meiji Period)*, Bessatsu Taiyo, no.70, Summer 1990, pp.97-101

141
Lamp, Late-Edo period
H. 47 cm
Private Collection

Lamps became very popular in Japan during the Meiji period (1868-1911), especially in the 1890s. They were regarded as symbols of Westernisation, but there are taller versions which are adapted for use in Japanese straw-matted rooms. This is perhaps one of the finest Meiji-period lamps and though the globe is lost, it shows skilfully executed engravings and gold-red colour overlay.

up of the first railway in Japan providing materials, technical know-how and even the initial capital. Edmund Morel (1841-1871) who led the team which built the first railway also encouraged the Japanese Government to pursue a policy of self-sufficiency in both materials and manpower. The first railway was officially opened in 1872.

LIT : Harada Katsumasa, 'Meiji Seifu no Tetsudo Seisaku' (The Railway Policy of the Meiji Government), in Yoshikawa and Mizuno 1990, pp.34-7

142
Model of a Train, c.1872
Kanagawa Prefectural Museum, Yokohama

Initially British locomotives and carriages such as these were used, but from the mid-1890s the Japanese started to manufacture their own locomotives. Japanese carriages had three classes of accommodation, like their British cousins.

143
Tokyo Station: Railway Centre in Japan
Postcard
Horesh Collection, London

LIT : Fujimori 1979, pp.143-7; Yoshikawa and Mizuno 1990

Cat.143

144
ICHIYOSAI KUNITERU (1829 - 1874)
Complete View of the Steam Engine Railway at Kanagawa (Kanagawa jokisha tetsudo no zenzu), 1870
Colour print from woodblocks
(two sheets from triptych), 37.8 x 50.6 cm
Bodleian Library, Oxford

LIT : Yokota 1989, p.58

The popularity of the new railway system is reflected in the astonishingly large number of Ukiyo-e prints (over 300) which relate to railways. Details, such as the design of the locomotives, are frequently incorrect and many of these prints were published even before the railway came into operation.

145
Japanese Illustrated Books

A. *One Hundred Beauties and Famous Spots of Tokyo (Tokyo Meisho Hyakunin Bijo)*, c. 1870's
Album of colour woodcuts, 36.4 x 27 cm
Mrs D. Wallis

B. *Fifty-three views of Tokaido Highway (Tokaido Gojusan Tai)*, c. 1870's
Album of colour woodcuts, 37 x 26 cm
Mrs C. A. Jamieson

C. *Famous Spots of Tokyo (Toto Meisho Cho)*, c. 1870's
Album of watercolours on silk, 36.2 x 25 cm
Mrs C. A. Jamieson

These items were brought back as souvenirs from Japan by two British engineers who participated in the setting up of the railway system in Japan and have come to light only recently.

NOTE
We are grateful to Mr Tom Richards for drawing our attention to these books.

THE AGE OF MODERN TRAVEL AND LEISURE

The railway between Yokohama and Shinbashi in Tokyo was regarded as one of the most potent symbols of Westernisation in Meiji- period Japan. For the Japanese Government the development of the railway network was an important tool to strengthen the centralist policy which they were pursuing. As Harada Katsumasa has argued, unlike other Asian countries, Japan organised its own railway system, thanks partly to the non-colonialist attitude of Britain towards Japan. However, Britain was instrumental in the setting

Tokyo Station (1907-14) was originally built by Josiah Conder's pupil, Tatsuno Kingo, utilising the layout planned by the German Franz Baltzer (1857-1927). It was bombed during the Second World War and reconstructed after the war. The three-storey building has been changed to two storeys and the roof line has undergone considerable changes, but the original elevation beneath it has been substantially retained. This old postcard gives a good impression of the original station.

POSTCARDS

Gradually the postcard replaced the coloured photograph as a popular tourist souvenir for Western visitors to Japan. There were many different types of postcard: hand-coloured photo reproductions, crudely hand-painted cards, prints by named artists, etc. Japan's victory over China in 1895 and over Russia in 1905 and the Anglo-Japanese Alliance of 1902 seem to have made Japan-related postcards very popular in Britain. They were often published by German or French companies for the British market. Some of them are fancifully designed with little understanding of the Japanese subjects they depict, but a great number of others are virtually indistinguishable from those published in Japan.

146
Album of Picture Postcards showing Japanese Street-Scenes,
27.5 x 37 cm
Horesh Collection, London

Display of eight colour postcards:

A. *Azumabashi, Tokyo*

B. *Entrance to Asakusa Temple, Tokyo*

C. *Sakae-machi, Kobe*

D. *Motomachi-dori, Kobe*

E. *Yoshidabashi, Yokohama*

F. *Jinpu-ro, Yokohama*

G. *Whole view of the Grand Hotel, Yokohama*

H. *Bentenbashi, Yokohama*

These postcards show major sights and streets in the three cities, Tokyo, Yokohama and Kobe, which were the cities most visited by foreigners. Jinpu-ro was a well-known house in the licensed quarter.

147
Nationalist-type Postcards

A. *Kimigayo (Japanese national anthem)*
Horesh Collection, London

B. *A Japanese Prince*
Horesh Collection, London

148
Military-type Postcards

A. H. MONTAGU LOVE
Three Postcards showing Japanese Officers
Horesh Collection, London

B. ANONYMOUS
Uniforms of the Japanese Army
Horesh Collection, London

C. *Four Postcards of Japanese Celebrities:*
(a) Marquis Yamagata. Famous Japanese Field Marshal
(b) Viscount Katsura. Prime Minister of Japan
(c) Admiral Togo. 'The Nelson of Japan'
(d) General Terauchi. Japanese Minister of War
Horesh Collection, London

D. *Three Satirical Postcards:*
(a) DUDLEY HARDY (1866-1922)
'Making Him Dance' c.1904/5
Japanese officer whipping a bear.
(b) WILLIAM HENRY ELLAM (FL.1900-14)
'Xmas Greeting. 'Jap' The Giant Killer, c.1904/5
Samurai with sword leaning on a Russian soldier.
(c) WILLIAM HENRY ELLAM
What The 'Sea Saw', c.1904/5
Japanese and Russian soldiers playing seesaw.
Horesh Collection, London.

Cat.160

Cat.158

Cat.159

THE AGE OF MODERN COMMERCE AND ADVERTISING

The first National Industrial Exhibition (Naikoku Kangyo Hakurankai) was held in 1877 in Tokyo. Throughout the Meiji period the Japanese Government tried to use these exhibitions to promote industry and commerce and their efforts culminated in the fifth and by far the largest National Industrial Exhibition of 1903 in Osaka. With the expansion of commerce, advertisements became more important and many companies used English texts in their advertisements to enhance their modern appeal and to reach foreign customers in cities such as Kobe and Yokohama.

WHAT THE "SEA SAW"

Cat.148

LIT : Yoshii Keiro, 'Daigokai Naikoku Kangyohaku no disupure' (The displays of the fifth National Industrial Exhibition), in Yoshida 1986, pp.287-306

149
Pair of Postcards commemorating the fifth National Industrial Exhibition (Naikoku Kangyo Hakurankai), 1903
Horesh Collection, London

150
TENGUYA TSUTIDA & CO., OSAKA
Set of Playing Cards for Japanese/English Use, c.1895
6 x 3.5 cm each, in original box and wrapper
Worshipful Company of Makers of Playing Cards, London

This set of playing cards is ingeniously designed so that with the same set both Japanese hanakaruta (flower cards) and Western cardgames can be played. The company called itself an overseas export and import trader and the set was probably marketed as an export item. It was awarded a prize at the fourth National Industrial Exhibition in Kyoto.

151
ANONYMOUS
Handbill (with Fukusuke) of C. Illies & Co., c.1880-90
Gallery Art Kamigata, Kyoto

This colourful handbill advertises 'ANILINE COLOURS'. The figure with the huge head is Fukusuke, a talisman for luck, a particularly popular character used in handbills.

152
ANONYMOUS
Handbill (with a butterfly) of Findlay, Richardson & Co., c.1880-90
Gallery Art Kamigata, Kyoto

153
ANONYMOUS
Handbill (with a boy playing the flute) of Cornes & Co., c.1880-90
Gallery Art Kamigata, Kyoto

154
ANONYMOUS
Handbill (with a gourd) of Cornes & Co., c.1880-90
Gallery Art Kamigata, Kyoto

155
ANONYMOUS
Handbill (with a Kabuto, Japanese military helmet) of H.C. Morf & Co., c.1880-90
Gallery Art Kamigata, Kyoto

156
ANONYMOUS
Handbill (with two Japanese women) of C Illies & Co., c.1880-90
Gallery Art Kamigata, Kyoto

157
ANONYMOUS
Handbill for the New Year, 1890
38.6 x 26.4cm
Inscribed: SHINTO THOKIE, PAPER HANGER, ENGLISH WALLPAPER, FOR SALE
Bodleian Library, Oxford

This is a handbill containing New Year greetings produced by a paper hanger in Kobe, who gives his name in English as 'Shinto Thokie'.

158
ANONYMOUS
'Happy Cigarettes', c.1902
Poster, 76.3 x 34.4 cm
Tobacco and Salt Museum, Tokyo

In this poster for 'Happy Cigarettes' of the Imperial Tobacco Co. Ltd, Britannia and the Japanese Goddess Amaterasu-omikami are riding together on a cloud which is 'on top of the world'!

159
DUDLEY HARDY (1866-1922)
AND JOHN HASSALL (1868-1948)
Nestlé's Milk, c. 1904
Handbill, 18.6 x 13.3 cm
Published by Waterlow & Sons Limited, London Wall, London
Gallery Art Kamigata, Kyoto

In this handbill a Japanese girl is holding the Union Jack and a British boy the Hinomaru (the Japanese flag). The Japanese text underneath extols the virtues of Nestlé's Swiss Milk. The boy is telling the girl that the best gift he could bring her is condensed milk, as nothing is more nourishing than this, and in England everybody drinks it. The handbill contains the signature of

Dudley Hardy and John Hassall, both very active poster designers at the time in Britain. Hardy designed many posters for the company Waterlow & Sons.

160
ANONYMOUS
Handbill (with a scene on the deck of an ocean liner) of a Merchant of Imported Goods, 1908
37.4 x 51.5 cm
Published by Nakajima Teijiro
Gallery Art Kamigata, Kyoto

This is a handbill issued by an import merchant from the Okayama prefecture, Ikeda Kuichiro. People are promenading on the deck of an ocean liner, most wearing Western clothes. In the background are a Chinese and a Korean.

161
KATAOKA TOSHIRO AND INOUE MOKUDA
Akadama Port Wine, 1922
Poster, 82 x 58 cm
Suntory Whisky Museum, Yamanashi Prefecture

LIT : *Nihon no posutashi ten* 1989, pp.19, 23; *Posters - Japan* 1989, p.94

This is perhaps one of the most famous examples in the history of the Japanese poster, the first time nude photography was employed. Though it is more suggestive than revealing, it was a most daring design then and won the first prize in a poster contest in Germany.

162
WADA SANZO (1883-1967)
Cascade Beer, c.1926
Poster, 94.5 x 63.7 cm
Kyoto University of Industrial Art and Textiles

Wada studied oil painting under Kuroda Seiki, and then travelled to France and other countries in 1909 until his return in 1915. During his stay abroad he became more and more interested in design. From 1932 until 1944 he was Professor of Design at Tokyo Bijutsu Gakko (Tokyo School of Fine Arts). He pioneered poster designs which use strongly fine-art orientated paintings, with Western subjects. It remained an experiment, but this poster for Cascade Beer from the Nichiei Jozo Kabushiki Gaisha (Anglo-Japanese Brewery Co. Ltd) is perhaps one of his most successful.

163
Official Programme : The Prince and Princess of Wales in the City
Crêpe paper handkerchief, 50 x 50 cm
Bodleian Library, Oxford

A popular export item from Japan which was widely available in the West was crepe paper on which decorative motifs and figures were printed. These were overprinted in the West and then turned into menus, theatre bills, invitations, souvenirs and handbills for various events. The paper company Isetatsu exported a massive quantity of these not only to Britain but also to other countries. This example carries the Izumi manufacturers' mark.

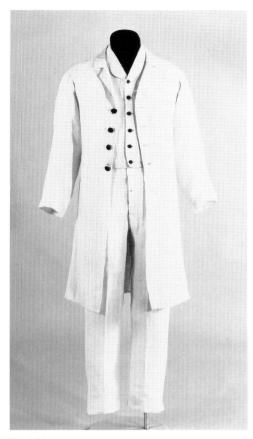

Cat.136

Cat.131
(see Section II)

164
BASIL HALL CHAMBERLAIN (1850-1935)
Three Books translated from Japanese Fairy-tales
(Barbican only)

A. *Urashima*, 1886
Illustrated by Sensai Eitaku (1843-1890)
Bodleian Library, Oxford

B. *Yamata-no-orochi*, 1886
Illustrated by Sensai Eitaku (1843-1890)
Bodleian Library, Oxford

C. *The Silly Jelly-Fish*, 1887
Illustrated by Kawabata Gyokusho (1842-1913)
Bodleian Library, Oxford

The translator of the above books, Basil Hall
Chamberlain, was a British Japanologist who
lived in Japan between 1873 and 1911 and was
regarded as one of the foremost experts on
Japanese culture. His very Eurocentric *Things
Japanese*, published in 1890, became one of the
most popular guides to Japanese culture and
the Japanese way of life. Eitaku was a principal
illustrator of these fairy-tale books, and Gyokusho,
who was apparently taught oil painting both by
Wirgman and Takahashi Yuichi, turned to
Japanese-style painting and later became
Professor at the Tokyo School of Fine Arts.

165
LAFCADIO HEARN (1850-1904)
Two Books from the 'Japanese Fairy-tale':

A. *The Boy who drew a Cat*, 1898
Book using crêpe paper, 19 x 13.8 cm
The Japan Society, London

B. *The Goblin Spider*, 1899
Book using crêpe paper, 15.5 x 10.5 cm
The Paper Museum, Tokyo

C. *Chin Chin Kobakama*, 1903
Book using crêpe paper, 19.5 x 14 cm
The Paper Museum, Tokyo

Towards the end of the nineteenth century crêpe
paper books in Western languages began to be
produced in Japan. According to L. Spanjer, there
exist editions in French, German, Danish and
Dutch, but the majority of them are in English.
The author of the above books, Lafcadio Hearn,
was a Greek-born British writer, who came to
Japan to teach English literature in 1890. He took
up Japanese citizenship in 1895, and adopted a
Japanese name, Koizumi Yakumo. His essays and
novels contributed greatly to the introduction of
Japanese culture and literature to Western readers.

LIT : L. Spanjer, 'Crêped paper books of Japan', in
Images of 19th Century Japan (sales cat.), Ukiyo-e Books,
Leiden n.d., n.p.

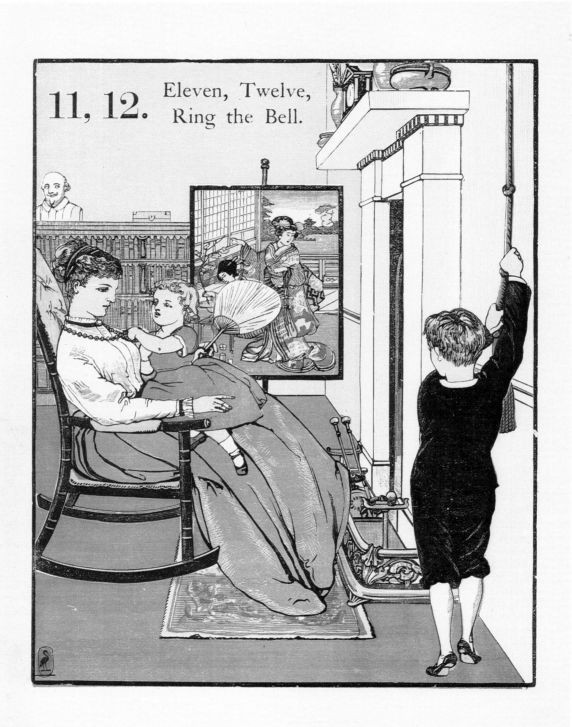

Cat.195 WALTER CRANE (1845-1915) *One, Two, Buckle My Shoe*, 1869

VIII. THE CULT OF JAPAN

DANTE GABRIEL ROSSETTI (1828-82)
(For a short biography see Section IV.)

166
ALGERNON CHARLES SWINBURNE (1837-1909)
Atalanta in Calydon. A Tragedy, London 1865
22.3 x 17.5 cm
Bodleian Library, Oxford

LIT : Schmutzler 1978, pp.25-8; Tanita 1985, pp.12-14, Watanabe 1991 B, pp.204-5

Rossetti's binding for Swinburne's poems shows an astonishing simplicity and elegance. In contrast to the tendency for symmetry and heavy ornamentation, he decorated the book only with gilt medallions placed asymmetrically near the edges of the white cover. While those on the right show Celtic and Greek motifs, those on the left are of note as they overlap and show the whirling curves of peacock feathers in a somewhat Japanese manner. Rossetti seemed to have been interested in simple book designs since the early 1860s. The binding for *The Goblin Market*, a collection of his sister Christina's poems, published in 1862, shows a similarly minimalist design. Here, he employed a combination of vertical and horizontal lines, which were unusual motifs at that time but common in Japanese designs. Rossetti's first contact with Japanese art has not been established, but as Tanita points out, the decorative principles employed by Rossetti indicate that he may have had some initial knowledge of it even before the 1862 International Exhibition.

CHRISTOPHER DRESSER (1834-1904)

An influential designer and writer on decorative arts, Dresser played a leading role in the adaptation of Japanese aesthetics to Western industrial design. His enthusiasm for Japanese art resulted in a visit to Japan in 1876-77, the first European designer to make the journey. Born in Glasgow and brought up in London, Dresser was trained as designer at the Government School of Design, where he was introduced to the ideas of design reformers such as William Dyce, Henry Cole and above all Owen Jones. Interested in the link between science and art, he first became a botanist with a doctorate from Jena University, but in the 1860s he was established as an industrial designer working in many different media. As a designer, Dresser shared the reformist view with Morris and the associates of the Arts and Crafts Movement but he rejected their mediaevalism and fully accepted the advantages of modern technology, stressing the importance of design rather than craftsmanship.

Dresser was one of those who were deeply affected by the Japanese display at the 1862 International Exhibition. In the same year, under the influence of Sir Rutherford Alcock, he began to collect Japanese art; in 1863 he lectured and wrote on Japanese ornamentation. Many of his pottery designs from the mid-1860s to the mid-1870s show Japanese influence in decorative details (Cat.167). However, Dresser's interest in Japan developed beyond its exotic and traditional values. Dresser organised the Japanese stand for the 1873 International Exhibition in London, and he was involved in the business of importing Japanese goods. His cross-cultural activities culminated in his visit to Japan in 1876 as a representative of the South Kensington Museum (today's Victoria and Albert Museum) bearing a gift of contemporary British products to the new Ueno Imperial Museum (today's Tokyo National Museum: see Section VI). While in Japan, he advised the Japanese how to adapt Western industrial techniques, and travelled the country extensively visiting artists and manufacturers of all kinds. He took nearly one thousand photographs, and bought Japanese articles on behalf of the South Kensington Museum and Tiffany's & Co. in New York. On his return, Dresser wrote a detailed account of the arts of the country, *Japan, Its Architecture, Art and Art Manufacturers*, which was published in 1882. Furthermore, he formed a partnership in 1878 with Charles Holme, the future founder of *The Studio* magazine, setting up the company Dresser & Holme for the importation of Japanese and other Oriental wares into Britain.

With deeper understanding of Japanese aesthetics, Dresser became more interested in simple, geometric and functional forms. He was particularly influenced by Japanese metalwork with exposed rivets and joints as 'functional' ornaments. Such ideas are reflected in his silverwork for Hukin & Heath (Cats 168-169), Elkington & Co., James Dixon & Sons, and some of their undecorated, austere styles anticipate Bauhaus design.

LIT : Halén 1990

167
WATCOMBE POTTERY CO.
Teapot with Lion on Top, c.1870-75
Terracotta with turquoise glaze, H. 14 , W. 17 cm
Andrew McIntosh Patrick,

LIT : FAS and H & W 1990 (19)

168
HUKIN & HEATH
Electroplated Kettle with Ebony Handle and Stand, 1878
Silver and ebony, H. 17.8 cm, W. 20.5 cm
Marks: registration mark for 6 May 1878 - same mark on all three pieces
Nicholas Harris Gallery, London

Angular ebony handles are one of the characteristics of Dresser's kettle designs. This type of handle, a solid construction of wood and metal joined together with exposed rivets, resembles a 'torii' (Japanese Shinto-shrine gate).

169
HUKIN & HEATH
Electroplated Teapot with Ivory Handle, c.1880
Silver and ivory, H. 14.5 cm, W. 17.5 cm
Marks: 2 H & H 21 10
Nicholas Harris Gallery, London

ATTRIBUTED TO CHRISTOPHER DRESSER (1834-1904)

170
MINTON & CO.
Vase, c.1872
Porcelain, decorated in imitation cloisonne with Japanese crests on a turquoise ground and four applied balls on gold band at the neck, H. 10 cm, D. 7.3 cm
Marks: impressed pattern number, maker Minton Haslam and Whiteway Ltd, London

171
MINTON & CO.
Small Footed Pot, c.1875
Porcelain with celadon glaze ground decorated with a gold key and floral motif in the Oriental manner, H. 9 cm, D. 12.5 cm
Marks: indistinct impressed mark, maker Minton Haslam and Whiteway Ltd, London

BRITISH ART INDUSTRY AND JAPAN

The Japanese designs displayed at the 1862 International Exhibition had a great impact on British manufacturers. The Japanese exhibits, especially porcelain and metalwork, were featured in John B. Waring's *Masterpieces of Industrial Art & Sculpture at the International Exhibition, 1862*, published in 1863. In the 1860s the porcelain makers, Minton's and the Royal Worcester Company, and the silversmiths, Elkinton's, began to experiment with Japanese styles, and other leading manufacturers soon followed suit. Throughout the 1870s and 1880s Japanese design characteristics, including an asymmetrical arrangement of bamboos, birds, fish, blossoms and fans, were widely used by British manufacturers of goods ranging from domestic tableware to decorative objects, and they became the principal motifs for the Aesthetic Movement in Britain. In this period, modern Japanese industrial goods were also imported into the country. Some British firms even collaborated with Japanese craftsmen to produce authentic Japanese design (Cats.178 and 204). The spoons (Cat.189) and napkin holders

(Cat.190) were made for Western use, but decorated with traditional Japanese motifs to appeal to the Western market. Furthermore, after 1876, when the possession of swords no longer allowed in Japan, vast quantities of 'kozuka' (small knives with rectangular hilts) were exported to the West. Due to their decorative quality 'kozuka' were used as cutlery handles by British metal manufacturers (see Cats.185-186).

172
MINTON & CO.
Tiles decorated with a Crane on a Pine-tree against the Sun, c.1874
Three ceramic tiles, 56.7 x 20.3 cm (overall)
Haslam and Whiteway Ltd

173
STEELE & WOOD
Pair of Tiles decorated with Japanese Motifs, c.1870s
Ceramic tiles painted in enamel,
25 x 45.5 cm (overall)
Haslam and Whiteway Ltd, London

Painting was applied, probably by a Japanese hand.

174
ENGLISH
Brooch decorated with a Lady with a Parasol, 1870s
Hand-painted on gold, 3 x 4.5 cm
Victor Arwas, London

175
MINTON & CO.
Pair of Moonflasks, c.1875
Porcelain with blue glaze simulating four panels of Japanese gold and silver lacquer,
H. 30.5 cm each, W. 23.5 cm each
Marks: Minton, 1348
Nicholas Harris Gallery, London

176
G. H. STOCKWELL
Oval Box decorated with Japanese Motifs, 1877-78
Mixed metal, 10 x 5 x 3 cm
Signed: Nobumasa
Haslam and Whiteway Ltd, London

177
ELKINGTON & CO.
Salver on Three Feet, 1879
Sterling silver engraved with Japanese motifs,
H. 2.5 cm, D. 25.5 cm
Marks: FE (Frederick Elkington), Birmingham, 1879
Nicholas Harris Gallery, London

178
G. H. STOCKWELL
Large Paper Knife with Japanese 'Shibiyama' Handle, 1880
Sterling silver blade engraved with Japanese motifs, with ivory handle decorated with ivory inlay, gold and silver, L. 30 cm
Marks: E.H. Stockwell, London, 1880
Nicholas Harris Gallery, London

The blade is mounted on a Japanese ivory hilt decorated with two 'shakudo' (alloy of copper and gold) figures of a seated merchant with a 'soroban' (abacus) and a samurai.

179
C. CHESHIRE
Aide-Mémoire, 1880
Sterling silver and three-colour gold engraved with Japanese motifs, 10.3 x 7.5 cm
Marks: C C (C. Cheshire), Birmingham, 1880
Nicholas Harris Gallery, London

180
SAMUEL MORDEN
Scent Bottle, 1881
Sterling silver and gilt engraved with bird, branch and blossom, H. 6 cm, D. 2.5 cm
Marks: Samuel Morden, London, 1881
Nicholas Harris Gallery, London

181
J & A. SAVORY
Three-piece Cruet Set on Stand, 1882
Sterling silver and gilt engraved with Japanese motifs, H. 14.5 cm, D. 12.5 cm (overall)
Marks: JS (J. Savory), AS (A. Savory), London, 1882, with initials RMS
Nicholas Harris Gallery, London

182
HENRY TITTERTON BROCKWELL
Jug and Pair of Beakers, 1883
Porcelain with gilt and silver Japanese-inspired decoration and sterling silver mounts,
Jug: H. 22.5 cm, D. 15 cm;
beakers: H. 13.7 cm each, D. 7.5 cm each
Marks: HTB (Henry Titterton Brockwell), London, 1883
Nicholas Harris Gallery, London

183
ELKINGTON & CO.
Dessert Spoons, 1884
Sterling silver and gilt decorated with Japanese motifs, L. 12.8 cm
Marks: FE (Frederick Elkington), Birmingham, 1884
Nicholas Harris Gallery, London

The spoons have been taken from a cased set comprising twelve teaspoons, four servers and one sugar spoon, similarly decorated with Japanese motifs.

184
MARTIN HALL AND SON
Bowl and Spoon Set, 1885
Silver decorated with fish, shells and seaweed in two-colour gold. In original box from the retailers Pearce & Sons, Huddersfield, Leeds 1885,
Bowl: H. 6.5 cm, D. 11 cm; spoon: L. 16.8 cm, W. 3.3 cm
Marks: Martin Hall and Son, London, 1880.
Engraved on base of bowl: Dorothy Charlotte Drummond Oct 18th 1885 and on reverse of spoon handle: monogram DCD
Haslam and Whiteway Ltd, London

185
J.H. POTTER
Knives with Japanese 'Kozuka' Handles, c.1885
Sterling silver blades engraved with Japanese-inspired motifs, with 'shakudo' handles,
L. 21.7 cm
Marks: JH Potter, Sheffield
Horesh Collection, London

186
HENRY TITTERTON BROCKWELL
Paper Knife with Japanese 'Kozuka' Handle, 1886
Sterling silver-gilt blade with 'shakudo' handle,
L. 21.5 cm
Marks: London 1886
Peter Jeffs at Nicholas Harris Gallery, London

187
ROYAL WORCESTER PORCELAIN CO.
Vase, 1889
Porcelain decorated with Japanese motifs in gold,
H. 23 cm, D. 14.5 cm
Marks: Royal Worcester mark impressed and printed, date and pattern number
Haslam and Whiteway Ltd, London

188
ROYAL WORCESTER PORCELAIN CO.
Vase, 1890
Porcelain decorated with Japanese motifs in gold and enamel,
H. 15 cm, D. 13 cm
Marks: Royal Worcester mark printed, date and pattern number
Haslam and Whiteway Ltd, London

189
JAPANESE
Pair of Spoons decorated with Flowers: Chrysanthemum and Hydrangea, c.1890
Gold and silver, L. 12 cm each
Andrew McIntosh Patrick

190
JAPANESE
Napkin Holders, c.1890s
Ivory decorated with birds, insects and flowers in gold and enamel, D.5 cm each
Horesh Collection, London

191
DAVID HERBERT & GEORGE EDWARD AND ALAN & DARWIN
Fruit Knives and Forks with Japanese 'Kozuka' Handles, 1898-1900
Knives: sterling silver blades by David Herbert & George Edward, with 'shakudo' handles, L. 21 cm; forks: sterling silver forks by Alan & Darwin, with 'shakudo' handles, L. 17.8 cm
Marks: (knives) David Herbert & George Edward, Sheffield, 1900; (forks) Alan & Darwin, Sheffield, 1898
Nicholas Harris Gallery, London

These have been taken from a cased set of thirty-six pieces, comprising eighteen knives and forks. Two of the knife-handles bear the signatures of Mitsumasa and Gyokuunsai, and one of the fork-handles is signed Ishiguro Masaaki.

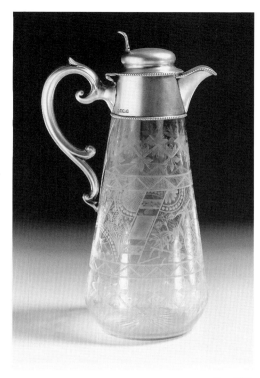

Cat.193

192
ENGLISH
Spoons with Japanese 'Kozuka' Handles, c.1890s
Copper spoons decorated with flowers and leaves,
with 'shakudo' handles, L. 20.2 cm
Horesh Collection, London

193
WALTER & CHARLES SISSONS
Claret Jug, 1899
Sterling silver-mounted glass jug with engraved
'Aesthetic' motifs, H. 27 cm, D. 15 cm
Marks: WS (Walter Sissons), CS (Charles
Sissons), Sheffield, 1899
Nicholas Harris Gallery, London

BRUCE JAMES TALBERT (1838-1881)

Born in Dundee. Trained as an architect in
Glasgow, Talbert was an influential designer,
especially of furniture. With his award-winning
Gothic dresser, exhibited at the Paris International
Exposition in 1867, and the publication of *Gothic
Forms Applied to Furniture*, in the same year,
he established himself as a leading furniture
designer in a simplified Gothic style. He also
designed metalwork, wallpapers and textiles.

194
Original Design for 'Sunflower' Wallpaper, 1878
Water and body colour on paper, 38.7 x 53.3 cm
Design made for Jeffrey & Co.
Trustees of the Victoria and Albert Museum,
London

LIT : Aslin 1981, pp.66-70 with pl.9

The most popular among his wallpaper designs
was the 'Sunflower' series, which was awarded a
Gold Medal at the Paris International Exposition
in 1878. Cat.194 is from this series, and it shows
the patterns of sunflowers and leaves, all boldly
outlined and flatly coloured, arranged against
Japanese-inspired wave and lattice patterns.

WALTER CRANE (1845-1915)

Alongside Kate Greenaway (see below), Walter
Crane was the foremost illustrator of children's
books, which experienced a golden age in the
1870s and 1880s. Born in Liverpool and trained
as a wood-engraver under W.J. Linton in London,
he began his career as a book illustrator in the
early 1860s for Edmund Evans, the pioneering
printer of popular colour books. Their venture
was extended to children's books in 1865 when,
with the publisher, Routledge, they began the
'Sixpenny Toy Series'. Richly coloured and well
designed, the Toy Books became extremely
popular: by 1875 Crane had published nearly
thirty picture books in this series. Most of them
were also available at one shilling mounted on
linen. Their success depended not only on the
accessible prices and technical advances, but also
on the growing demand for 'tasteful' nursery
books reflecting the aesthetic climate at the time.
As Ellen Terry recalled later, her and E. W.
Godwin's children were not allowed to have
'rubbishy books' but 'Japanese prints lined on the
nursery walls and Walter Crane was their classic'.1

Crane was a versatile artist, who also designed
textiles, tiles, ceramics and stained glass, and
painted in the Pre-Raphaelite manner. Sharing

the reformist and socialist views of William
Morris, he was the principal advocate of the
Arts and Crafts Movement.

NOTE
1 E. Terry, *Memoirs*, London 1933, p.66, quoted by
Aslin 1981, p.160; Smith and Hyde 1989; Watanabe
1991G, pp.208-9

LIT : Spencer, 1975

195
One, Two, Buckle My Shoe, 1869
From the 'Sixpenny Toy Series'
Wood-engraving by Edmund Evans, published
by George Routledge & Sons, London, Glasgow,
New York, 24.5 x 18.5 cm
Hornby Library, Liverpool (Hugh Frederick
Hornby Bequest)

LIT : Spencer 1975, pp.52-3 with fig. on p.53,
p.192 for notes

The illustration to 'Eleven, Twelve, Ring the
Bell' shows a typically 'Aesthetic' interior: a
mother is sitting on an 'Anglo-Japanese'-style
chair, holding a Japanese fan, and a screen is
decorated with a picture based on a Japanese
woodcut. Crane had some prints by Toyokuni,
which he had been given probably in 1867 by
a family friend who had returned from Japan.
Spencer informs us that Crane included, in the
same year, a Japanese folding screen in the first
illustration to *The Argosy* by Anne Hereford.
Towards the end of the 1860s, his style became
more decorative, and he acknowledged 'Japanese
colour prints' as 'an important factor' for the
evolution of his bold outlines and flat and
delicate colours, as seen in this illustration.

Cat.194

196
The Fairy Ship, 1870
From the 'Sixpenny Toy Series'
Wood-engraving by Edmund Evans, published
by George Routledge & Sons, London, Glasgow,
New York, 24.5 x 18.5 cm
Hornby Library, Liverpool
(Hugh Frederick Hornby Bequest)

197
The Frog Prince, 1874
From the 'Shilling Series'
Wood-engraving by Edmund Evans, published
by George Routledge & Sons, London, Glasgow,
New York, 27 x 23.5 cm
Hornby Library, Liverpool

LIT : Spencer 1975, pp.59-60 with ill. on p.61;
Aslin 1981, p.161

Walter Crane's 'Shilling Series' began in 1874.
The format was larger, and the pictures were
separated from the texts and printed in a wider
range of colours. They were also available

mounted on linen at two shillings. The cover
shows Japanese-inspired details, including a
crane, standing against bamboo and the sun,
and the wave and scale patterns decorating the
border. In many illustrations Crane used
variations of a crane, a pun on his name, as his
signature in the same way that Whistler used
the butterfly. Furthermore, he placed the crane
and his name, with the horizontal hatching
disappearing towards the centre, in a manner
similar to that of Japanese woodcut artists.

198
Aladdin; or The Wonderful Lamp, 1875
From the 'Shilling Series'
Wood-engraving by Edmund Evans, published
by George Routledge & Sons, London, Glasgow,
New York, 27 x 23.5 cm
Hornby Library, Liverpool

LIT : Aslin 1981, p.161 with pl.98

An Arabian fantasy is here represented in an
extraordinary juxtaposition of 'exotic' images

from Japan, China and other Oriental countries.
A page shows an Arabic princess dressed in a
kimono and 'geta' (Japanese sandals), attended
by Japanese maids and African servants who are
holding a Japanese fan and a parasol. In this
picture, while Aladdin, watching the princess
behind the door, is dressed in Chinese style,
architectural details show Japanese motifs in the
lacquer screens of the doors and in painted tiles.
A vase with hydrangea is seen in the foreground
in the Japanese manner.

199
Jack and the Beanstalk, 1875
From the 'Sixpenny Toy Series'
Wood-engraving by Edmund Evans, published
by George Routledge & Sons, London, Glasgow,
New York, 24.5 x 18.5 cm
Hornby Library, Liverpool

KATE GREENAWAY (1846-1901)

Studied in London at the Islington School of Art
and the Slade and began her career as a designer
of Christmas cards and children's books in the
early 1870s. Her style was characterised by
prettily dressed children, playing in rustic
settings, which were painted in soft, delicate
colours. In 1878 she established her reputation
with *Under the Willow*, a collection of her drawings
and verses, which was printed by Edmund Evans
and published by Routledge. With their
distinctive bonnets and frocks, the image of
'Greenaway-style' children became extremely
popular, and they were the model for children's
fashions at that time.

200
T. & R. BOOTE
*Four Tiles representing the Four Seasons with
Japanese-style Border Design inspired by 'Mon'*, 1883
Earthenware, transfer-printed and hand-coloured,
15.2 x 15.2 cm each
Trustees of the Victoria and Albert Museum,
London

LIT : Aslin 1981, pp.163-4 with pl.105

Greenaway hardly used Japanese motifs directly
in her illustrations. Nevertheless, her effective
use of space and asymmetrical composition, seen
in *Under the Willow*, indicates her knowledge of
Japanese art. In these tiles, the Japanese-inspired
motifs, discs and scroll patterns, are used as
border decoration.

WILLIAM J. NEATBY

201
Plate with Japanese-style Lady, 1887
Ceramic plate, D. 32 cm
Andrew McIntosh Patrick

Cat.198

130

ARTHUR LASENBY LIBERTY
(1843-1917)

The founder of Liberty's in Regent Street, London, he was instrumental in fostering the 'cult of Japan' in Britain, an integral part of the Aesthetic Movement in the 1870s and 1880s. Born in Chesham, Buckinghamshire, he began as a shop assistant in Farmer & Roger's Great Shawl and Cloak Emporium in Regent Street in the year of the International Exhibition of 1862. At the close of the exhibition, Farmer & Rogers bought a large portion of the Japanese exhibits, and based on this they opened a new Oriental Warehouse next door. Liberty joined them and became manager in 1864. His Oriental Warehouse was the most popular part of the shop and he steadily established long-standing customers drawn mainly from London's artistic circles, including Whistler, Rossetti, William Morris, Burne-Jones, Albert Moore, Ruskin, Norman Shaw, E.W. Godwin and Ellen Terry. Encouraged by this success, Liberty opened his own shop in 1875. Liberty's staff included a Japanese boy and the shop's balcony was decorated with Japanese Buddhist statues.

Liberty's intuition was proved correct. The popularity of 'things Japanese' was rapidly growing. By 1878, as *The Furniture Gazette* of that year announced, 'Everything is already Japanese', the 'cult of Japan' was in full swing, and Liberty was the 'most progressive tradesman in Regent Street'. 1 In the early days, Liberty specialised in imported goods, ancient and modern, from the East, but in the 1880s Liberty began to commission designs from contemporary British artists. His ideal was to produce 'useful and beautiful objects at prices within the reach of all classes', 2 and the designers who worked for Liberty's include those featured in this exhibition, E.W. Godwin, Christopher Dresser, Walter Crane and Arthur Silver.

Liberty's success depended not only on his business instinct but also on his own enthusiasm for Japanese art. Since the 1862 Exhibition, Liberty had been a great admirer of Japanese craftsmanship, and he was a close friend of Dresser. Liberty visited Japan in 1889-90, accompanied by his wife, Emma, and his artist friend, Alfred East (see Section) as well as Dresser's partner, Charles Holme. It was Dresser who gave advice and put Liberty in touch with his Japanese contacts before Liberty's visit. While in Japan, Liberty visited Japanese manufacturers and gave a talk at the Ueno Imperial Museum (today's Tokyo National Museum) on the mutual influences in art and design between Japan and the West. On his return, in 1890, he delivered a lecture at the Society of Art in London on *The Industrial Arts and Manufacturers of Japan*. It was a comprehensive survey of contemporary Japanese art, and for this paper Liberty received a Silver Medal. From this year onwards, Yokohama appeared in the list of Liberty's branches.

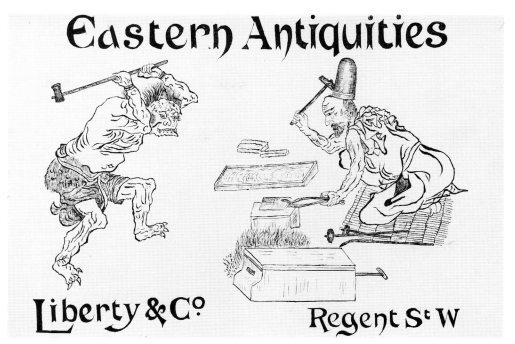

Cat.202

LIT : Adburgham 1975; V & A, *Liberty's* 1975; Morris 1989

NOTE
1. *The Furniture Gazette* 1878, p.277
2. Fleming & Honour 1977, p.468

202
LIBERTY'S & CO.
Eastern Antiquities, 1880s
27.5 x 18.5 cm
Barbara Morris, Brighton

LIT : Morris 1989, p.76 with ill.

The cover shows a Japanese blacksmith, assisted by an 'oni' (a demon) on the left, probably copied from a Japanese picture. Out of 137 items in this catalogue, sixty-four are Japanese including pottery, metalwork, lacquer work and 'netsuke' (ivory carving), with prices ranging from seven shillings and six pence for an eighteenth century iron 'tsuba' (sword guard) to 50 guineas for a late nineteenth century 'hiramakie' (gold lacquer) partitioned box, made in Kyoto.

203
ARTHUR AND EMMA LIBERTY
Japan, A Pictorial Record, 1910
Photographic album in cloth binding,
26 x 36.5 cm
Liberty's Archives

The album comprises fifty Japanese photographs taken by Emma Liberty on her visit to Japan with her husband in 1889-90. The pictures, including scenes from Kyoto, Nara, and Nikko, were selected from over a thousand photographs taken by her in Japan.Later the photographs were edited, with a descriptive text by Arthur Liberty, based on which 200 hundred copies of an album were printed in 1910. This copy is number 96.

204
JAPANESE
Set of Six Spoons and Matching Sugar Tongs,
c.1894
Sterling silver
Marks: Maker's mark LY & Co.
Andrew McIntosh Patrick

LIT : Morris 1989, pp.79-80 with ill. on p.80

Until the late 1890s, when they began to introduce their own ranges of metalwork, Liberty's relied on foreign products. Japanese wares predominated, including swords, 'tsuba' (sward guards), bronze vases and statues. They also commissioned Japanese manufacturers, including Konoike of Yokohama, to produce silverware for Western use, and some of them bore Liberty's own maker's mark, LY & Co., which was registered in 1894. This set of spoons and sugar tongs, decorated with plant motifs, was imported from Japan in 1894, and some of the spoons bear Liberty's mark. The Victoria and Albert Museum also has a silver teapot and a set of silver spoons with the LY & Co. mark, which were imported from Japan in the 1890s.

205
LIBERTY'S & CO.
A Japanese Year Book, 1915
15.4 x 22.7 cm
Liberty's Archives

This gift diary contains twelve colour pictures, each representing one month. Selected by a Japanese, Ken Hoshino, they illustrate old Japanese tales.

Cat.210

ARTHUR SILVER (1853-96)

Born in Reading. On leaving Reading School of Art, Silver went to London, where in the 1870s he was apprenticed to the furniture and carpet designer, Henry Batley. Batley, an Aesthetic designer, was strongly influenced by Japanese art, and almost certainly Silver was introduced to it at Batley's workshop. In 1880 Silver opened his own studio in Hammersmith and began to supply designs for many manufacturers. Above all, the Silver Studio was closely associated with Liberty's: Arthur Silver was responsible for Liberty's famous 'Peacock Feather' design, which was displayed at the Manchester Royal Jubilee Exhibition in 1887. His designs were shown at many exhibitions, including every Arts and Crafts Society Exposition from 1889 to 1896, the Paris International Exposition of 1889 and the Chicago World's Columbian Exhibition in 1893.

Japanese art was an integral part of Arthur Silver's life and a primary source of influence. Silver's house was decorated with Japanese woodcuts, porcelain, lacquer wares and screens, and from 1888 he was a subscriber to Seigfried Bing's magazine, *Artistic Japan* (Section XI, cat.297). He was also an early member of the Japan Society. Furthermore, his close study of Japanese design was evident in his large collection of books on Japanese art, samples of Japanese fabrics, stencil sheets and parchment papers, which can still be seen today in the Silver Studio Collection in London.

After Arthur Silver's early death in 1896, the Silver Studio was taken over by its designers, Harry Napper and J.R. Houghton, and from 1901 by Arthur Silver's sons, Rex and Harry, and it continued until 1963.

LIT : Turner et al. 1980-81

206
Design for the Decoration of a Door and Wall, c.1885
Pencil and body colour on paper, 38 x 28 cm
Middlesex Polytechnic, London
(Silver Studio Collection)

LIT : Turner et al. 1980-81 (49); Turner & Hopkins 1988, p.16 with pl.7 on p.18

This drawing shows a complete interior scheme with a wall divided into three sections, dado, filling and frieze, which was fashionable at the time. Japanese motifs are used in the door panels, the dado paper and the frieze.

207
Design for a Textile with Japanese Patterns, 1891
Gouache on cartridge paper, 59.6 x 38 cm
Inscribed: No.809
Middlesex Polytechnic, London
(Silver Studio Collection)

Silver was interested in Japanese stencilled patterns, and they were often incorporated into his textile and wallpaper designs. The plant and flower motifs in Cat. were probably taken from an original Japanese stencil. In collaboration with Rottmann and Co., the importers of Japanese stencils and parchment papers (see below), the

Silver Studio exhibited stencilled decorations in 1895, and Silver gave a lecture on *The Modern Stencil and Its Application to Interior Decoration* at the Architectural Association in London in 1896.

208
Design for a Wallpaper with Pine-tree Branches and Flowers, 1892
Watercolour on cartridge paper, 61 x 44.8 cm
Inscribed: No.1579
Middlesex Polytechnic, London (Silver Studio Collection)

LIT : Turner et al. 1980-81 (118)

209
Design for a Wallpaper with Irises and Water Rings, 1895
Gouache on cartridge paper, 57.5 x 46.5 cm
Inscribed: No.1531
Middlesex Polytechnic, London (Silver Studio Collection)

ATTRIBUTED TO ARTHUR SILVER
(1853-96)

210
Design for a Christmas Card, 1890
Pen and wash with a gouache border on cartridge paper, Signed: t.l.; with monogram also shows Japanese signature b.r.: Yamakawa Rinpo
Inscribed: (t.r.) Merry/Xmas;
(bottom) Best 1890-91 Wishes
Middlesex Polytechnic, London (Silver Studio Collection)

LIT : Turner et al. 1986 (30)

This design, with frogs having a party on a giant lotus leaf shows the artist's great familiarity with Japanese motifs and artistic conventions. All Japanese details, including a 'shamisen' (Japanese music instrument), played by the frog on the far left, and a gourd-shaped bottle in the centre, are accurately depicted. It is tempting to think that the drawing was produced by a Japanese designer, called Yamakawa Rinpo. His name is seen at bottom right, and several drawings in the Silver Collection also bear the same name. Nevertheless, at present there is no record of a Japanese designer having been employed in the Silver Studio.

211
ATTRIBUTED TO JOHN ILLINGWORTH KAY
Trade Card for Rottmann & Co., 1894
28 x 21.5 cm
Middlesex Polytechnic, London
(Silver Studio Collection)

Established in 1883, Rottmann & Co. were based in the City, specialising in the importation of Japanese papers and stencils. This card, probably designed by Kay, a Silver Studio designer, shows a Japanese-inspired design with Mt Fuji and the rising sun. In 1894, Silver formed a business partnership with Alexander Rottman, the company's managing director, to produce stencilled friezes on grass (handmade Japanese) paper.

THE 'JAPANESE CRAZE' IN THE THEATRE

Japanese fashion also pervaded London's theatre world. A Japanese-inspired costume design was seen in the Gaiety Theatre as early as 1870, and there was a 'Grand Japanese Ballet' at the Alhambra Theatre in 1877. Fans, parasols and blossoms were often used as decorative motifs in theatre bills and programmes. The Japanese vogue culminated in Gilbert and Sullivan's opera, *The Mikado*, originally performed at the Savoy Theatre in 1885 with Japanese costumes and make-up. Set in the imaginary town of Titipu, with characters with Japanese-sounding names such as Ko-Ko and Nanki-Poo, it was a fanciful representation of Japan. Nevertheless, with the sumptuous costumes made of Japanese fabrics and with easily understandable music and words, it popularised the image of Japan. *The Mikado* was performed one thousand times between 1885 and 1896. Japanese themes continued to be popular around the turn of the century, further encouraged by the Anglo-Japanese Alliance of 1902 and 1905. During this period, many Japanese-inspired productions were mounted, including the musical comedies, *The Geisha* (1896), *The White Chrysanthemum* (1905) and *The Mousme* (1911), as well as the play, *The Darling of the Gods* (1903).

NOTE
We are grateful to John Culme for pointing out the Japanese influence on the early Gaiety Theatre and the Edwardian theatre.

212
Mr J.L. Toole's New Song, 'STILL I AM NOT HAPPY', c.1870-71
Sheet music cover, coloured lithograph, 34.5 x 24.5 cm
John Culme

Here Japanese elements are combined with mediaeval ones. The tall head-dress worn by the singer is a Japanese 'eboshi', and his face is depicted like a Japanese Noh theatre mask.

WILLIAM JOHN CHARLES PITCHER
(1858-1925)

213
Costume Designs for the Original Production of 'The Mikado',
Savoy Theatre, London, 14 March 1885:

A. *Nanki-Poo*, 1885
Pencil, watercolour and body colour on paper, 28.2 x 19 cm
Signed and dated b.l.: Wilhelm/85
Trustees of the Victoria and Albert Museum, London (Theatre Museum)

B. *Goto*, 1885
Pencil, watercolour and body colour on paper, 23.1 x 19.1 cm
Signed and dated b.l.: Wilhelm/85
Trustees of the Victoria and Albert Museum, London (Theatre Museum)

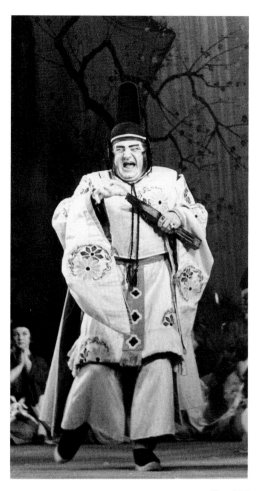

Cat.215

C. *Chorus*, 1885
Pencil, watercolour and body colour on paper, 28 x 19.5 cm
Signed and dated b.l.: Wilhelm/85
Trustees of the Victoria and Albert Museum, London (Theatre Museum)

D. *Chorus*, 1885
Pencil, watercolour and body colour on paper, 23 x 19 cm
Signed and dated b.l.: Wilhelm/85
Trustees of the Victoria and Albert Museum, London (Theatre Museum)

The Mikado was one of fourteen comic operas created by the playwright, W.S. Gilbert (1836-1911), and the composer, Arthur Sullivan (1842-1900), for Richard D'Oyly Carte's company. Gilbert had tight control over stage and costume designs, working closely with designers. Pitcher's costume designs show Gilbert's eagerness for the accurate representation of Japanese dresses. Pitcher, who signed 'Wilhelm', was also known as a landscape painter in watercolour. He also produced the designs for *The Mousmé* (1911; see Cat.221). Authentic Japanese fabrics were supplied by Liberty's, who had sent a delegation to Japan to study materials and designs. 'Liberty's Art Fabrics' were advertised in the programme of the original performance.

214
JOHN HASSALL (1868-1948)
Poster for the Tour of the First Revival Production of 'The Mikado', 1895
Lithograph
Trustees of the Victoria and Albert Museum, London (Theatre Museum)

This poster was used for the tour of the first revival production, which had been staged at the Savoy Theatre from 6 November 1895. The design is identical to that used for the performance at the Savoy, with the dominant figure of Mikado against bright red. In this poster blanks were left for overprinting. The design was based on a photograph of Frederic Federici who had played the role in New York.

NOTE
We are grateful to Cathy Haill at the Theatre Museum for providing this information.

215
CHARLES RICKETTS (1866-1931)
Costume for the Mikado, c.1926
Robe, trousers and head-dress
Trustees of the Victoria and Albert Museum, London (Theatre Museum)

Cat.220

133

Designed by Charles Ricketts (see Section XI for a short biography and some of his work), this costume was worn by Donald Adams as The Mikado for the revival production at the Savoy Theatre in 1926.

216
The George Edwarde's Gaiety Theatre Programme, 1891
20.5 x 9.6 cm
John Culme

LIT : Garner 1974, pp. 78-80 with pl.91 on p.86

217
The Geisha, 1896
Sheet music cover, 36 x 26 cm
John Culme

LIT : Garner 1974, pp. 78-80 with pl.92 on p.87

Here the star, Marie Lloyd, is presented as 'a Geisha, Japaneasy, free and easy Tea house girl'. From this period onwards, with the stereotyped image of a Japanese woman, the word 'geisha' began to be used in a sexually provocative context as seen in many Edwardian pin-ups (see below).

218
DUDLEY HARDY (1866-1922)
The George Edwarde's Birthday Book, 1897
23 x 18.5 cm
John Culme

The Geisha was a great success. To commemorate its anniversary performance, about 1,200 copies of the birthday book, designed by Dudley Hardy, were produced and presented to the audience on 26 April 1897.

219
MAKINO YOSHIO (1869-1956)
Souvenir Programme of 'The Darling of the Gods',
His Majesty's Theatre, London, 1903
22.5 x 16.3 cm
The Corporation of London (Guildhall Library)

Written by David Belasco and John Luther Long, *The Darling of the Gods* was a five-act play, set in feudal Japan, with Sir Herbert B. Tree (see below) in the leading role, Zakkuri, a Cruel Minister of State. With the costumes and settings produced with 'the utmost accuracy' and the entertaining scenes including 'a band of lovely Geisha girls', the play was greatly popular. One of the notable effects of the play was that certain Japanese phrases, including 'I break my bones towards you (hone o oru)' meaning 'Sorry to trouble you', became incorporated into the slang of London's fashionable society. Illustrated by the Japanese painter, Yoshio Makino (see Section XIV for a short biography and some of his work), this souvenir programme shows seven scenes depicted in bright colours.

220
CHARLES BUCHEL (FL.1898-1917)
Sir Herbert B. Tree as Zakkuri, a Japanese Minister of State, c.1903
Charcoal and Chinese white, 50.8 x 31.8 cm
Trustees of the Victoria and Albert Museum, London

This is probably a design for the poster for *The Darling of the Gods*. Buchel was a portrait painter who lived in London. He exhibited at the Royal Academy between 1898 and 1917.

221
WILLIAM JOHN CHARLES PITCHER (1858-1925)
Costume design for Hana in 'The Mousmé',
Shaftesbury Theatre, London, 1911
Watercolour on paper, 25.7 x 17.2 cm
Signed and dated b.l. vertically, simulating Japanese characters: Ue (in Japanese character) :
Wilhelm : 1911
Inscribed tr.: Hana/Act I
John Culme

Cat.224

222
Three Magazines featuring the Japanese Gaiety Theatre

A. *The Play Pictorial*, 1905 (Vol.6, No. 39)
30 x 22.2 cm
John Culme

The Play Pictorial was a monthly theatre magazine. This number features *The White Chrysanthemum* with the cover showing Isabel Jay.

B. *The Playgoer and Society*, 1911 (Vol.5, No.26)
25.3 x 20.3 cm
John Culme *The Playgoer and Society* was another major theatregoers' magazine. This number features *The Mousmé* with the cover showing Cicely Courtneidge and Florence Smithson.

C. *The Play Pictorial*, 1911 (Vol. 19, No.113)
30 x 22.5 cm
John Culme

The Mousmé was also featured in *The Play Pictorial*. The cover shows Florence Smithson playing a 'shamisen' (Japanese stringed instrument).

223
Four Edwardian 'Japanese' Pin-up Postcards

A. *Four Postcards from the Original Performance of 'The Geisha'*,
John Culme

B. *Three Cabinet-size Cards from 'The Geisha'*
John Culme

C. *Five Postcards from 'The Mousmé'*
John Culme

D. *Three Postcards of Edna May*
John Culme

224
Six Edwardian 'Japanese' Postcards

A. *Girl in a Kimono*, 1904
Horesh Collection, London

B. S. HARDY. P.H.
'*A Japanese Greeting*', 1900s
Horesh Collection, London

C. *Japanese Couple with Lantern*, 1904
Horesh Collection, London

D. *Girl serving Tea in a Japanese Room*, 1904
Horesh Collection, London

E. *Two Japanese Girls with an Umbrella*, 1907
Inscribed bottom: Dainty little ladies, from scholastic/ troubles free, Each a little bit/ afraid is, wondering what the world can be
Horesh Collection, London

F. *Japanese-style Lady with a Fan*, 1911
Horesh Collection, London

With the renewed interest in Japan following the conclusion of the Anglo-Japanese Alliance of 1902, a vast number of 'Japanese' postcards were produced around that time. Most of the pictures show 'exotic' Japanese manners and customs, or fragile flower-like images of young Japanese girls.

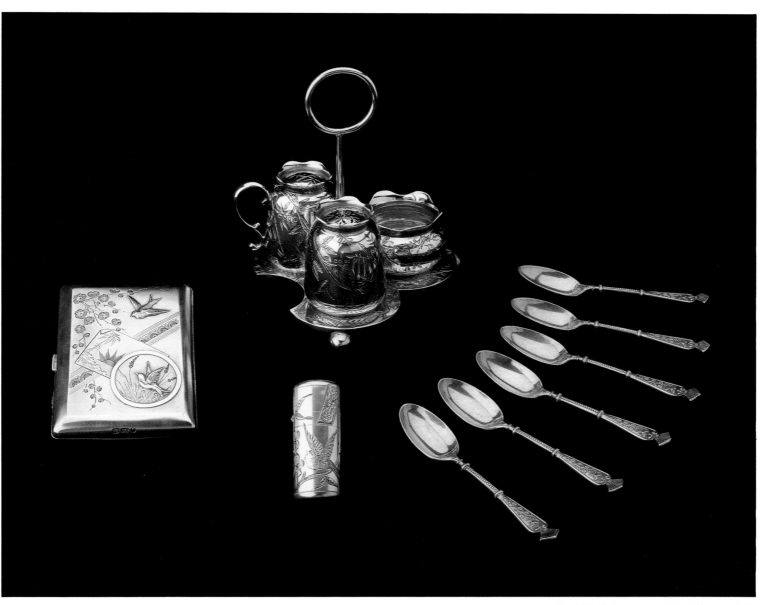

Cat.179 C. CHESHIRE *Aide-Mémoire*, 1880
Cat.180 SAMUEL MORDEN *Scent Bottle*, 1881
Cat.181 J & A. SAVORY *Three-piece Cruet Set on Stand*, 1882
Cat.183 ELKINGTON & CO. *Dessert Spoons*, 1884

Cat.264
TAKASHIMA HOKKAI
(1850-1931)
Farmhouse at Doncleigan (?)
(Sukottorando Donkuraigen Noka),
1906

IX. JAPANESE PAINTERS AND BRITAIN

CHARLES WIRGMAN (1832-1891)

Little is known about the early life of Wirgman, who was born in London. His younger brother Theodore Blake Wirgman became quite a successful portrait painter and was a member of the Royal Society of Portrait Painters. Wirgman himself was sent to China as a correspondent for *The Illustrated London News* in 1857 and then to Japan in 1861. He sent back to London vivid images of Japan in turmoil. These illustrations in *The Illustrated London News* were very influential in forming the Victorian image of Japan. He married a Japanese in 1863 and settled in Japan, apart from occasional trips abroad. In about 1863 he formed a partnership with the photographer Felix Beato to sell photographs and photographic reproductions of his own paintings. 1 This partnership may have lasted until about 1867. In Japan he is regarded as the first Western teacher of oil painting. He was linguistically gifted, could converse with the Japanese easily, and seems to have had an informal demeanour, often verging on eccentricity. His wit and humour are amply expressed in the pages of *Japan Punch* which he published between 1862 and 1887 at irregular intervals. *Japan Punch* was very popular among Westerners in the treaty ports and laid the foundation for future newspaper cartoons in Japan.

NOTE
1 Saito Takio in Yokohama Kaiko Kinenkan 1987, p.177 mentions that, according to a Hong Kong directory, 'Beato and Wirgman, Artists and Photographers' is already listed under Yokohama in 1864. This means the partnership was probably in existence by 1863. John Clark (1989, p.16) refers to *The Chronicle and Directory, Shanghai* of 1865 in which 'Beatto [sic] and Wirgman, artists and photographers' is listed under Yokohama.

LIT : Clark 1989, pp.4-94; *Charuzu Waguman* 1990

225
Sitting Japanese Lady
Watercolour, 30.4 x 22.8cm
Tokyo University of Fine Arts

226
Portrait of a Young Woman
Oil on board, 48 x 36 cm
Tochigi Prefectural Museum of Art, Utsunomiya

A young woman is standing in front of an entrance of a modest house. With the accuracy of a reporter's eye, the artist prominently painted a tear in the paper of the sliding door without trying to hide it.

227
A Highway, 1872
Oil on canvas, 34.8 x 62.7 cm
Kanagawa Prefectural Museum, Yokohama

228
A Post Town, 1872
Oil on canvas, 34.8 x 62.7 cm
Kanagawa Prefectural Museum, Yokohama

A Highway and *A Post Town* were both recently cleaned and show clearer colours and details.

LIT : *Charuzu Waguman* 1990, pp.211-12

229
The Five-storey Pagoda, c.1874-80
Watercolour on paper, 16.5 x 21.5 cm
Trustees of the British Museum, London

Okabe Masayuki pointed out the similarity of this watercolour and that by Goseda Yoshimatsu (Cat. 243) in the Kanagawa Prefectural Museum. They are so close that either the artists painted the scene together or Yoshimatsu based his on Wirgman's watercolour.

230
A View at Odah
Watercolour on paper
Trustees of the British Museum, London

231
A Seaside Landscapex
Watercolour on paper, 39 x 51 cm
Tochigi Prefectural Museum of Art, Utsunomiya

Wirgman uses here a quite adventurous composition with a high viewpoint. Comparisons with old photographs indicate that this watercolour depicts the Honmoku beach area.

232
A Sketchbook of Japan, 1884
Lithographic album, 20.2 x 26.3 cm
E.I. Wirgman, London

233
Sketchbook, c.1876
Watercolour, pencil, pen and ink, 24.6 x 37 cm
E. I. Wirgman, London

234
Illustrations to 'Artistic and Gastronomic Rambles in Japan from Kioto to Tokyo by Tokaido', 1872
Pen and ink drawings, approx. 14 x 21 cm each
E.I. Wirgman, London

A. *You must be tired*

B. *The Jin Riki sha*

C. *The Kago*

D. *Hakone Pass, Tokaido*

E. *Bay of Owari*

F. *Misaka*

These sketchbooks and drawings were kept within the Wirgman family and are shown to the public for the first time here. In 1872 Wirgman travelled to Kyoto and in *The Illustrated London News* (19 October 1872) reported on the second

Kyoto Exhibition. 1 This exhibition was also important, because it was the first occasion on which Westerners were allowed freely to enter Kyoto, the traditional seat of the Emperor until he moved to Tokyo. The illustrations to 'Artistic and Gastronomic Rambles in Japan from Kioto to Tokyo by Tokaido' were probably sketched on the way back from this visit.

LIT : Clark 1989, pp.38(A.1.1, A.1.2), 39 (A.1.7)

NOTE
1. The Kyoto Exhibition Wirgman visited was the second and not the first as stated in *Charuzu Waguman* 1990, p.223. Foreigners were not allowed to attend the first one which took place in 1871. See Maruyama Hiroshi, 'Meiji Shoki no Kyoto Hakurankai' (Early Meiji Period Kyoto Exhibitions), in Yoshida 1986, pp.221-48

GOSEDA YOSHIMATSU (1855-1915)

Goseda was the son of the Western-style painter, Goseda Horyu. Horyu ran an active painting workshop in Yokohama catering for Western demand and Yoshimatsu's sister Yuko was also a Western-style painter. Yoshimatsu became Wirgman's pupil as early as 1865 or 1866 and was, by all accounts, regarded as a child prodigy. His works while under the tutelage of Wirgman show freshness and a keen sense of observation. Wirgman himself is said to have regarded Yoshimatsu as better than himself and way above Kawakami Togai or Takahashi Yuichi, two of the more senior oil painters of the time. 1 In 1876 he became a student of Antonio Fontanesi at the Tokyo School of Fine Arts, though he does not seem to have been happy there and left the School the following year. In 1880 Yoshimatsu went to Paris and studied under Léon Bonnat (1833-1922), who later became head of the Ecole des Beaux-Arts. During this time he suffered poverty, but managed to get his works accepted at the Salon. He spent most of the year 1887 in Britain, then travelled to America and returned to Yokohama in 1889. In 1890 he went to America with his father, Horyu, for about five months. It is generally conceded that Yoshimatsu did not fulfill his promise as a child prodigy and his works after his return from the West are on the whole disappointing.

LIT : *Meiji no Kyutei Gaka* 1986; Aoki 1987

NOTE
1 Aoki Shigeru, 'Yoshimatsu to Gosedaha no Keifu' (The genealogy of Yoshimatsu and the Goseda School), in *Charuzu Waguman* 1990, pp.150-9; p.154

235
Portrait of a Woman (Yokohama Style), 1871
Oil on canvas, 37 x 29 cm
Tokyo University of Fine Arts Museum

236
Portrait of a Boy
Oil on paper, 32.5 x 23 cm
Kanagawa Prefectural Museum, Yokohama

237
Portrait of a Family
Watercolour on paper, 15 x 23.5 cm
Sealed b.r.: Goseda Yoshimatsu
Kanagawa Prefectural Museum, Yokohama

238
Goseda Family Portrait
Watercolour on paper, 25 x 36.2 cm
Kanagawa Prefectural Museum, Yokohama

The figure looking towards us is probably
Yoshimatsu himself. The girl in the painting
could be his sister Yuko. As a painter she is
known as Watanabe Yuko (1856-1942) and
published collections of lithographs (1886).
and engravings (1887).

239
Horyu drawing
Watercolour on paper, 11.8 x 16.3 cm
Sealed b.l.: Goseda Yoshimatsu
Kanagawa Prefectural Museum, Yokohama

240
Portrait of Goseda Horyu I
Ink on paper, 16.6 x 24 cm
Inscribed b.l.: Ryuo no zo
Sealed b.l.: Goseda Yoshimatsu
Kanagawa Prefectural Museum, Yokohama

The two drawings of his father (Cat.239-240)
by Yoshimatsu show his skill in the handling of
the brush. In the inscribed version, the beard,
something which is usually drawn in a linear
manner, is broken up into small flat grey and
white parts like a net, yet still looks like a beard.

241
The Village of Nishiota in Yokohama, 1872
Watercolour on paper, 17.7 x 42.3 cm
Inscribed b.r.: Meiji gonen Yokohama Nishiota
no sonraku (Meiji 5 [1872] The Village of
Nishiota in Yokohama)
Kanagawa Prefectural Museum, Yokohama

242
Theatre at Takashima-cho in Yokohama
Watercolour on paper, 18.3 x 45.8 cm
Titled b.l.: Yokohama Takashima-cho Gijo
(Theatre at Takashima-cho in Yokohama)
Kanagawa Prefectural Museum, Yokohama

This theatre was built in 1872 and is said to
have survived until about 1882.

243
The Five-storey Pagoda
Watercolour on paper, 16.6 x 25.9 cm
Kanagawa Prefectural Museum, Yokohama

Compare this with Cat.229

244
Asakusa Nio Gate
Watercolour, 18.2 x 24.4 cm
Kanagawa Prefectural Museum, Yokohama

TAKAHASHI YUICHI (1828-1894)

Yuichi was born in Edo, the son of a low-ranking
samurai. He decided to give up the life of a
samurai pursuing the military arts and instead
to become a painter. He was trained in the
traditional Kano-School manner, but one
day came across a Western lithograph. In his
autobiography he writes that he was so inspired
by its realism that he decided at once to study
Western-style painting. Much later, in 1866, he
visited Wirgman in Yokohama and became his
pupil. In 1869 he even tried unsuccessfully to
ask the authorities whether Wirgman could leave
Yokohama and live with him in Tokyo. Later on
he was also taught by Antonio Fontanesi (1818-
1882), the Italian painter who was invited to
Japan by the Meiji Government. Yuichi was
considerably older than most of Wirgman's other
pupils. Most of his early works use self-taught
techniques and his compositions are heavily
reliant on traditional models. Nevertheless,
his works express his strong will and struggle to
confront Western-style oil painting head on. In
1873 he opened a painting school, Tenkairo (the
name was changed to Tenkaisha in 1875 and to
Tenkaigakusha in 1879), and throughout his life
he tried to advance Western-style art in Japan.
He exhibited his paintings both at the 1867 Paris
Exposition Universelle and at the 1873 Vienna
Weltausstellung.

LIT : Aoki 1984; Haga 1984; Aoki 1987

245
Hitoyoshi on Fire, 1877
Oil on canvas, 65.7 x 121.3 cm
Inscribed: Meiji junen gogatsu yokka Hitoyoshi
Ryujin-cho yori Kumagawa o nozomu. Ishii
Retsuzo zukomo' (10th Meiji [1877] May 4th.
A View of the Kuma River from Ryujin Town in
Hitoyoshi. Copy of a sketch by Ishii Retsuzo)
Private Collection

LIT : Aoki and Haga 1979 (17)

In 1877 the Seinan rebellion, the largest and also
the last of the military uprisings against the Meiji
Government, took place in Kyushu. This painting
depicts the scene when the government troops
set the city of Hitoyoshi in Kumamoto prefecture
on fire. A pupil of Yuichi, Ishii Retsuzo,
accompanied the troops and made several
sketches of the conflict. This is a copy by Yuichi
of one of Ishii's sketches, but the painting does
not have a strong element of reportage and is
more like an exploration into landscape painting.

246
Books and Objects, c.1875-76
Oil on canvas, 36.3 x 57.8cm
Kotohira Shrine Museum

LIT: Aoki and Haga 1979 (9); Takashina 1980, pp.63-7

This powerful still-life depicts household objects,
most of which probably belonged to one of his
daughters, including a lantern, a calligraphy
block, a battledore for a New Year's game, small
bean-bags for juggling and a school textbook. In
1872 the Japanese Government introduced a

general education system but official textbooks
were issued only in 1874. Takashina Shuji
identified the textbook in the painting as *Shoga
ku Nyumon Otsugo* (Primary School Introduction,
Issue Otsu) published in summer 1874.
Takashina proposed a probable date for this
painting of about January 1875, because of the
battledore which is normally used by girls during
the New Year's festivities and because of the age
of Yuichi's second daughter Tetsu, who was born
in 1868. As Takashina mentions in his book,
this painting has different and inconsistent
viewpoints, but the vivid colours and the
loving details create a naive charm.

YAMAMOTO HOSUI (1850-1906)

In 1865 Hosui, inspired by Hokusai Manga,
decided to become a painter, just at the time
that these works were also inspiring the avant-
garde painters in Paris. However when he saw
a Western-style painting by Goseda Horyu in
Yokohama, he decided to become a Western-
style painter and in 1869 became a pupil of
Horyu. At this time also, Horyu's son,
Yoshimatsu, was one of Wirgman's best pupils.
Either directly or indirectly Hosui must have
learnt the Western technique of painting from
Wirgman. After a short period with Antonio
Fontanesi he went to Paris in 1878, where he
became a student of Jean-Léon Gérôme at the
Ecole des Beaux-Arts. Hosui mixed with many
Parisian intellectuals, such as Théophile and
Judith Gautier and Victor Hugo and encouraged
Kuroda Seiki, the future leader of Japanese oil
painting, to become a painter. In 1887 he
returned to Japan and opened an art school,
Seikokan Gagakko, the first to introduce
French-style art education, in 1889.

LIT : Takashina 1980, pp.367-80;
Paris autour de 1882 1982

247
Portrait of Mrs Sonoda Kei, 1885
Oil on canvas, 61 x 50.8 cm
Signed and dated at bottom: Yamamoto 1885
Inscribed on back: February Meiji 18
(1885)/ Eikoku Rondon
Koriyama City Museum of Art

Mrs Sonoda is here portrayed in an elegant
Victorian dress. Her husband, Sonoda Kokichi,
was a diplomat who was stationed in London as
Japanese Consul between 1881 and 1888 and
later became director of the Yokohama
Commercial Bank (Yokohama Shokan Ginko).
How and where this portrait was commissioned
has not been fully established, but from the date
and inscription on the painting it is tempting to
think that the painting was produced in London.
Although no document has been found
concerning Yamamoto's visit to Britian, it is not
inconceivable that he visited London at the time
he was active in Paris. He had been living in Paris
since 1878 and had a one-man exhibition at the
Georges Petit Gallery in 1885.

NOTE
We are grateful to Murata Tetsuo at the Koriyama City Art Museum for introducing us to the painting and for supplying information.

HYAKUTAKE KANEYUKI (1842-1884)

He was born in Saga and became a close retainer of Nabeshima Naohiro, the last feudal lord of the Saga clan (see Cat.134). In 1871 he travelled to the West with Naohiro and from the following year studied economics in Britain. In 1874 he returned to Japan for a brief period, but went back to Britain the same year. During his second stay in Britain he studied painting under Thomas Miles Richardson Jr (1813-1890) and this seems to be the first time that he showed a serious interest in painting. Already in 1876 he managed to get a painting called *View near Yokohama, in Japan* accepted at the Royal Academy. In 1878 he went to Paris where he studied painting for about a year under Léon Bonnat (1833-1922), as did Yoshimatsu after him. From 1880 until 1882 he was in Rome where Cesare Maccari (1840-1911) was his teacher. After his return from the West he held a position at the Ministry of Agriculture and Trade, but died shortly afterwards. Miwa Hideo's study shows that Hyakutake gradually changed his own style to reflect the styles of his teachers, but his shifts from impressionistic landscape to academic historical painting show an independent mind and indicate the direction he felt was needed for the development of oil painting in Japan.

LIT : Miwa 1978; Miwa 1988

248
Barnard Castle, c.1878
Oil on canvas
The Imperial Collection, Tokyo

There is an oil study (40.5 x 55.5 cm) in the Saga Prefectural Museum. The finished painting shows how well, within a short period of time, Hyakutake managed to master the techniques of English landscape painting.

MIYAKE KOKKI (1874-1954)

Miyake studied oil painting at Soyama Sachihiko's (1859-1892) studio, but the exhibition of works by John Varley Jr (fl.1870-1895, d.1899) which he visited in 1891 inspired him to pursue watercolour painting. Then in 1894 he saw the exhibition of watercolours by Alfred Parsons (see Cat.286h), which further stimulated him to concentrate on watercolour. In 1897 he went to America, and in 1898 to Britain, where he visited Alfred East (1849-1913) and Parsons. He also went to Paris but returned to Japan in the same year. After this first visit he frequently returned to the West. Miyake championed the art of watercolour painting in Japan and was one of the leaders of this movement.

249
Forest in Hampstead, 1898
Watercolour, 15.7 x 26.2 cm
Tokyo University of Fine Arts Museum

This watercolour was painted during Miyake's stay in England in 1898 and shows his sensitive and delicate use of the watercolour medium. It also shows clearly how his approach to painting intentionally differed from traditional Japanese painting techniques, which also used water-soluble pigments.

MINAMI KUNZO (1883-1950)

Minami studied Western-style painting at the Tokyo School of Fine Arts under Okada Saburosuke (1869-1939) and immediately after graduation in 1907 went to London where he studied at the South West Polytechnic under Ernest Borough Johnson (1867-1949). In 1909 he went to France and returned to Japan in 1910. Some of his works show the strong influence of Whistler's Nocturnes. Recently a considerable number of his works was bequeathed by his family to the collection of the Tokyo University of Fine Arts Museum.

LIT : *Minami Kunzo Ten* 1983; *Minami Kunzo Shuga Sakuhin Ten* 1989; 1908/09 *Rondon no Seishun: Zengo* 1990

250
A Night Scene
Watercolour, 30.0 x 10.3 cm
Tokyo University of Fine Arts Museum

LIT : *Minami Kunzo Shuga Sakuhin Ten* 1989 (51)

Watercolour painting was very important for Minami and here we can see Whistler's influence in his tonal use of paint and in the flat composition.

251
A Farmhouse with White Walls, 1908
Oil on canvas, 75.5 x 101 cm
Hiroshima Prefectural Museum of Art

In 1908 Minami stayed for about three weeks at a small village, North Moreton, between Didcot and Wallingford. He obviously enjoyed his stay and it was a productive trip for him.

SHIRATAKI IKUNOSUKE (1873-1960)

Shirataki first studied art at Seikokan Gagakko (Seikokan Art School) run by Yamamoto Hosui. Later he studied with Kuroda Seiki and in 1904 travelled to America. Before his return to Japan in 1911 he went to Paris, but spent more than three years in London. Though he is better known for his oil paintings, during his stay in London Shirataki produced a considerable number of memorable watercolours.

LIT : 1908/09 *Rondon no Seishun: Zengo* 1990

252
Suburbs of London, 1907
Watercolour on paper, 21.2 x 30 cm
Otani Memorial Art Museum, Nishinomiya

253
Suburbs of London (View with Bridge), 1907
Watercolour, 18.4 x 26.8 cm
Otani Memorial Art Museum, Nishinomiya

254
London in the Morning, 1907
Watercolour, 18.3 x 27 cm
Signed: I. Shirataki
Otani Memorial Art Museum, Nishinomiya

This at first sight unassuming watercolour beautifully depicts the rising sun through a morning mist. His technique of handling washes is reminiscent of Turner's so-called 'Colour Beginnings'.

255
London - near Kew Garden, 1907
Watercolour on paper, 18.5 x 27 cm
Signed: I. Shirataki
Otani Memorial Art Museum, Nishinomiya

HARA BUSHO (1866-1912)

Hara studied Western-style painting at Kyoto-fu Art School under Koyama Sanzo (1860-1927) and Tamura Soryu (1846-1918), an erstwhile Wirgman pupil. He gained a high reputation as a portrait painter, but was not satisfied with his own progress. In 1904 he travelled to London to further his study of oil painting and stayed there until 1907. With unusual concentration he tried to master the art of oil painting mostly by copying, especially at the National Gallery. One day he was taken by his friend Makino Yoshio to the critic and editor of the *Magazine of Art*, Marion H. Spielmann (1858-1949), and through him Hara was able to meet a number of British artists, such as Solomon J. Solomon (1860-1927), who gave him instruction in painting. Spielmann also mentioned Hara in the magazine *Graphic* (1 September 1906, 12 January 1907) and praised his progress very highly. He was perhaps the most accomplished British-trained Japanese painter, but sadly died of cancer shortly after his return to Japan.

256
Woman, 1903
Oil on canvas, 151.2 x 60 cm
Inscribed b.l.: After Harry van der Weyden
By H. Busho 190
Keio University (Kojun-sha), Tokyo

This is a copy of a painting by Harry van der Weyden (1868-?), a painter born in Boston, who was one of the group of Americans then active in Paris. According to Tan'o Yasunori, this painting was not copied during his stay in the West, but just before. He was expecting to study oil painting in London by copying and this was a preparatory exercise. Tan'o quotes a passage from Hara's diary of 1 November 1903, where he writes: 'At Iwasaki Villa in Fukagawa I copied paintings by the Englishman Wotaro and by the Frenchman Widen'. 'Wotaro' must be the Royal Academician, Sir Ernest Albert Waterlow (1850-1919), and Hara's copy is extant in the collection of the Tokyo University of Fine Arts Museum. 'Widen' is obviously Weyden, as inscribed on the painting. Iwasaki Villa in Fukagawa was an Elizabethan-style building by Josiah Conder completed in 1889, the first of Conder's many villas.

LIT : Tan'o 1984, pp.12-13, 15; Tan'o 1987, August, p.19; *Treasures from the Keio-Gijuku Collection*, Kume Museum, Tokyo 1990 (29)

257
Nude Woman, 1906
Oil on canvas, 130.5 x 97.8 cm
Signed and dated b.r.: B.K. Hara 1906 London
Tokyo University of Fine Arts Museum

LIT : Tan'o 1987, September, p.18

This is one of the few major nude pictures by a Japanese painted during the Meiji period. The body of the model is depicted with subtle nuances and the balance of the contrapposto of the figure is deft. The face is shown contre-jour and the use of the body's shadow on the wall is very unusual within the tradition of Japanese oil painting. The figure trying to draw on the wall suggests that the model is meant to be his Muse. A photograph of his studio with the artist, the model and this painting exists. The canvas comes from Winsor and Newton.

258
The Chandos Portrait of Shakespeare, 1906-7
Oil on canvas, 53.3 x 45.7 cm
Tokyo University Library

LIT : Tan'o 1984

For Hara, copying seems to have been more than anything the direct route to unravelling the secrets of oil painting. As Tan'o's research on this painting shows, Marion Spielmann, who was very supportive of Hara, wrote the definitive article on the portraits of Shakespeare in the *Encyclopaedia Britannica* (11th ed. 1911). Hara's decision to copy the so-called 'Chandos' portrait of Shakespeare from the early seventeenth century, now in the National Portrait Gallery in London, must have had something to do with Spielmann. Whatever the initial reason for painting this picture, the finished painting is not strictly a copy. The original seems to have a larger, fuller and warmer face, whereas Hara's Shakespeare has a more compact face and a penetrating gaze. The contrast of the highlights is stronger and the brush strokes more flickering. As Tan'o indicates, Hara was probably aware of the history of the many versions of the Chandos portrait and this was his own contribution to this tradition.

259
Lady Montague, 1907
Oil on canvas
Tokyo National Museum

This portrait dating from Hara's last year in Britain shows how far he had developed as a painter. Compared with this fluent and original painting, his portraits prior to his visit to Britain look rather stiff, even though they are some of the best portraits painted in Japan at that time.

SHIMOMURA KANZAN (1873-1930)

Kanzan was one of the leading Japanese-style painters of the Meiji and Taisho periods. He was trained under Kano Hogai (1828-1888) and Hashimoto Gaho (1835-1908). In 1903 he was sent by the government to Britain to study watercolour. While there, he copied a number of paintings, and in April 1904 he organised an exhibition of his works at the Club for the Japanese in London. He also attended the opening of the Whistler Memorial Exhibition in 1905, where about 750 of Whistler's works were exhibited. He returned to Japan in 1905. His paintings were frequently shown at International Exhibitions abroad including the 1910 Anglo-Japanese Exhibition, where he showed his masterpiece *Autumn Forests*, now in the Tokyo Museum of Modern Art.

LIT : Shimomura 1981

260
Copy of J.E. Millais's Knight Errant, c.1904
Watercolour on paper, 101 x 75.5cm
Signed b.r.: Kanzan sha (Copied by Kanzan)
Sealeded b.r.: Kanzan
Yokohama Museum of Art, Yokohama

This is a copy of *Knight Errant* (1870) by the Pre-Raphaelite artist John Everett Millais (1829-1896) now in the Tate Gallery. The original large painting belongs to the period when Millais was a successful Academician. Quentin Bell referred to it as representing 'Millais's final and complete abandonment of Pre-Raphaelitism'. 1 The painting certainly does not show the fully lit and sharp details of Millais's early works.

NOTE
1 Quentin Bell, *A New and Noble School: The Pre-Raphaelites*, London 1982, p.100

261
London by Night, 1904
Ink and gold on silk (hanging-scroll),
124.5 x 50.5 cm
Yamaguchi Eiichi, Yokohama

262
Diogenes sitting in Meditation
Ink and watercolour on silk (hanging-scroll),
H. c.225 cm
Trustees of the British Museum, London

While in London, Kanzan sent several paintings back to Japan including *London by Night* and *Diogenes* for an exhibition in Japan, the fifteenth Kaiga Kyoshinkai of 1903. The *Diogenes* received

the Silver Medal. Recently a *Diogenes* painting by Kanzan has come to light which seems to be the one exhibited in Japan. Here the Greek philosopher and friend of Alexander the Great is depicted as if he were an Oriental sage. It reminds us that within the progressive *Rangaku* circle during the Edo period, several portraits of another Greek, Hippocrates, the father of Medicine, were painted. Cat.262 was in the collection of Kanzan's friend and Japanophile, Arthur Morrison.

TAKASHIMA HOKKAI (1850-1931)

Takashima studied geology and botany and gained a position within the Department of Forestry at the Ministry for Agriculture and Trade. In 1884 he was sent to Scotland to visit the International Forestry Exhibition. From 1885 he studied forestry in Nancy for three years. There he became a friend of the designer Emile Gallé (1846-1904) and was a strong influence on him. He was a self-taught painter in the traditional style. In 1899 he resigned his post and after a short teaching period decided to become a professional painter. He followed an active life as a painter until his death in 1931. His achievements were neglected, until it was discovered that Hokkai was actually the mysterious Japanese friend of Gallé.

LIT : *Takashima Hokkai Gashu* 1976; *Takashima Hokkai Ten* 1986

263
Mount Suriof (?) in Scotland (Sukottorando Suriofu-zan), 1906
From *One-Hundred Hokkai Sansui*
Ink and watercolour on silk (hanging-scroll),
136.4 x 54.5 cm
Signed and sealed b.r.: Hokkai
Freer Gallery of Art, Washington, D.C.
(Gift of Mr Taniguchi Toyosaburo)

264
Farmhouse at Doncleigan (?) (Sukottorando Donkuraigen Noka), 1906
From *One-Hundred Hokkai Sansui*
Ink and watercolour on silk (hanging-scroll),
136.4 x 54.5 cm
Signed and sealed b.r.: Hokkai
Freer Gallery of Art, Washington, D.C.

In 1884 Hokkai travelled to Scotland to visit the International Forestry Exhibition. One can therefore assume that he knew what Scottish landscapes looked like. At first sight this landscape by Hokkai give the impression of a Japanese or a Chinese scene, but closer scrutiny of the small buildings reveals that they are not Far-Eastern huts but Scottish cottages, one of them merrily spouting smoke out of a chimney! Hokkai uses the traditional Japanese perspective of vertically piling-up hills and mountains alternately from right and left to express distance.

Cat.262 SHIMOMURA KANZAN (1873-1930) *Diogenes sitting in Meditation*

X. BRITISH ARTISTS VISIT JAPAN

FRANK DILLON (1823-1909)

Frank Dillon visited Japan in 1876. He was
a topographical painter, who had travelled
extensively, especially in Egypt, where he had
depicted pharaonic ruins and the interiors of
houses in Cairo. His activities in Japan are not
well documented, but it is known that he stayed
there for more than a year. On his return to
London in 1877, his Japanese paintings were
exhibited and sold at Agnew's and the remaining
works were sold at Christie's in 1911. 1 How
he became attracted to Japan is not clear, but it
is likely that as with many of his contemporaries
this evolved from an interest in Orientalism. He
was a friend of George Price Boyce, who had
shared a studio with him in Egypt in 1861-62.
As we saw in Section IV, Boyce was a member
of Rossetti's circle and apparently a Japanese
enthusiast. It is also worth noting that the period
of his visit to Japan overlaped with that of
Dresser's (see Section VIII: Dresser's Japonisme
also developed out of his interest in the Egyptian
and Islamic arts), and it is highly unlikely that
they did not know each other: both had a high
profile in London's artistic world at the time.
Nevertheless, whether they met in Japan or
even in London remains complete speculation.
Although Japanese art does not seem to have
affected his stylistic development, Dillon's
interest in Japan was beyond mere exoticism.
He published *Drawings by Japanese Artists* in
1880, which was accompanied by fifteen colour
reproductions of Japanese paintings. In the
introduction, Dillon compares Japanese painting
with Chinese, and discusses at length the
characteristics of Japanese painting, including
the decorative use of flowers and birds, attitudes
to nature and human figures, and calligraphy
and brush techniques.

NOTE
1 *Art Journal* 1909, p.223

265
A Japanese Interior, c.1877
Gouache on paper, 38 x 54 cm
Signed b.r.: F. Dillon
Mr and Mrs Broughton, Lincoln

This painting shows a room identical to that of
The Stray Shuttlecock in the Victoria and Albert
Museum (fig.4). However, while the V & A
version takes a view facing the 'tokonoma'
(ornamental alcove) and a 'stray shuttlecock' is
seen by a little girl standing by the 'shoji' screen
on the left, Cat.265 shows a view diagonally
across the room and two Japanese women eating
and drinking tea by the open window. The
decorative details also differ between the two.
For instance, this picture shows a hanging-scroll
with a peacock and an incense-burner on a
wooden stand under the shelves on the right, but
the V & A version shows a picture of a crane and

fig. 4 Frank Dillon
The Stray Shuttlecock
Victoria and Albert Museum

a large ceramic vase which replaces the incense-
burner and stand. Reflecting Dillon's careful
observation of Japanese architectural features and
objects,
the depiction of both scenes is convincing.
Nevertheless, one finds subtle inconsistencies
in manners and seasonal symbolism, including,
for example in *The Stray Shuttlecock*, a pair of 'zori'
(outdoor sandals) worn by the girl indoors, which
represent summer, while the shuttlecock
conflictingly represents New Year, and therefore
winter. It indicates that these interiors were
painted from memory, either while Dillon was
in Japan or after his return, based on his sketches.
The decorative objects were probably painted
from life, as it is known that they were in Dillon's
collection and that several articles seen in these
interiors, including the scrolls, were lent to the
Bethnal Green Museum in London in 1884 and
then donated to the museum in 1916 after
Dillon's death.

NOTE
We are grateful to Lionel Lambourne at the Victoria and
Albert Museum for introducing us to these paintings
and for supplying information.

JOSIAH CONDER (1852-1920)
See Section VI for a short biography and some of
his architectural work.

266
AFTER KAWANABE KYOSAI (1831-1889)
Owl on Cherry Blossom Branch (Mimizuku zu),
c.1883-89
Ink on silk (hanging-scroll), 59 x 27.3 cm
Signed l.r.: Kyoei hitsu
Sealed c.r.: Kyoei
Private Collection, London

LIT : *Rokumeikan no yume* 1991, p.31

267
AFTER KAWANABE KYOSAI (1831-1889)
A Shrike (Mozu zu), c.1883-89
Ink and watercolour on silk (hanging-scroll),
63.2 x 27.5 cm
Signed b.r.: Kyoei hitsu
Sealed b.r.: J. Conder
Kawanabe Kyosai Memorial Museum

LIT : *Rokumeikan no yume* 1991, p.30

Conder began to learn 'nihonga' (traditional
Japanese painting) under Kawanabe Kyosai
(see below) around 1881. Lessons were given
privately at Conder's house every Saturday,
and were principally devoted to the copying
of Kyosai's work. Conder was a skilful
watercolourist, and soon became Kyosai's
favourite student. In 1883 Conder was given the
artist's name 'Kyoei', and he signed his 'nihonga'

with this name from this time onwards. In 1884, Conder became the first foreign exhibitor at the second *Naikoku kaiga kyoshin-kai* (National Painting Exhibition), and one of his exhibits in particular, *A Heron in the Rain* (Uchu no sagi), was highly praised by *The Tokyo Nichinichi Shimbun* . 1 Cats 267 - 268, copied from Kyosai's examples, show Conder's understanding of Eastern calligraphic techniques.

NOTE
1 S. Yamaguchi, 'Eshi Kyoei to Kyosai', *Rokumeikan no yume* 1991, pp.46-7

268
Portrait of Kyosai (Kyosai Sensei), 1885
Watercolour on paper, 21.5 x 27.7 cm
Signed, dated and inscribed b.l.: J. Conder
August 1885 Kyosai Sensei at Nikko, August 5th
Sealed: J.Conder/Pinxit
Kawanabe Kyosai Memorial Museum

LIT : Iijima, No.3, 1984, pp.127-42; S. Yamaguchi, 'Eshi Kyoei to Kyosai', *Rokumeikan no yume* 1991, pp.44-9 with ill. on p.49

Conder went on a sketching tour to Nikko with Kyosai in early August 1885. This portrait was made while Kyosai was drawing in a room at the Io-in Temple, their accommodation in Nikko.

KAWANABE KYOSAI (1831-1889)

Kyosai was first trained under the Ukiyo-e-school artist, Utagawa Kuniyoshi (1797-1861), and then under the Kano-school painters, Maemura Towa and Kano Tohaku. Kyosai was a versatile artist, whose work included not only Kano-style paintings of flowers and birds, but also Ukiyo-e-style illustrations and satires.
Despite his arrest in 1870 for his political satires, Kyosai was one of the most successful artists at the time. His work was exhibited at the International Exhibition of 1873 in Vienna, in which the Meiji Government joined for the first time. His quick and fluent brush drawings, which captured momentary movements of humans and animals, were extremely popular, especially among Western visitors and collectors, including Emile Guimet, the founder of the Musée Guimet, William Anderson, Ernest Fenollosa, and Mortimer Menpes (see below). Francis Brinkley, a British sea Captain and chief-editor of *The Japan Mail*, was Conder's fellow student under Kyosai. Kyosai's work was widely introduced to other countries by their writings, especially by Conder's comprehensive thesis, *Paintings and Studies by Kawanabe Kyosai*, published in 1911.

LIT : Conder 1911; Iijima, No.3, 1984; S. Yamaguchi, 'Eshi Kyoei to Kyosai',*Rokumeikan no yume* 1991, pp.44-9

Cat.266

269
Studies for the Use of British Students (Eikokujin Gacho Shitae), c.1887
Ink on paper (hand-scroll), 27 x 1,162 cm
Kawanabe Kyosai Memorial Museum

These drawings were used by Kyosai's British students, Conder and Brinkley, as models for copying. As stated in *Kyosai's Lecture on Drawing (Kyosai Gadan)* (Cats 270 - 271), it was Kyosai's teaching principle that first of all art students should learn how to copy the truthful form of the object. 1

NOTE
1 Iijima, 1984, pp.178-9

270
URIU MASAYASU (1823-1893)
Kyosai's Lecture on Drawing (Kyosai Gadan)
Published in Tokyo 1887
Illustrated book, 25.5 x 17.5 cm
Signed: Kyosai Kawanabe Toiku
Kawanabe Kyosai Memorial Museum

271
URIU MASAYASU (1823-1893)
Kyosai's Lecture on Drawing - Copies of Western Drawings (Kyosai Gadan - Seiyo Gamo)
Published in Tokyo 1887
Illustrated book, 25.5 x 17.5 cm
Signed: Kyosai Kawanabe Toiku
Kawanabe Kyosai Memorial Museum

Written by Uriu Masayoshi, *Kyosai's Lecture on Drawing (Kyosai Gadan)* was published in 1887 in four volumes. According to the publisher's note, this book was the compilation of Kyosai's drawings copied from works of Old Masters, and it was intended to be 'the compass and instructor of the future students of painting'. 1 The text was written in a manner which sought to capture Kyosai's conversational style. 2 The volume shown features Conder's pictures of a heron and a carp.

NOTES
1 K. Iijima, No.3, 1984, pp.142-3
2 Ibid., p.142

MORTIMER MENPES (1860-1938)

Menpes was born in Port Adelaide, Australia, and moved to London in the mid-1870s. He studied under Poynter and in the early 1880s he became Whistler's assistant. His formative period coincided with the height of the 'Japanese craze' in London, which, alongside Whistler's Japonisme, undoubtedly fostered Menpes's enthusiasm for Japanese art. It was in the spring of 1887 that Menpes went to Japan to learn 'all the methods of Japanese art' and to study the condition of modern art in that country. 1 During his eight-month stay, he was introduced to Kawanabe Kyosai (see above) at Francis Brinkley's house. There he observed the complete process of Kyosai's work and he was deeply impressed by his theory of 'a painting from memory...a true impression', which was

first composed in his mind and then depicted in minimal and swift strokes of his brush. 2 A detailed account of this meeting was published on his return in his article 'A Personal View of Japanese art - A Lesson from Khiosi [sic]' in *The Magazine of Art* (April 1888). Kyosai's diary (*Kawanabe Kyosai Enikki*, 30 April 1887) also includes a record on 'Igirisu eshi' (an English painter), who is almost certainly Menpes. 3 Menpes's work from Japan was exhibited at the Dowdeswell Galleries in New Bond Street in London, which included 137 oils and 40 prints. However, Whistler was enraged by his disciple's visit to Japan without his permission. From that time onwards their relationship became strained, but Menpes's love for Japan was unflagging. He lived in a Japanese-style house, which was designed by Arthur Mackmurdo (1851-1942) and completed in 1895. The fittings for the interior were all executed in Japan. 4 Menpes visited Japan again in 1896, and his writings on Japanese art were published in the volume *Japan. A Record in Colour* in 1901, accompanied by 100 colour illustrations.

NOTES
1 Menpes 1888, p.192
2 ibid., p.195
3 S. Yamaguchi, 'Eshi Kyoei to Kyosai', *Rokumeikan no yume* 1991, p.48
4 Lasden 1981, p.336 with pls 403-5. The house is now preserved as a staff building for the Peter Jones Department Store at 25 Cadogan Gardens, London

272
Dolce Far Niente, 1886
Oil on panel, 21.6 x 12.6 cm
Hunterian Art Gallery, University of Glasgow

This small oil shows Maud Franklin, Whistler's model, in a kimono. She was also his long-time mistress, referred to as 'Mrs Whistler', until his marriage to Godwin's widow, Beatrix, in 1888.

273
A Japanese Boy, c.1887-88
Oil on panel, 16.2 x 12.3 cm
Michael Whiteway

274
Japanese Children, c.1887-88
Oil on panel, 10.8 x 15 cm
Private collection

275
A Potter of Japan, c.1887-88
Colour print, 11.5 x 13.3 cm
Andrew McIntosh Patrick

276 (Setagaya only)
Watching the Play, Kyoto, c.1887-88
Etching, 21 x 29.5 cm
Yokohama City Art Museum

LIT : Shuyu *Menpes* (12)

277 (Setagaya only)
Under the Bridge, c.1887-88
Etching, 20.3 x 20.3 cm
Yokohama City Art Museum

LIT : Shuyu *Menpes* (16)

278 (Setagaya only)
By the Light of a Lantern, c.1887-88
Etching, 24 x 19 cm
Yokohama City Art Museum

LIT : Shuyu *Menpes* (30)

279 (Setagaya only)
Japanese Carpenter, c.1887-88
Etching, 27 x 20.5 cm
Yokohama City Art Museum

LIT : Shuyu *Menpes* (36)

From his numerous sketches, paintings and etchings, we know that Menpes travelled extensively, not only to Tokyo but also Osaka, Kyoto and Nagasaki. Menpes was fully aware of Western influences which had begun to change the texture of Japanese culture, 1 but his pictures of children, craftsmen, actors, workers, and street-scenes recorded the life of ordinary Japanese people who were still little affected by Westernisation.

NOTE
1 Menpes 1888, p.192

ALFRED EAST (1849-1913)

East was born at Kettering, Northamptonshire. After training at the Glasgow School of Art and the Ecole des Beaux-Arts in Paris, he settled in London around 1883. East was a landscape painter, and his style evolved from the influences of Corot and the work of the 'plein-air' Barbizon School which was influential during his time in Paris. He was a successful artist, who exhibited regularly at the Royal Academy from 1883 for over twenty years and received a Gold Medal at the Exposition Universelle in Paris in 1889 for the watercolour, *The New Neighbourhood*. In 1889-90, East visited Japan with his friends, Arthur and Emma Liberty and Charles Holmes (see Section VIII). During this visit, he produced numerous watercolours and at least five large oil paintings including *Haru-no Yuki (Snow in Spring)*, which was to be exhibited at the Japan-British Exhibition in London in 1910 (see Section XIII). Furthermore, while in Japan, as a result of introductions from Josiah Conder (see above), he gave lectures and exhibited his work in Tokyo at the Meiji Bijutsukai, the first society of *yoga* painters. Stylistically his work is not obviously Japanese, but it was the Japanese tradition which prompted him to apply the principles of decorative design to landscape painting. East contributed to a revival of the traditional values of 'English' landscapes and wrote many articles and books including *The Art of Landscape Painting in Oil Colour* (1906).

LIT : McConkey 1988

280
Kioto Scene with a Shrine, c.1889-90
Watercolour on paper, 33.2 x 49.4 cm
Signed and inscribed b.l.: Alfred/East Kioto
Sealed in Japanese b.c.: Arufredo Iisto
Whistler type gilt frame
Rosemary Newall

Cat.280 is one of the watercolours exhibited at the Fine Art Society in New Bond Street on his return from Japan in 1890. The picture shows the precinct of a shrine in Kyoto with Japanese figures.

JOHN VARLEY JR (FL.1870-1895 D.1899)

A landscape painter, based in London, the son of Albert Fleetwood Varley (1804-1876), a teacher of drawing, and a grandson of John Varley Snr (1778-1842), a landscape painter and architectural watercolourist. He exhibited at the Royal Academy from 1870 to 1895, and specialised in Oriental subjects including street-scenes, genre and landscape. He travelled to Egypt and India, and visited Japan in 1890.

281
A Japanese Street-scene, 1890
Watercolour on paper, 26.5 x 36 cm
Andrew McIntosh Patrick

GEORGE HENRY (1858-1943)

A 'Glasgow Boy', Henry was born in Ayrshire and studied at the Glasgow School of Art. In 1881 he joined James Guthrie (see Cat.289), Joseph Crawhall (1861-1913) and E.A. Walton, to paint 'en plein-air' at the village of Brig o'Turk in the Trossachs. He met Edward Atkinson Hornel (see below) in 1885, and they soon became close friends. They shared a studio and together developed a highly decorative style in bright, flat colours, as seen in his first acclaimed work, *A Galloway Landscape* (1889; Glasgow Art Gallery and Museum). They worked also on two collaborative projects, *The Druids* (1890; Glasgow Art Gallery and Museum) and *The Star in the East* (1891; Glasgow Art Gallery and Museum). During this period, Henry and Hornel developed a serious interest in Japan. Japanese fashion was in full swing in the city and Whistler's *Ten O'Clock Lecture* was the 'Glasgow Boys'' gospel. 1

Henry's and Hornel's enthusiasm culminated in their visit to Japan in 1893-94. They were financed by the art dealer, Alexander Reid, and other patrons. Travelling to Tokyo, Yokohama, Nagasaki and other towns, they spent nearly fourteen months there. While in Japan, both Henry and Hornel produced a large number of oils and watercolours, mainly of children, Geisha-girls, street-scenes and interiors. Unfortunately, many of Henry's canvases stuck together on the journey back to Britain and were subsequently destroyed, and this may explain the high proportion of his watercolours remaining from this period. 2 At the turn of the century, Henry moved to London and became a successful portrait painter, but in later years he often returned to Japanese subjects. 3

LIT : Buchanan 1978-79; Buchanan 1980; Billcliffe 1985

NOTES
1 Buchanan 1980, p.292
2 Billcliffe 1985, pp.257-623. ibid., p.263

282 (Barbican only)
Koto Player, Kyoto Tokyo, 1894
Watercolour on paper, 71 x 48.3 cm
Signed and dated c.r.: George Henry Tokio/94
Glasgow Art Gallery and Museum

LIT : Buchanan 1978-79 (62); Billcliffe 1985, p.261 with pl.242

283
A Japanese Lady with a Fan, 1894
Oil on canvas, 61 x 40.6 cm
Signed: George Henry Tokio/1894
Glasgow Art Gallery and Museum

LIT : Buchanan 1978-79 (60); Billcliffe 1985, p.261 with pl.243

EDWARD ATKINSON HORNEL (1864-1933)

Hornel was born in Australia but lived mostly at Kirkcudbright. He studied in Edinburgh at the Trustees Academy and in Antwerp under Verlat. In 1885 he met George Henry (see above), through whom he was introduced to the 'Glasgow Boys'. Hornel's early work shows a strong Belgian influence, especially of the landscapes by Maris and Mauve, but through his friendship with Henry he developed a more colourful decorative style. Hornel visited Japan with Henry in 1893-94, and in 1895 he had a successful exhibition of his Japanese work at Reid's Gallery in Glasgow. Stylistically, his Japanese paintings show his great interest in the purely decorative effects of surface textures and colour arrangements. After the visit to Japan, Hornel retreated to Kirkcudbright, where, from 1901, he lived in a seventeenth-century mansion, Broughton House (today's Hornel Art Gallery and Library). He decorated the house with plaster casts from 'the marbles of the Parthenon' and Japanese fans and prints, which reflected Whistler's aesthetic principles, and over the years he created a Japanese garden. He repeatedly painted Japanese themes and later travelled to Asia again, to Ceylon in 1907, and to Burma and Japan in 1922.

284
Two Japanese Girls, 1894
Oil on panel, 73.4 x 47.5 cm
Signed and dated b.l.: E A Hornel/94
Hunterian Art Gallery, University of Glasgow
(Macfie Collection)

285
The Fish Pool, 1894
Oil on canvas, 45.7 x 35.6 cm
Signed and dated b.r.: E A Hornel 1894
Glasgow Art Gallery and Museum

LIT : Billcliffe 1985, p.260 with pl.237

ALFRED WILLIAM PARSONS (1847-1920)

A landscape painter, watercolourist and illustrator, Parsons was born in Beckington, Somerset. He worked as a Post Office clerk, while studying at South Kensington Art School, where he later became Professor. He began to exhibit at the Royal Academy from 1871. In 1905 he was elected a member of the Royal Society of Painters in Watercolours. He visited Japan in 1892, and exhibited his work at the Tokyo School of Fine Arts (today's Tokyo University of Fine Arts), which inspired many Japanese art students including Miyake Kokki (see Section IX).

286
On the Tenryugawa, Near Kajima, 1896
Ink wash on heavy card, 26.5 x 36.5 cm
Signed: Alfred Parsons
Inscribed in pencil beneath drawing: Wanderings in Japan / On the Tenryugawa near Kajima/ Boats sailing up
Trustees of the Victoria and Albert Museum, London

Parsons' records of Japan were published in the book, *A. Parsons' Notes in Japan*, in 1896. This drawing is the illustration for page 213.

ROBERT WEIR ALLAN (1852-1942)

Born in Glasgow, the son of a lithographer, he studied in Paris at the Académie Julian and under Alexandre Cabanel. Allan was a landscape and seascape painter and watercolourist, who painted, mainly on the north-east coast of Scotland, fishing villages and boats in the 'plein-air' style. He exhibited at the Glasgow Institute in 1873 and at the Royal Academy from 1875 onwards. Allan lived in London from 1881, but travelled extensively in Europe, Asia and North Africa. He visited Japan in 1907.

287 (Barbican only)
Nikko, Japan, c.1907
Watercolour, 38.5 x 53.7 cm
Signed and inscribed: Robert W. Allan / Nikko, Japan
Glasgow Art Gallery and Museum

Sada Yacco

Cat.314 WILLIAM NICHOLSON (1872-1949) *Sada Yacco*, c.1900-01

XI. TURN OF THE CENTURY BRITAIN

LAWRENCE ALMA-TADEMA (1836-1912)

Alma-Tadema was born at Dronryp, Holland, and studied in Belgium under Louis de Taye at the Antwerp Academy and under Baron Leys. Having fled from the Franco-Prussian War, he arrived in London in 1870 and took British citizenship in 1873. Alma-Tadema was a dedicated amateur archaeologist, and painted scenes from ancient Greek and Roman life with remarkable accuracy of deetail. He was also a 'Japoniste' and one of the earliest customers of Liberty's. Alma-Tadema's Japanese taste at the time is reflected in the portrait of Laura Theresa Epps (1871; Van Gogh Museum), where his English wife poses with a Japanese fan, admiring a Japanese print. He was close to the Aesthetic circle including Whistler and James Tissot, and had a major one-man exhibition at the Grosvenor Gallery in 1882. His interest in Japanese art continued until the turn of the century, and he was actively involved in the promotion of Japanese culture. In 1892 he became a charter member of the Japan Society, London, and in 1895 its Vice-President. He also worked on the 1904 exhibition of Japanese war art.

LIT : Swanson 1990

288
A Japanese Woman, c.1890s
Watercolour on paper, 27 x 19.5 cm
Signed b.l.: L. Alma Tadema
Peter Pantzer, Bonn

With his close involvement in Japanese culture, his Japonisme reached its peak in the 1890s. His paintings became more decorative with the use of brighter colours, a tendency dating from about 1880. This watercolour shows a fanciful representation of a Japanese lady with a parasol, typified in Gilbert and Sullivan's *The Mikado*, and the Japanese influence is also seen in the treatment of trees and blossoms in the foreground.

JAMES GUTHRIE (1859-1930)

Guthrie was born in Greenock, Scotland. He gave up law in 1877 to take up painting. He was essentially self taught, but strongly influenced by Jules Bastien-Lepage (1848-1884). In 1879 he formed a group with Edward Arthur Walton (1860-1922) and Joseph Crawhall (1861-1913), who were later joined by George Henry (see Section X), to paint in the 'plein-air' style. His first important work, *A Funeral Service in the Highlands* (1881-82; Glasgow Art Gallery) was shown at the Royal Academy in London, and in the 1880s Guthrie was preoccupied with peasant and rustic subjects. From the mid-1880s, however, he took up portraiture, and by the early 1890s he had established himself as a leading

Cat.288

portrait painter. He was President of the Glasgow Art Club from 1896 to 1898.

LIT : Billcliffe 1985

289
Miss Helen Sowerby, 1882
Oil on canvas, 160 x 61 cm
Signed and dated b.r.: J. Guthrie/.82
Inscribed t.l.: Helen/Sowerby
Andrew McIntosh Patrick

LIT : Billcliffe, 1985, pp.61-3 and fig.53

Cat.289 is one of the earliest portraits by Guthrie. Little is known about the background of this painting, or the family who commissioned it, but the work shows a new influence, notably from Whistler (see Section III). In this painting, the model is placed in a shallow, undefined space against a floral-patterned background. As Billcliffe points out, this kind of simple composition and decorative treatment is not seen in the work of Guthrie and his circle before this date, 1 but this style recalls Whistler's work from the 1870s, especially the portraits of *Cicely Alexander* (1872-74; National Gallery, London) and *Mrs. F.R. Leyland* (1873; Frick Collection, New York). Guthrie was in London in the summer of 1882: at the time, Whistler was again prominent in London's art world following his return from Venice, and Whistler's paintings were exhibited at the Grosvenor Gallery, where they might have been seen by Guthrie.

NOTE
1 Billcliffe 1985, p.63

JOHN LAVERY (1856-1941)

Lavery was born in Belfast, but having been orphaned, was brought up in Ulster and Ayrshire. In the 1870s he was apprenticed to J.B. McNair, a photographer and portrait painter in Glasgow, and this experience led to his interest in photography. He was also trained at the Glasgow School of Art and at Heatherley's Art School in London. In the early 1880s he lived in Paris, where he studied under William Adolphe Bouguereau at the Académie Julian. He was influenced by Bastien-Lepage and worked in the 'plein-air' style at Grez-sur-Loing in 1883 and 1884. His small outdoor piece, *Les Deux Pêcheurs*, was exhibited at the 1883 Salon next to Manet's *Un Bar aux Folies-Bergère*. After his return to Glasgow in 1885, Lavery became a leader of the 'Glasgow Boys', and together with Edward Arthur Walton (1860-1922), he was the first Glasgow painter to be associated with the New English Art Club in 1887. In 1888, he was commissioned to paint Queen Victoria's State Visit to the Glasgow International Exhibition, which established his career as a portraitist. In 1896 he moved to London, where he was a friend of Alfred East (see Cat.280) and Whistler (see Section III) and became a highly fashionable portrait painter. In the late 1890s, together with Whistler and the watercolourist, Francis Howard (1874-1954), he was involved in setting up the International Society of Sculptors, Painters and Carvers, which involved a scheme for regular exchanges with French artists. Their first show in 1898 included works by Degas, Fantin-Latour, Manet, Monet, Puvis de Chavannes and Toulouse-Lautrec.

LIT : K. McConkey, *Sir John Lavery*, exh. cat., Belfast and London 1984-85

290
Hokusai and the Butterfly, 1889
Oil on canvas, 61 x 46 cm
Signed b.r.: J Lavery
Inscribed b.r.: Hokusai And The Butterfly Nov' 29 1889
National Galleries of Scotland

LIT : Buchanan 1978-89, pp.6-8; McConkey op. cit. (44); Billcliffe 1985, pp.287-8, pl.271

Painted on the occasion of the Grand Costume Ball at the Glasgow Art Club in November 1889, this portrait shows E.A. Walton costumed as Hokusai and his fiancée, Helen Law, as Butterfly. A surviving photograph of the Ball shows the efforts made by Walton to dress as a Japanese, wearing a kimono, a wig, a pair of zori (sandals), and holding a fan. By that time, the cult of Japan had reached Scotland, and Whistler was the hero of the 'Glasgow Boys'.

WILLIAM KENNEDY (1860-1918)

Kennedy was born in Glasgow, where he was trained at the Paisley School of Art and possibly at the Glasgow School of Art. 1 In the early 1880s he studied in Paris under Bouguereau, Fleury, Bastien-Lepage and Raphael Collin, and formed a friendship with John Lavery (see Cat.290). He was influenced by Bastien-Lepage's naturalist style, and painted outdoors at Fontainebleau and with Lavery at Grez-sur-Loing. Back in Britain, he was active in Glasgow, Stirling and in the South of England. Throughout the 1880s he painted landscape and genre subjects in the naturalist style established in Paris, but towards the end of the decade, like many of the 'Glasgow Boys', he was influenced by Whistler.

NOTE
1 Billcliffe 1985, p.23

291
The Fur Boa, c.1890-91
Oil on canvas, 53.3 x 28.6 cm
Signed b.l.: William Kennedy
Glasgow Art Gallery and Museum

LIT : Billcliffe 1985, p.202, pl.193

Cat.291 is one of his few portraits. With a Japanese print in the background, the picture demonstrates Kennedy's homage to Whistler. In this period, the studios of his friends, Walton, Lavery and other 'Glasgow Boys' were all decorated with Japanese prints.

BESSIE MACNICOL (1869-1904)

MacNicol is regarded as the most important woman painter in Glasgow at the turn of the century. Born in Glasgow, she studied at the Glasgow School of Art under the figurative painter, Francis Newbery (1855-1946), and also in Paris at the Académie Colarossi. Back in Britain, she was active in Glasgow. In 1896 she visited Kirkcudbright, a popular venue for the Glasgow School artists, and met Edward Atkinson Hornel (see Section X), whose strong colours deeply impressed her. Her style reflects the influences of Bastien-Lepage and the works of the 'Glasgow Boys', and her subjects are mainly young girls, women and babies. She exhibited at the Royal Academy, London, the Glasgow Institute of Fine Arts and the Glasgow Society of Artists. In 1899 she married Alexander Frew, a physician and painter, whom she had met at Kirkcudbright, but five years later she died prematurely in childbirth.

LIT : A. Tanner, 'Bessie MacNicol (1869-1904)', in Burkhauser 1990, pp.192-200

292
Portrait of E.A. Hornel, 1896
Oil on canvas, 76 x 61 cm
Signed b.l. in Japanese style: B MacNicol;
on back: B. MacNicol 175 St Vincent
E.A. Hornel Trust, Kirkcudbright

LIT : Tanner, op. cit., pp.194-5, fig.258; Tanner, 'Portrait of a Portrait', *The Scots Magazine* 1990, pp.192-202

MacNicol was closely associated with Hornel in 1896-97. Nine of her letters to Hornel from this period survive in Broughton House, Kirkcudbright (Hornel's former residence). This portrait was painted in Hornel's studio in 1896 and his influence is seen in the use of bright colours. Hornel's Japanese taste is indicated by a large Japanese picture in the background, in the same manner as Van Gogh's *Portrait of Père Tanguy* (1887; Musée Rodin, Paris). She also signed the portrait in a style inspired by Japanese woodcuts. The Japanese picture used here is one of the large-scale paintings illustrating Kabuki scenes, which were probably theatre bills brought back from Japan by Hornel. The portrait was shown at the Glasgow Institute of Fine Arts in 1897, and in the same year it was exchanged with Hornel's painting, which she called 'The Kite Flyer Picture' (probably *Kite Flying, Japan*, c.1894, now in the Scottish National Galleries, Edinburgh). 1

NOTE
1 Tanner, 'Portrait of a Portrait' 1990, p.201

PHILIP WILSON STEER (1860-1942)

Steer was born in Birkenhead and trained at the Gloucester School of Art under a watercolourist, John Kemp (fl.1868-1876). In 1882-84 he studied in Paris, first at the Académie Julian under Bouguereau and then at the Ecole des Beaux-Arts under Cabanel. Back in London, he became a leading promoter of Impressionism in Britain: in 1886 he was a founder-member of the New English Art Club, whose hanging policy was strongly Impressionist-oriented, and in 1889 he organised the 'London Impressionists' exhibition at the Goupil Gallery. During this period, he also exhibited at the Society of British Artists under the presidency of Whistler, whose influence is seen in some of Steer's portraits and coastal scenes painted at that time. From the late 1880s to the mid-1890s he experimented with various French Impressionist styles, and he was invited twice, in 1889 and 1891, to exhibit with Les XX in Brussels. In 1893 he became an assistant of Frederick Brown (1851-1941) at the Slade School, where he was to teach for nearly forty years.

LIT : Laughton 1971

293
The Kimono, c.1894
Oil on canvas, 61 x 21.6 cm
York City Art Gallery

LIT : Laughton 1971 (161), pp.62-3

Cat.293 is the first of two studies for *The Japanese Gown*, which was first shown at the New English Art Club in November 1894; its repainted version (1896; National Gallery, Victoria, Melbourne) was exhibited at the Goupil Gallery in 1896. 1 In this study, Rose Pettigrew, who met Steer through Whistler and became his favourite model from

the late 1880s onwards, poses in a kimono, holding her hand under her chin. Her standing figure is rendered in a narrow format with Whistlerian loose brush strokes. Their subdued tonal arrangement is contrasted with the bright red lining of the kimono and white and yellow patterns on the fabric. The model's relationship with the surrounding space is ambiguous here, but the second study (c.1894; Private Collection), painted in a broader format, introduces a mirror on the right, where the model's profile and her back are reflected, and this spatial arrangement is repeated in the larger version, *The Japanese Gown*.

NOTE
1 Signed and dated 1896, this painting shows various alterations to the 1894 version, which is known only from the reproduction in *The Studio* (December 1894), including the model's face (Steer's relationship with Rose Pettigrew terminated around 1895) and the details of the interior. Laughton suggests that the picture in Melbourne is a replica of the first study of 1894, which was painted in a new style.

JAMES HAMILTON HAY (1874-1916)

Hay was a landscape painter and printmaker, who was active in Liverpool until 1912 when he moved to London. Born in Birkenhead, he studied at the Liverpool Art Schools, and then under various painters including Julius Olsson (1864-1942), David Muirhead (1867-1930), and Augustus John (1878-1961), with whom Hay formed a friendship. He exhibited at the Liverpool Autumn Exhibition from 1895, and at the Royal Academy, London, from 1900. His work in this period shows Whistler's influence. In 1904 he organised an exhibition in Liverpool which included Hornel, Whistler, Augustus John and Manet, and around 1908 he joined the Sandon Studios Society, a group of avant-garde artists in the city. In 1910 he had a one-man exhibition in London at the Baillie Gallery. In 1912 he settled in London, where he became strongly influenced by the Post-Impressionists. Most of Hay's prints, etchings and drypoints were produced in 1913-16. Their subjects consist mainly of landscapes and cityscapes, especially of London, and his decorative style shows the influence of Japanese woodcuts, as seen in *Wimborne* and *Japanese Effect with Trees*, both produced in 1914.

LIT : Walker Art Gallery, *Merseyside Painters, People & Places: Catalogue of Oil Paintings - Text*, Liverpool 1978, pp.111-112; K.M. Guichard, *British Etchers 1850-1940*, London 1981, p.42

294
The Lady in the Japanese Gown - Portrait of Miss Enid Rutherford, (Barbican only) c.1905-07
Oil on canvas, 198.8 x 122 cm
Walker Art Gallery, Liverpool

LIT : Walker Art Gallery, op. cit., p.112 (2511)

Enid Rutherford was the daughter of Sir W.W. Rutherford, MP and Lord Mayor of Liverpool in 1902-03. Trained at the Liverpool School of Art, she was an artist who exhibited at the Liverpool

Academy and the Sandon Studios Society. She married Hay in 1907 but died in 1911. Before their marriage, Hay produced this large Whistlerian portrait of Enid, who posed against a simple grey wall, wearing an Oriental gown, which Hay called 'the Japanese gown', over a white chiffon dress. The wall is decorated with a Japanese print, showing two women with an umbrella, a fan placed on the skirting-board and a spray of hanging leaves arranged asymmetrically. The frame is decorated with a Japanese-inspired design with leaf-patterns and crests, which also reflects Whistler's influence. Whistler had died in 1903, but he was still a highly influential figure in British art. In 1905 there was a large memorial exhibition at the New Gallery, London, which Hay might have seen.

DAVID YOUNG CAMERON (1865-1945)

Born in Glasgow, Cameron was the son of a Scottish minister. He decided to be an artist at the age of twenty after abandoning a business career. He attended the Glasgow School of Art, while working, and then moved to Edinburgh to start full-time training at the Life School of the Royal Scottish Academy. Subsequently he became a landscape artist in oils, watercolours and prints, and his style was influenced by Whistler and the Barbizon painters. He was a prolific printmaker, and his reputation as an etcher was established in the 1890s. His work from this period includes a series of Scottish landscapes and the Thames scenes, where Whistler's influence is evident. He travelled extensively, not only in Britain but also on the Continent and in the Near East, which resulted in numerous etchings, including the 'North Holland Set' (1892), 'North Italian Set' (1896), 'Belgian Set' and the Egyptian series of 1909-10.

LIT : K.M. Guichard, *British Etchers 1850-1940*, London 1981, p.32; W. Smith, *A Picture of Flemings*, London n.d., p.47

295
The Steps, 1892
Etching, 25.2 x 7.5 cm
Andrew McIntosh Patrick

JOHN HASSALL (1868-1948)

Hassall was a farmer in Manitoba, but left Canada to train as an artist. He studied in Antwerp and Paris and was active in London as a painter, illustrator and poster designer. From 1894 to 1901 he exhibited three works at the Royal Academy, and he was a member of the London Sketch Club. Alongside the Beggarstaff Brothers (see Cat.312), Hassall was a leading poster artist at the turn of the century, and his bold, simple design seen, for instance, in *Skegness is So Bracing* for the Great Northern Railway (1909) was influential.

LIT : Wood, 1978, p.209; Farr 1984, pp.323-4

296
A Seated Woman, c.1890s
Pencil, watercolour, chalk on paper, 59 x 49.5 cm
Signed b.l.: Hassall
Victor Arwas, London

A red-haired woman in a voluminous gown is sitting against a wall covered with prints, photographs and curious objects, such as a Japanese figure on the far right (probably a paper cutting) and two small Japanese heads (masks or dolls' heads). Her fixed expression, common to the image of a 'femme fatale' at the time, and the dark, monochromatic tone, create a decadent atmosphere. The picture's flat colours and well-defined outlines reflect his style as a poster designer.

SIEGFRIED BING (1838-1905)

Siegfried Bing was one of the most influential figures in disseminating Japonisme in Europe and America in the late nineteenth century. He was an art dealer from Hamburg, who cultivated close Japanese contacts following his first trip to Japan in 1880 - 81. 1 He opened a shop in Paris to sell Japanese objects, which was a great success, and was followed by branches not only in Paris but also in New York. His regular customers included Bonnard, Van Gogh, Gauguin and Toulouse-Lautrec. Bing also promoted Japanese art through exhibitions and publications. He was the organiser of successful exhibitions of Japanese woodcuts in Paris: the first was at his own shop in 1888; the second, a major show at the Ecole des Beaux-Arts, displaying more than 700 prints; and the third at the Durand-Ruel Gallery in 1893. In 1888 he launched a publishing venture with the highly influential periodical, *Le Japon artistique* (see Cat.297), which had simultaneous editions in German, French and English, and advocated the incorporation of Japanese design into Western applied arts. In 1895 Bing opened a new shop in Paris, called, L'Art Nouveau, to foster modern Arts and Crafts, and it became identical with a highly decorative style evolved at the turn of the century, commonly called, 'Art Nouveau'. He became known, erroneously, as Samuel Bing, following his death.

LIT : Weisberg 1986; Meech & Weisberg 1990, pp. 22-9

NOTE
1 Meech & Weisberg 1990, p.23

297
Artistic Japan. A Monthly Illustrated Journal of Arts and Industries
English edition edited by Marcus B. Huish, published by Sampson, Low, Marston and Company Ltd., London, 1888-91
Two vols. including nos. 1-6, 8-12, 26-28 and 1, 30-31, 34-36
David Elliott, Oxford

LIT : Meech & Weisberg 1990, pp.26-9

Cat.297 is a collection of the English edition of Bing's monthly magazine, *Le Japon artistique*. A total of thirty-six numbers were issued between May 1888 and April 1891. Edited by Bing himself, each issue featured specialist essays contributed by international authors, accompanied by luxurious illustrations introducing Japanese art, including high-quality reproductions of woodcuts. As it was published in three European languages, it was far reaching and highly influential, and contributed to the popularisation of Japanese art.

AUBREY VINCENT BEARDSLEY (1872-1898)

In spite of his early death at the age of twenty-five, Beardsley was remarkably prolific and one of the most influential artists around the turn of the century. He was principally a book-illustrator whose medium was pen and ink, and his highly stylised black-and-white drawings, commercially reproduced through the line-block process, became the image of the 'decadent Nineties'. Born in Brighton, Beardsley began his artistic career in London, while working as a clerk in the City. He was largely self taught: the only formal training he had received was in 1891-92 when he attended Frederick Brown's night classes at the Westminster School of Art. His style evolved from his personal response to a variety of influences ranging from Burne-Jones and Puvis de Chavannes, whom he met in 1891 and in 1892 respectively, to Whistler and Japanese woodcuts. In 1892 he was commissioned by the publisher, D.M. Dent, to illustrate and design Sir Thomas Malory's *Le Morte D'Arthur* (Cat.299), which established his reputation. In his short life, the peak of his career came in 1894: his illustrations for the English edition of Oscar Wilde's *Salomé* (Cats 300-303), published in that year, achieved a *succès de scandale*, and he founded *The Yellow Book* (Cat.304), 'a new literary and artistic quarterly' with his friend, Henry Harland. By that time he had established his mature style characterised by the skilful balance of black and white, the complete flatness without shading and eloquent line, which reflects the influence of Japanese prints. In 1895, however, following the arrest of Oscar Wilde on homosexual charges, Beardsley, whose public image was associated with Wilde through his illustrations, was dismissed from *The Yellow Book*. In his last years, he was still productive, involved in another new magazine, *The Savoy*, with Arthur Symons and other work including *The Rape of the Lock* and *Lysistrata*, but his health declined rapidly with advanced tuberculosis and he died at Menton, in the South of France in 1898.

LIT : Wilson 1983; Reade 1987

298
Carl Maria von Weber, c.1892
Ink drawing, 27.9 x 11.1 cm
Titled t.l.: Carl Maria Von Weber
Princeton University Library

LIT : Reade 1987 (29) with pl.30

When Beardsley came to London in 1888, the Japanese fashion was at its peak, and London offered a variety of opportunities to introduce him to Japanese art, including exhibitions and publications. In the summer of 1891, he visited Leyland's House, where he was deeply impressed by Whistler's famous Peacock Room and the painting, *La Princesse du Pays de la Porcelaine*. 1 Japanese effects had begun to appear in his work by the summer of 1892. In the autumn of that year, he wrote to his former headmaster at Brighton that he had evolved 'a new style and method of work which was founded on Japanese art' and that he had shown Puvis de Chavannes twenty drawings produced in this style on his visit to Paris in June of the same year. 2 Cat.298 was executed in this new style, which was termed 'japonesque' by Beardsley, and it introduced an effective use of black areas which were placed asymmetrically, decorated by Japanese-inspired motifs and textured by scratching and rubbing.

NOTES
1 Wilson 1983, p.12
2 We are grateful to Professor Kawamura Joichiro for a copy of Beardsley's letter to Mr Marshall (autumn 1892).

299
SIR THOMAS MALORY
Le Morte D'Arthur (3 vols)
Published by J.M. Dent & Co., London, 1893-94
Illustrated by Aubrey Beardsley
Reading University Library

Le Morte D'Arthur was Beardsley's first major commission, as a result of which he attracted the critical attention of the art world for the first time. For this work he produced nearly 470 designs, including initial letters and a cover. The majority of his designs reflect the influence of Burne-Jones's Kelmscott books, but some drawings, including *How King Arthur Saw the Questing Beasts and thereof had great marvel* (frontispiece to vol.I) and *How Sir Tristram Drank of the Love Drink* (facing p.334 in vol.I), reveal his knowledge of the characteristics of Japanese motifs and composition.

300
J'ai baisé ta bouche Iokanaan, 1893
Ink with green watercolour wash, 27.8 x 14.8 cm
Signed b.r.: Aubrey Beardsley, with his emblem
Inscribed l.l.: J'Ai Baisé Ta Bouche/Iokanaan/
J'Ai Baisé Ta Bouche
Princeton University Library

LIT : Wilson 1983, p.19 with fig.10; Reade 1987 (261) with pl.272

Beardsley produced this drawing after reading Oscar Wilde's *Salomé*, which was originally written in French and published in Paris in

February 1893. 1 Taken from the last scene of the play, Beardsley condensed the image of Salome in the evil- looking figure holding the severed head of John the Baptist, stemming from the pool of blood. This shocking drawing was featured in the first number of *The Studio* (April 1893) among his other illustrations, accompanied by Joseph Pennell's article, 'A New Illustrator: Aubrey Beardsley'. There Beardsley was introduced as 'an artist whose work is quite as remarkable in its execution as in its invention', and the originality of his style and medium, which was suitable for mechanical reproduction, was fully recognised. 2 The appearance of this article led to his next major commission from the publishers, Elkin Mathews & John Lane, to illustrate the English translation of Wilde's *Salomé* (Cat.301), which was published in 1894 For this book, Beardsley produced a re-worked version of this drawing, entitled *The Climax*, in which the composition remained basically the same but simplified with the omission of peacock-feathers and other details. The scale pattern seen in both drawings was one of Beardsley's favourite motifs in this period, which was probably inspired by Whistler's peacocks which he had seen in 1891, and by Japanese prints. It is also worth noting that Hokusai's 'Toryu no Fuji'(Fuji and Ascending Dragon) from *One Hundred Views of Mount Fuji* shows a dragon whose scales and claws have a striking similarity to those in Beardsley's drawing such as *How King Arthur Saw the Questing Beasts and thereof had great marvel* for *Le Morte D'Arthur*.

NOTES
1 Wilson 1983, p.21
2 J. Pennell, 'A New Illustrator: Aubrey Beardsley', from *The Birth of The Studio 1893-1895*, Woodbridge, n.d., p.9

301
OSCAR WILDE
Salomé
Translated by Lord Alfred Douglas,published by Elkin Mathews & John Lane, London, 1894
Illustrated by Aubrey Beardsley
De luxe edition (limited to 100 copies), bound in green silk with cover and spine stamped in gold, with Beardsley bookplate, 18 x 23.25 cm
The Collection of the late Brian Reade

LIT : R. Ross, 'A Note on "Salomé"'from *Salomé* 1930, pp.xiii-xviii

302
The Toilet of Salomé, 1893
Pen and ink on paper, 21 x 16 cm
Signed b.r. with the emblem
Trustees of the British Museum

LIT : Wilson 1983, pl.14; Reade 1987 (281) with pl.281

303
The Black Cape, 1893
Pen and ink on paper, 22.4 x 15.9 cm
Signed b.r. with the emblem
Princeton University Library

LIT : Reade 1987 rev.ed.(278) with pl.278

The two drawings above (Cats 302-303) were produced as illustrations to *Salomé* by Oscar Wilde (Cat.301), which was translated by Lord Alfred Douglas and published in London by Elkin Matthews & John Lane in 1894. Both works display the accomplishment of his 'japonesque' style, with economy of line and a powerful contrast between black masses and space. The then current Japanese fashion is also reflected in the 'Anglo-Japanese'-style table and the screen seen in *The Toilet of Salomé* (Cat.302).

304
The Yellow Book
Published by Elkin Mathews & John Lane, London, and Copeland & Day, Boston Vols I (April 1894), II (July 1894) and III (October 1894), 21.6 x 16.5 cm
Chelsea College of Art and Design Library, London

LIT : F. Harrison, *The Yellow Book. An Anthology*, London 1974; Wilson 1983, pl.19

In 1894 'a new literary and artistic quarterly', *The Yellow Book*, was founded by Beardsley together with the writer, his friend, Henry Harland. As stated in the prospectus for the magazine, their aim was 'to depart as far as may be from the bad old traditions of periodical literature, and to provide an Illustrated Magazine which shall be beautiful as a piece of bookmaking'. 1 The magazine ran for three years, from April 1894 to April 1897, and the first three volumes were issued under Beardsley's art editorship. Beardsley not only contributed drawings but also designed the covers and entire layout.

NOTE
1 Harrison, op.cit., p.4

CHARLES DE SOUSY RICKETTS
(1866-1931)

Ricketts was a versatile artist, painter, sculptor, wood-engraver, book-illustrator and stage designer. He also wrote on art, and together with his friend Charles Shannon (1863-1937) built up an exquisite art collection ranging from antiquities and Old Master drawings to Japanese paintings and prints. Born in Geneva, Ricketts travelled Europe extensively with his family. After his return to England around 1880, he studied wood-engraving and life drawing at the South London (now City and Guilds) Technical Art School in Lambeth, where he met his life-long companion, the painter Charles Shannon. From the late 1880s he contributed pen and ink drawings to magazines and books, which culminated in the designs for Oscar Wilde's books in the early 1890s, including *A House of Pomegranates* (1891), *Poems* (1892) and *The Sphinx* (Cat.306). His early work reflects a variety of influences including Dürer, Rossetti, Gustave Moreau, and above all Whistler and Japanese prints. Ricketts and Shannon's house, The Vale, in Chelsea, was bought from Whistler, and its walls were decorated with prints by Hokusai. 1

In 1889 he founded with Shannon an art magazine, *The Dial* (Cat.305), which was published sporadically until 1897, and its typography and design owed a debt to Whistler, such as *Mr Whistler's 'Ten o'Clock'*, published in 1888. 2 In 1894 he launched the Vale Press with his own types and designs, and by 1904, when it was closed, he had produced in total more than forty works, together with a thirty-nine volume edition of Shakespeare. 3 From the 1900s onwards he was active as a painter, especially of romantic subjects. In the same period he also took up stage design and was involved in more than fifty productions, including Oscar Wilde's *Salomé* (Cat.307-308), Bernard Shaw's *St Joan* (1924) and Gilbert & Sullivan's *The Mikado* (Cat.309). From his student days onwards, he was an enthusiastic collector of Japanese prints, which amounted to more than 350, under joint ownership with Shannon, by the end of his life. 4 His Japanese collection, including the hanging-scrolls by Motonobu and Sesshu, was admired by a visiting Japanese scholar, called Kohitsu, who was 'the hereditary expert of the Shogun family', 5 and they met in 1902 through Laurence Binyon, Ricketts' friend and the Oriental expert at the British Museum. The principal part of Ricketts' and Shannon's large Japanese collection is now in the British Museum, and the other part, including European drawings and antiquities, in the Fitzwilliam Museum, Cambridge.

LIT : Calloway 1979; Darracott 1980

NOTES
1 Calloway 1979, p.12
2 ibid., p.13
3 ibid., p.58
4 Darracott 1980, p.138
5 Ricketts' diary of 1902 quoted by Darracott, ibid., pp.140-1

305
The Dial
No.I, The Vale, London 1889, 32.5 x 25.5 cm
Reading University Library

LIT : Calloway 1979, pp.12-13; I.Fletcher, 'Decadence and the Little Magazine', from *Decadence and the 1890s* (Stratford- upon-Avon Studies 17), 1979, pp.191-2

The first number of *The Dial* appeared in 1889, which was followed by four more issues between 1892 and 1897. Designed and edited by Ricketts and Shannon, the magazine was the first project over which they had complete artistic control. Their collaborators included John Gray, Sturge Moore and Lucien Pissarro, Arthur Symons and W.B. Yeats, who were all interested in contemporary French art and the unity of all the arts, and the magazine helped to introduce French Symbolist works into Britain. Ricketts' design for the magazine is highly eclectic. *The Great Worm* featured in the first number, for instance, shows a curious combination of Symbolist and Japanese influences: a standing female figure is virtually borrowed from Gustave Moreau, while the landscape, with the tonal graduation in the sky, owes much to Japanese woodcuts.

306
OSCAR WILDE
The Sphinx
Published by Elkin Mathews & John Lane, London 1894
Designed by Charles Ricketts
Vellum blocked in gold, 22.5 x 17.8 cm
The Syndics of Cambridge University Library

LIT : Calloway 1979, pp.44-9

The exotic and timeless atmosphere of Wilde's poem, *The Sphinx*, is here evoked by Ricketts' overall design for the book, including illustrations, layout, binding and the selection of materials. Combined with Greek and Celtic elements, Japanese design principles are now re-interpreted in his drawing style, which is characterised by sinuous lines and exquisite details, contrasted with blank spaces. On the cover he used the Japanese architectural features of sliding screens and wooden-floor patterns to give a subtle feeling of asymmetry.

307
Stage design for 'Salomé', 1919
Watercolour and body colour, 21.1 x 40 cm
The Syndics of the Fitzwilliam Museum, Cambridge

LIT : Darracott 1979 (A 18) with pl.1

308
Costume design for the Young Syrian in 'Salomé', 1920
Watercolour, 26.67 x 21.59 cm
Trustees of the Victoria and Albert Museum, London

LIT : Calloway 1979, p.83 with pl.95

Ricketts' interest in the theatre began in the 1890s through his friendship with Oscar Wilde. The idea of designing Wilde's *Salomé* was conceived in his early days at The Vale through discussions with Wilde, and Ricketts was

involved in two productions, one by the Literary Theatre Society in 1906 and another in Tokyo in 1920. 1 Cat.307 shows Ricketts' stage setting for the Tokyo showing and Cat.308 is a replica of a costume design for the same performance.

NOTE
1 Calloway 1979, p.23; Darracott 1979 (A 18) with pl.1

309
Costume designs for 'The Mikado', c.1926
Pencil, charcoal, watercolour and gouache on paper, 35.2 x 50.9 cm
Titled b.l. in pencil: Mikardo [sic]
Royal Albert Memorial Museum, Exeter

Ricketts undertook the designs for the revival production of *The Mikado* by the D'Oyly Carte

Cat.308

Cat.311

Company, which was staged at the Prince's Theatre, London, in September 1926. Ricketts' deep knowledge of Japanese art was suited to this project, and he regarded it as 'the most successful I have so far done'. 1 This drawing shows two costumes, one of which with a tall head-dress is for the Mikado, a role taken by Donald Adams, as seen in Cat.215 (see Section VIII).

NOTE
1 Quoted in Darracott 1980, p.187

310
Costume design for the Witch Dancer for a projected production of 'Itto', c.1920s
Pencil and watercolour, 37.7 x 27.1 cm
Inscribed t.r.: Witch Dance/ Itto
The Ashmolean Museum, Oxford

LIT : Calloway 1979, p.76 with pl.88

Ricketts' interest in the Noh theatre, which he shared with his friend William Butler Yeats, is reflected in this design. The mask-like face with a pair of horns and the dress seem to have derived from one of the Noh theatre's classical programmes, *Kurozuka*.

T. H. ROBINSON (dates unknown)

311
Five drawings from 'Old-World Japan. Legends of the Lands of the Gods... Re-told by Frank Rinder',
London, 1895
Victor Arwas, London

A. *The Love of the Snow-White Fox*, c.1895
Pen and ink on cardboard, 37.9 x 28.1 cm

B. *The Island of Eternal Youth*, c.1895
Pen and ink on cardboard, 38.2 x 28.1 cm
Inscribed b.r.: Soon He Came to its/ Shores and Landed as one in a dream/Island of Ethernal Youth

C. *The Souls of the Children*, c.1895
Pen and ink on cardboard, 38.2 x 28.1 cm

D. *Nedzumi*, 1895
Pen and ink on cardboard, 17.7 x 28.1 cm

E. *The Sparrow's Wedding*, 1895
Pen and ink on cardboard, 17.3 x 27.7 cm

Towards the end of the nineteenth century, a large number of Japanese fairy-tale books were published in Europe and America, translated and compiled by Western authors. One of them, *Old-World Japan. Legends of the Land of the Gods*, was published by George Allen, London, in 1895, accompanied by T.H. Robinson's exquisite illustrations. Cat.311 A-E are Robinson's original pen drawings for the book.

WILLIAM NICHOLSON (1872-1949)

Born at Newark-on-Trent, Nicholson attended Herkomer's School of Art at Bushey, and then went to Paris, where he studied at the Académie Julian in 1889-90. Around 1893 he formed a partnership with his brother-in-law, the Scottish artist James Pryde (1869-1941), and together they designed posters under the pseudonym of the Beggarstaff Brothers from 1894 to 1899. Their bold and simplified style, owing much to Toulouse-Lautrec, revolutionalised not only British but also European graphic art. In 1896 Nicholson took up the woodcut without formal training, and produced a series of portraits, and also popular prints for the publisher Heinemann. His uncluttered and strongly outlined designs reflect his earlier poster designs and also Japanese influence. Later on, he concentrated on painting landscapes, still-lifes and portraits; his style contrasting light and dark evolved from his print-making.

LIT : Colin Campbell, *The Beggarstaff Posters*, London 1990

312
London Types
Published by William Heinemann, London 1898
Album of colour lithograph from woodblocks,
34 x 29 cm
The Corporation of London (Guildhall Library)

London Types is one of the colour woodcut series commissioned by William Heinemann. It features thirteen types of Londoners, ranging from a Beefeater to a Barmaid. Although the subject is in the English tradition of popular prints, Nicholson's bold outlines, silhouettes and flat colours reflect Japanese woodcuts. Only a limited de-luxe edition was printed on Japanese vellum direct from the original woodblocks, and then hand-coloured. Cat.312 is a popular edition, printed from the woodblocks onto lithographic transfer paper and transferred to lithographic plates.

313
James McNeill Whistler, late 1890s
Colour lithograph from woodblocks, 24.4 x 22.3 cm
Titled at bottom: James McNeill Whistler
Victor Arwas, London

314
Sada Yacco, c.1900-01
Colour lithograph from woodblocks, 24.2 x 22.3 cm
Titled at bottom: Sada Yacco
Victor Arwas, London

Cats 313-314 are from a series of portraits produced by Nicholson at the turn of the century. Sada Yacco, portayed in Cat.314, was a leading Japanese actress, who visited London twice, in 1900 and 1901.

CHARLES RENNIE MACKINTOSH (1868-1928)

Mackintosh was a Glaswegian architect and designer, whose astonishing clarity of design and rationalist and functionalist principles had an international influence on the new art and design movement at the turn of the century. Trained in Glasgow under an architect, John Hutchison, and at the Glasgow School of Art, he began to work in 1889 as a draughtsman at a major architectual firm in Glasgow, Honeyman & Keppie. In 1891 he travelled in Italy, France and Belgium after winning the Alexander (Greek) Thomson Travelling Scholarship with the design of a Public Hall in early classical style, and having delivered his first paper, 'Scottish Baronial Architecture', to the Glasgow Architectural Association. By the mid-1890s, he had formed the group 'Four' with his friends from the Glasgow Art School, Herbert MacNair (1868-1953) and the two Macdonald sisters, Margaret (later Mrs Mackintosh: 1865-1933) and Frances (later Mrs MacNair: 1874-1921) and together they designed graphic work, repoussé metalwork and textiles in a distinctive curv-linear style, inspired by Celtic motifs, Beardsley, Jan Toorop and Japanese art. Their work was introduced by *The Studio* magazine and shown at the Vienna Secession exhibition in 1900 and at the International Exhibition of Decorative Art, Turin in 1902. In 1897 Mackintosh was given the commission to build the new building of the Glasgow School of Art (completed in 1909), for which he became famous. Parallel to this, he was also involved in other major projects, such as Miss Cranston's Tea Rooms (Cats 315-318), Windyhill (1899-1901) and the Hill House (1902-03). By this period, he had fully evolved his mature style, a unique harmony of rationality, which is found in his spatial arrangements, and fancifulness in his designs of furniture and decorative details. Among others, Japanese design elements contributed to his interior design scheme significantly, especially in his uncluttered open plan, simple furnishing and the plain light-coloured walls, which are characteristic of Japanese domestic architecture. His furniture and metalwork also demonstrate his knowledge of Japanese motifs and construction methods. Although he did not acknowledge Japanese influence (and any other influences) openly, his interest in Japanese culture was evident in his home at 120 Mains Street, which was decorated with Japanese woodcuts and flower arrangements. Furthermore, as an architectural student, he could have come across important publications on Japanese architecture, such as Christopher Dresser's *Japan, its Architecture, Art and Art Manufacturers* (1882) and E.S. Morse's *Japanese Houses and their Surroundings* (1886). In 1914 he left Glasgow before settling in Chelsea, London, where he concentrated on furniture and textile designs. In 1923 he retired to Port Vendres in the South of France, and devoted the rest of his life entirely to watercolour.

LIT : Howarth 1952; Billcliffe 1979; Buchanan 1980; *Charles Rennie Mackintosh*, 1985

315
*Round Card Table for Argyle Street Tea Rooms,
Glasgow*, 1897
Oak, H: 70.5 cm, D: 76 cm
Glasgow School of Art

LIT : Billcliffe 1979 (1897.14)

By the turn of the century, tea-rooms had
become an important cultural feature in Glasgow.
Associated with the Japanese habit of tea-
drinking, the tea-rooms in Glasgow were soon
compared with those in Japan, and the city was
described as 'a very Tokio for tea rooms'. 1 Miss
(Catherine) Cranston was a pioneer of this new
pursuit, and first opened her small teashop at
114 Argyle Street in 1884; Mackintosh met her
in 1896 through Francis Newbery, the director
of the Glasgow Art School. In the following year,
when her Argyle Street tea-room was refurbished,
Mackintosh was commissioned to design the
furniture. Miss Cranston became one of
Mackintosh's most loyal patrons, and he was to
undertake a series of interior designs for her
new tea- rooms at Ingram Street (Cat.317) and
the Willow Tea Rooms at Sauchiehall Street
(Cat.318). This card table, designed for Miss
Cranston's Argyle Street Tea Rooms, shows a
simple and solid design. The four side panels
are decorated with a distinctive circular pattern,
which bears a similarity not only to a Celtic motif
but also to a Japanese 'mon' (crest) or 'tsuba'
(sword-guard). Mackintosh used this decorative
motif in many other designs. A variation of this
table, painted in white with a square top, was
used in his own drawing room at 120 Mains Street.

NOTE
1 J.M. Muir, *Glasgow in 1901*, 1901, p.166

316
*High-backed Dining Chair with Oval Backrail for
Argyle Street Tea Rooms*, 1897
Oak, stained brown; horsehair upholstery,
136.8 x 50.5 x 46.2 cm
Glasgow School of Art

LIT : Billcliffe 1979 (1897.23); *Charles Rennie Mackintosh*,
1985, p.60 (22)

Designed for the Luncheon Room at Miss
Cranston's Argyle Street Tea Rooms, Cat.316
is the first of Mackintosh's high-backed chairs.
This visually striking design was at the same
time functional. The tall back was intended to
create an individual space for a diner, separate
from other tables. 1 This idea is similar to the
Japanese use of screens: portable screens were
commonly used in traditional tea-houses and
eating places to create a private space in a tatami-
matted open room, although it is not known
whether Mackintosh was aware of this or not.
The stylised 'flying bird' motif, used in the
oval panel at the top of the back, seems to have
derived from a Japanese decorative pattern.
Pleased with this design, Mackintosh used it also
in his own dining room at 120 Mains Street and
exhibited it at the Vienna Secession Exhibition
in 1900.

NOTE
1. Billcliffe, 'Mackintosh's Designs for Furniture',
from *Charles Rennie Mackintosh*, 1985, p.55

317
*High-backed Dining Chair for Ingram Street Tea
Rooms*, 1900
Oak, stained brown; horsehair upholstery,
151 x 47.5 x 43.3cm
Glasgow School of Art

LIT : Billcliffe 1979 (1900.55); *Charles Rennie Mackintosh*,
exh. cat. Tokyo 1985, p.64 (26)

318
Waitress Stool for Willow Tea Rooms, 1903
Oak, ebonised; horsehair upholstery,
63.5 x 45.6 x 45.2cm
Glasgow School of Art

LIT : Billcliffe 1979 (1903.13); *Charles Rennie Mackintosh*,
1985, p.74 (36)

Cat.318 is one of four stools produced for Miss
Cranston's famous Willow Tea Rooms, which
was opened at Sauchiehall Street in 1904.
Here Mackintosh used a lattice-work cube
construction, obviously inspired by a Japanese
architectural motif. The lattice-work was used on
a large scale in 1911 for the wooden screens of the
'Chinese Room' at Miss Cranston's Ingram Street
Tea Rooms. The same theme was also used in his
designs for other furniture for the Willow Tea
Room, such as the clock (1903; Glasgow School of
Art) and the curved lattice-back chair for the
order desk (1904; Glasgow School of Art).

AGNES MIDDLETON RAEBURN
(1872-1955)

Agnes Raeburn was a Glasgow painter and
graphic designer. Trained at the Glasgow School
of Art under Francis Newbery, she was a friend
of Jessie M.King, the Macdonald sisters and C.R.
Mackintosh, and a member of the Glasgow
Society of Lady Artists. Together with her
friends, she was a contributor to *The Magazine*
(1893-96), a ladies' art and literary magazine
founded by her sister, Lucy Raeburn (1869-1952).
In 1901 she was elected to the Royal Scottish
Society of Painters in Watercolours. Her works,
mainly landscapes and flowers, were exhibited
in Paris, the United States, as well as in Britain.

LIT : I. Monie, 'The Magazine',
from Burkhauser 1990, p.76

319
The Glasgow Lecture Association, c.1897
Colour lithograph poster, 93.5 x 57.4 cm
Signed vertically l.c.: A.Raeburn.
Titled: The Glasgow Lecture/Association
Hunterian Art Gallery, Glasgow

LIT : Burkhauser 1990, p.96 with fig.115

The Glasgow style is reflected in this poster by
Raeburn. While the hieroglyphical form of a
snake entwining the stem of a flower recalls the
poster designs by 'The Four' (the Macdonald
sisters, C.R. Mackintosh and Herbert MacNair),
her bold outlines and the partitioning of the flat
space shows the influence of Japanese design.

HARRY CLARKE (1889-1931)

320
L. D'O. WATERS
The Year's at the Spring, London, 1920
Illustrated by Harry Clarke
Bodleian Library, Oxford

321
EDGAR ALLAN POE
Tales of Mystery and Imagination, London 1923
Illustrated by Harry Clarke
Bodleian Library, Oxford

Many graphic artists in the early twentieth
century were influenced by the designers of 'the
Nineties', especially Aubrey Beardsley. The list
of his followers is long and international,
including Charles Robinson, John Austen,
Alastair, Willy Poganyi, Kay Nielsen. The
Dublin-born stained-glass designer Harry Clarke
also illustrated at least six books 1 including Cats
320-321, and his linear style
and decadent images owe much to Beardsley.

LIT : Nichola Gordon Bow, *The Life and Work of Harry
Clarke* Blackrock, Co. Dublin 1989

NOTE
1 J.White, 'Introduction', from *The Stained Glass of
Harry Clarke 1889-1931*, exh. cat 1988, FAS,
London, n.p.

MAXWELL ARMFIELD (1881-1972)

Armfield studied at the Birmingham School of
Art and came under the strong influence of the
Birmingham Group of painters, such as Arthur
Gaskin and Joseph Southall. His tempera
paintings are in the style of the Pre-Raphaelite
revival of the turn of the century. His activities
ranged widely and he was involved in painting
as well as illustration, decorative arts and writing.
His text book *Rhythmic Shape*, where he uses
Japanese examples such as Hokusai, clearly
shows his lifelong interest in the teaching of
design principles.

322
*Rythmic Shape. A Text-book of Design,
The Syntax of Art*
Book Four, Berkeley, California 1920
21.2 x 15.2 cm
Toshio Watanabe, Oxford

LIT : N.G. Bowe, 'Maxwell Armfield, 1881-1972: an
account of his decorative art', *Journal of the Decorative
Arts Society*, no.12, 1989, pp.26-37

Cat.350 ATTRIBUTED TO AIHARA UNRAKU (1878-1954) *Flower Stand*, 1909

XII. TURN OF THE CENTURY JAPAN

AOKI SHIGERU (1882-1911)

Aoki studied Western-style art under Mori Miyoshi (1872-1913) in Kurume together with Sakamoto Hanjiro (1882-1969). It is known that Mori used English artbooks to teach. Aoki then went to Tokyo and studied under among others Koyama Shotaro (1857-1916) and Kuroda Seiki (1866-1924), but developed a more independent style strongly influenced by Albert Moore, the Pre-Raphaelites, such as Rossetti and Burne-Jones, and by French painters, such as Puvis de Chavannes, Moreau and Fantin-Latour. Unlike most other Western-style painters of note he never went abroad and absorbed Western art mostly through illustrations in publications. His paintings with Symbolist overtones are regarded as the pinnacle of Meiji romanticism. Aoki, though regarded very highly in Japan now, failed to gain full recognition during his lifetime .

LIT : Kawakita 1972; Nakamura 1976, pp.189-242; *Shigeru Aoki* 1983

323
Paradise under the Sea
(Wadatsumi no Irokonomiya), 1907
Oil on canvas, 181.5 x 70 cm
Signed and dated b.r.: S. Awoki. 1907
Ishibashi Museum of Art, Kurume

This subject is taken from Japanese mythology: Yama Sachihiko is looking in the sea for the lost fish-hook of his brother Umi Sachihiko and meets Princess Toyotama, the daughter of the God of the Sea and his future wife. When it was exhibited, the critics recognised the influence of Burne-Jones and Aoki wrote that such influences were what he himself expected.

324
The Hot Spring (Onsen), 1910
Oil on canvas, 70.8 x 36 cm
Signed and dated b.l.: T.B.S. Aoki. 1910
Private Collection

This painting is said to have been painted at a spa near Saga called Furuya. It has been rightly pointed out that the gesture of the woman combing her hair is very close to that of *The Mermaid* (1910) by John William Waterhouse (1849-1917), but it should also be pointed out that the whole setting (not the technique) of this painting is similar to Roman bath scenes by Lawrence Alma-Tadema (1836-1912) or by some other late Victorian Neo-classicists. Haga draws our attention to a poem by Aoki, which was inspired by Waterhouse's famous painting *Hylas and the Nymphs* of 1897. 1 It has also been argued that the 'T.B.' in his signature may mean 'True Brotherhood', as in 'P.R.B.' for the Pre-Raphaelite Brotherhood, though another theory is that it represents the initials of his artist's name 'Tozan-an Bokushu'. 2

NOTES
1 Haga 1984, pp.396-7
2 *Takehisa Yumeji - Aoki Shigeru*, Art Gallery Japan vol.12, Tokyo 1986, p.75 (Comments by Hashimoto Hiroki)

325
Illustrations for 'Old Testament Stories', 1907

A. *Let There Be Light*
Oil on board, 23.5 x 33 cm
Signed b.l.: S. Aoki
Private Collection

B. *Moses at the Red Sea*
Oil on board, 33 x 23.5 cm
Private Collection

C. *Jael killing Sisera*
Oil on board, 33 x 23.4 cm
Private Collection

D. *King Solomon and Jerusalem*
Oil on board, 23.4 x 33 cm
Private Collection

E. *Nebuchadnezzar and Daniel*
Oil on board, 33 x 22.9 cm
Signed and dated b.r.: S. Aoki. 1906
Private Collection

F. *Esther and Haman*
Oil on board, 23.5 x 33 cm
Signed t.r.: S.A.
Private Collection

They belong to a group of eight oil sketches, discovered in 1961, which were painted as illustrations for *Old Testament Stories* and published in 1907. Because of his delay, Aoki was apparently helped by his friends, Masamune Tokusaburo and Morita Tsunetomo, but it has not been established who was responsible for which subject.

FUJISHIMA TAKEJI (1867-1943)

Initially Fujishima wished to study Western-style painting, but then decided to study Japanese-style painting under Kawabata Gyokusho (1842-1913). After winning several prizes, he returned to the study of Western-style painting under Soyama Sachihiko (1859-1892) and subsequently under Yamamoto Hosui (1850-1906). He travelled to Europe in 1906 where he studied in Paris under Fernand Cormon (1845-1924) and in Rome under Emile Auguste Carolus-Duran (1838-1917). He returned to Japan in 1910. Fujishima went through considerable stylistic changes from the plein-airism of his friend Kuroda Seiki (1866-1924), and from Symbolist romanticism to decorative figures influenced by Italian Renaissance portraits. His mature works show the fusing of Post-Impressionism and the Far Eastern tradition. Fujishima became one of the most admired painters of his generation.

LIT : Kumamoto 1967

326
Reminiscence of the Tempyo Era
(Tempyo no Omokage), 1902
Oil on canvas, 197.5 x 94 cm
Ishibashi Museum of Art, Kurume

The eight-century Tempyo period with its monumental temples and sculptures is often regarded as the classical period in Japan. Here Fujishima looks back to this era as a golden period of cultural harmony, much as Albert Moore did in his paintings of figures from the Western classical period. When this painting was exhibited, the poet Kanbara Ariake (1876-1952), a fervent admirer of Rossetti, published a poem, which is reminiscent of Swinburne's poem about Whistler's painting (Cat.64). Fujishima's work shows clearly the influence of Puvis de Chavannes, but also of Albert Moore, who was well known in Japanese art circles at the time. In this painting a single brooding woman in loose drapery stands on a shallow stage within a tall vertical format. The background with a flat decorative tree is divided into horizontal bands. All these features are also shared by many of Moore's paintings. However, Fujishima transcended these influences and created a work which indicates a tendency towards decorative monumental painting.

327
Designs for the magazine 'Myojo' (Morning Star)
(reproduction)
Sheffield University Library

LIT : Nakamura 1976; Takumi 1979, pp.39-277; Haga 1981

Cat.334

Fujishima also made major contributions towards the illustration of the arts magazine *Myojo*, which was a cultural torch-bearer of late Meiji romanticism between 1900 and 1908. Some of Fujishima's illustrations show the influence of Art Nouveau, especially of Alphonse Mucha (1860-1939), and also of the Pre-Raphaelites, such as Rossetti and Burne-Jones.

ILLUSTRATIONS FOR PUBLICATIONS BY NATSUME SOSEKI (1867-1916)

Natsume Soseki is regarded as one of the greatest writers of modern Japan. He travelled to Britain and stayed there from 1900 to 1902. Soseki visited museums and art galleries enthusiastically during his stay. It has been convincingly argued by various scholars that in writing his novels he was strongly inspired by the Pre-Raphaelites. The illustrations of his novels by various artists are also permeated by Pre-Raphaelite taste. The design of his books broke new ground in their de luxe presentation and in their richness and high quality of illustrations.

LIT : Eto 1975; Takumi 1979, pp.279-94; Sadoya 1982; Haga 1984, pp.491-518

HASHIGUCHI GOYO (1880-1921)

Hashiguchi studied both Western and Japanese-style painting, but became more involved in graphic design and later printmaking, producing some of the most beautiful prints of the *Shinhanga* movement. He was involved in book designs for, among others, Tanizaki Junichiro, Shimamura Hogetsu and Izumi Kyoka, but most notably for Soseki. His designs have strong affinities with those by Walter Crane (1845-1915) and particularly those by C.F.A. Voysey (1857-1941).

328
Illustration of the story 'Maboroshi no Tate' (The Phantom Shield) in the magazine 'Hototogisu' (The Cuckoo), April 1905 (reproduction)
Museum of Modern Japanese Literature, Tokyo

329
Illustrations for the collected stories, 'Yokyo-shu', by Soseki Natsume:

A. *Yokyo-shu frontispiece and bookplate*
First edition (17 May 1906)
Museum of Modern Japanese Literature, Tokyo

B. *Kairoko frontispiece*
(reproduction)
Museum of Modern Japanese Literature, Tokyo

Yokyo-shu by Soseki, published in 1906 contains seven short stories including 'Rondon To' (Tower of London) and 'Karairu Hakubutsukan' (Carlyle's House). Both illustrations and the text relate very much to Britain and British culture. For example, 'Kairo-ko' (An Elegy) is a very Pre-Raphaelite story.

330
Front and back cover of 'Higansugi made' by Natsume Soseki, 1912
First edition
Museum of Modern Japanese Literature, Tokyo

This design with its silhouetted animals, stylised flat trees and decoratively spread-out motifs relate especially to Voysey's designs.

YAMANA AYAO (1897-1980)

Yamana studied Western-style painting. In 1923 he joined the company Puraton-sha and participated in the design of the magazines *Josei* and *Kuraku*. Some of Yamana's early designs for these magazines show the strong influence of Beardsley. From 1929 he was involved in designing advertisements for the large cosmetic firm Shiseido. He also taught at Tama University of Art.

LIT : *Design in Transition*, 1988, p.172

331
Frontispiece of the magazine 'Josei' (Woman), March 1924 (reproduction)
Museum of Modern Japanese Literature, Tokyo

332
Frontispiece of the magazine 'Kuraku' (Joys and Sorrows), October 1927 (reproduction)
Museum of Modern Japanese Literature, Tokyo

ASAI CHU (1856-1907)

Asai was one of the favourite pupils of Antonio Fontanesi. He went to France in 1900 and stayed there until 1902. He was one of the major oil painters of the Meiji period, but when he was appointed the first Professor of Design at the Kyoto High School of Crafts, he became more involved with design and design education.

333
Roses, 1902-07
Watercolour on Japanese paper, 10.7 x 11.4 cm
Chiba Prefectural Museum of Art

While in Paris, Asai was impressed by Art Nouveau design and after his return to Japan promoted such design in Japan in his teaching and in his own work. The pattern here evokes the Rose design of the Mackintosh circle.

SUGIURA HISUI (1876-1965)

Sugiura studied Japanese-style painting, but also became a friend of the leader of Western-style painting, Kuroda Seiki (1866-1924). In 1908 he joined the large department store Mitsukoshi and produced many memorable posters for the store. Some of his early posters show an affinity with the late Art Nouveau style of the Mackintosh circle and others, though on the whole he was a French-orientated designer. He travelled in France from 1922 to 1924. After his return he

formed the design study group, *Shichi'nin-sha*, and in 1927 founded the journal for the study of poster, *Affiches*. He is perhaps the best-known pre-war poster designer in Japan.

334
New Annexe Building for Mitsukoshi Fabrics Shop, 1914
Poster, 106 x 77 cm
Tokiko Sugiura

335
Mitsukoshi Fabrics Shop, 1914
Poster, 106 x 77 cm
Tokiko Sugiura

TAKEHISA YUMEJI (1884-1934)

Takehisa was a painter, a designer and a poet. In his paintings and designs he developed a characteristic type of woman with large eyes, an elongated sinuous body and an ethereal expression. His works are very popular in Japan and are regarded as the epitome of Japanese Art Nouveau. His depiction of somewhat unreal women can be interpreted as a form of escapism, as can the children created by the Victorian children's book illustrator Kate Greenaway (1846-1901). In the illustration 'Tukushinbo', his use of space, words and motifs within a page of a children's book is similar to that of Greenaway.

336
Horsetails (Tukushinbo), 1916
Illustration for the fairy-tale, *Nemunoki*, 16.5 x 12.8 cm
Yayoi Art Museum, Tokyo

FUKIYA KOJI (1898-1979)

Fukiya was an illustrator, a painter and a writer. From 1925 to 1930 he lived in France and exhibited at the Salon d'Automne in Paris. He is best known for the many illustrations he provided for the first magazines produced for girls. He was a friend of Yumeji and in his song-book cover illustration 'Yume no Okuni' Fukiya also shows a Japanese version of a Greenaway child daydreaming.

337
Cover for Dreamland ('Yume no Okuni'), 1926
From the series *Kinnohoshi Children's Song Book*, 21.8 x 15.3 cm
Yayoi Art Museum, Tokyo

THEATRE BILLS FOR SHAKESPEAREAN PLAYS

The popularity of Shakespeare during the late Meiji period can be gauged from the many theatre bills issued during this time. The Shakespeare adaptations by the Kawakami troupe with the famous star 'Sadayacco' stirred the theatre world of Tokyo. The troupe had just returned from the West, where they had performed, for example, 'Sairoku', an adaptation of *The Merchant of Venice*, in Boston. According to Dr Chiba Yoko's research, it so happened that Henry Irving and Ellen Terry were also appearing in *The Merchant of Venice* in a different theatre there and they both advised Kawakami Otojiro and Sadayakko on the playing of Shylock and Portia! Dr Chiba argues that nevertheless it was a crude adaptation and 'Sairoku' was, according to Kawakami himself, more of a satire on mercantile greed in Western society which had yet to percolate to Japan than a serious attempt to present Shakespeare. 1 The task of properly introducing Shakespeare to Japan was undertaken by the leading writer of the Meiji period and translator of Shakespeare, Tsubo'uchi Shoyo (1859-1935).

NOTE
1 . Yoko Chiba, 'W.B. Yeats and Noh: From Japonisme to Zen', unpublished Ph.D. thesis, University of Toronto, 1988, pp.69-71. Grateful thanks are due to Dr Chiba for giving us access to her thesis. She will discuss these issues in her forthcoming book on Japonisme in the theatre.

338
TORII KIYOTADA (dates unknown)
Othello, 1903
Theatre bill for the performance by Sadayakko and Kawakami Otojiro at Meijiza, February 1903
Waseda University Theatre Museum, Tokyo

339
Othello, 1906
Theatre bill for the *Shingeki* performance by Ito Fumio, from 23 September 1906
Waseda University Theatre Museum, Tokyo

340
King Lear
Theatre bill for the Shuraku-kan Theatre, Kobe, commemorating overseas performances
Waseda University Theatre Museum, Tokyo

341
Hamlet, 1907
Theatre bill for the Meijiza Theatre, 1907
Waseda University Theatre Museum, Tokyo

TAKEDA GOICHI (1872-1938)

Takeda studied architecture at the Tokyo Imperial University and became Assistant Professor there. In order to study design he travelled to London in 1901. He studied at the Camden School of Art and Science and also went to Glasgow, where he saw many works by Mackintosh and his circle. From 1902 onwards he travelled in Europe and North America, returning to Japan in 1903. He was appointed Professor of Design at the Kyoto High School of Crafts, as successor to Asai Chu. Many of his and his students' designs there show deep sympathy with the late Art Nouveau style of the Mackintosh circle and the Viennese Secession.

He remained an active architect and was also involved with the conservation of historic buildings.

LIT : *Takeda Goichi* 1987; *Japanese Aesthetics*, 1990, pp.161-70

342
Study of an Interior Design, 1902
Watercolour on paper (four sketches),
18.5 x 23.5cm; 18.5 x 23.5cm;
18.5 x 31.5cm; 18.5 x 31.5cm
Kobe University (Department of Architecture)

This strongly Glaswegian interior design apparently won a prize while he was in Britain, but it has not yet been established what the competition or exhibition was.

343
Study for a Cabinet Design, 1902
Watercolour on paper (four sketches),
16.0 x 23.5cm; 21.0 x 16.5cm; 30.0 x 16.0cm;
19.5 x 22.5cm
Kobe University (Department of Architecture)

The cabinet design here shows affinities with the works of C.F.A.Voysey (1857-1941), for example his design for a clock case of 1895 at the Royal Institute of British Architects in London. Adachi Yuji's research shows that Takeda had studied the design theories of Voysey and Walter Crane, whom he knew personally. 1

NOTE
1 Adachi Yuji, 'Takeda Goichi to Aru Nuvo - Takeda Goichi Kenkyu' (Art Nouveau and Modern Architecture in Japan. A study of Goichi Takeda Part 2), Nihon Kenchiku Gakkai Keikakukei Ronbun Hokoku-shu (Proceedings of the Society of Japanese Architects), No.357, November 1985, pp.97-111; p.99

344
Design for a Shop-front I, 1902
Watercolour on paper, 29.4 x 40.5cm
Kobe University (Department of Architecture)

345
Design for a Shop-front II, 1902
Watercolour on paper, 18.0 x 35.5cm
Kobe University (Department of Architecture)

346
Wallpaper Design, 1902
Watercolour on paper, 27.0 x 52.0cm
Kobe University (Department of Architecture)

347
Flower Stand for the Shibakawa Residence, 1912
Wood, 86.8 x 29.3 x 29.8cm
Shibakawa Matahiko, Nishinomiya City

348
Chair for the Shibakawa Residence, 1912
Wood, 79.3 x 53.3 x 51.4 cm
Shibakawa Matahiko, Nishinomiya City

These two Mackintosh-inspired pieces of furniture were designed for the residence of Shibakawa Mataemon in Hyogo Prefecture, built in 1912, in which Takeda used both Western and Japanese elements.

Cat.347

KONOIKE-GUMI MAIN OFFICE, OSAKA, 1909

The rare Art Nouveau interior of this building has only recently been discovered. It was built for the founder of the construction company Konoike-gumi, Konoike Chuzaburo. The architect is Kubota Shozaburo, who also supervised the building of another house with a splendid Art Nouveau interior, the Matsumoto Residence by Tatsuno Kingo, almost at the same time as he was building this one (see Section VI). The interior design and the flower stand are both attributed to Aihara Unraku (1878-1954), a sculptor and designer trained by Takamura Koun (1852-1934). Unraku was also involved with the designing of the Matsumoto Residence. The Konoike-gumi Main Office is currently undergoing restoration.

LIT : *Japanese Aesthetics*, 1990, pp.171-2

349
ATTRIBUTED TO AIHARA UNRAKU (1878-1954)
Interior of the Study (First Floor)
(reproducton)

350
ATTRIBUTED TO AIHARA UNRAKU (1878-1954)
Flower Stand, 1909
Wood, 116 x 42 x 41cm
Konoike-gumi Collection, Osaka

Cat.360
OKADA SABUROSUKE (1869-1939)
Portrait of a Lady standing against Bush Clove, 1908

XIII. THE ANGLO-JAPANESE EXHIBITION OF 1910

In 1910 the large-scale Anglo-Japanese Exhibition took place at the White City in Shepherd's Bush, London. Many exhibits from both Britain and Japan were shown and a number of Japanese gardens laid out in the grounds. The White City itself became the major exhibition site in Britain between 1908 and 1914. Before the Anglo-Japanese Exhibition it had already hosted huge shows such as the Franco-British Exhibition of 1908 and the Imperial International Exhibition of 1909. The gleaming white Court of Honour in what was called the 'Mohamedan-Hindoo' style had been built in 1908 and created a strange centrepiece for the Anglo-Japanese Exhibition. As Paul Greenhalgh argued, in these White City exhibitions the educational and philanthropic flavours of the earlier South Kensington shows were replaced by those of the theatre and fairground. 1 An enormous quality of souvenirs was produced and many postcards, published on this occasion, showed a Japanese girl and a British boy (not usually the other way around) in 'Anglo-Japanese Alliance'. The shared ethos of Imperialism was an important ingredient of this exhibition in the year of the annexation of Korea by Japan. In the 'native villages' sections, a characteristic feature of White City shows, Japan contributed examples of work from Formosa and the Ainu people.

NOTE
1 Greenhalgh 1988, p.91

351
1910 Anglo-Japanese Exhibition Guidebook
The Corporation of London (Guildhall Library)
352
Selection of Souvenir Postcards related to the 1910 Anglo-Japanese Exhibition
Peter Pantzer, Bonn
Horesh Collection, London

MIYAGAWA KOZAN (1842-1916)

Miyagawa was a leading potter of the Meiji period, producing many pieces for export, and his works were extensively seen at international exhibitions. Miyagawa was the son of a Kyoto

Fig. 5 *Kyoto Pavilion at the Japan - British Exhibiton*, 1910

Cat.354

potter, Makuzu Chozo, but around 1870 he went to Yokohama, where he set up his kiln, producing a great variety of pieces known as Makuzu ware.

353
Vase and Cover, c.1900-10
Supported by an elephant-head stand
H. 32 cm, D. 13.3 cm
Trustees of the Victoria and Albert Museum, London

This piece was bought by Kenneth Dingwall at the Anglo-Japanese Exhibition. Another piece also by Miyagawa sold to Dingwall at this exhibition has a receipt which states that it was sold for £1.10s by a salesman called Hayashi on 7 July on behalf of Miyagawa Heinosuke of Kanagawa, and was donated to the Victoria and Albert Museum on 19 September 1910.

YABU MEIZAN

354
Vase, early 20th century
Cream-coloured earthenware, painted and gilt
Mark: 'Yabu Meizan' in a square gilt panel
H. 32 cm, D. 15.5 cm
Trustees of the Victoria and Albert Museum, London

Satsuma-style ceramics, which were highly and minutely decorated with flowers, landscapes and figures, such as this piece from Osaka, were extremely popular in the West. This piece was originally bought by Kenneth Dingwall at the Anglo-Japanese Exhibition and he paid £10 for it.

UDAGAWA NIGYO (DATES UNKNOWN)

355
Mother and Child, c.1910
Bronze sculpture with wooden bench,
H. c.59 cm
Ashmolean Museum, Oxford

A nearly identical piece to this was exhibited at the Anglo-Japanese Exhibition in the section 'Modern Craft' with the title 'Countrywoman nursing her baby'. The bronze part shows only very minor differences from the photograph in the exhibition catalogue, but the wooden bench is quite different. A *gebori* (ivory sculpture) version of this piece was auctioned on 6 June 1990 at Christie's in London.

KAMISAKA SEKKA (1866-1943)

Kamisaka studied traditional Shijo-School painting, but became a pioneer designer in Kyoto and was active in both designing and design education. He taught at Kyoto City School of Arts and Crafts. He promoted new types of design which were developed from traditional Japanese versions, and was wary of slavishly following new Western design trends.

356
Hyakka (hundreds of flowers), early 20th century
Silk damask, 70 x 100 cm
(Reproduction of a detail of a piece of curtain fabric woven in 1908 and exhibited in 1910)
Kawashima Textiles Museum

Kawashima Jinbei II, the head of Kawashima Orimono (Kawashima Textiles), explored possibilities of utilising traditional techniques of textiles for new uses within the context of Western-style interiors, such as curtain fabrics and framed pictures made out of textiles. This particular piece was developed from a type of Noh costume fabric and was woven on a broad loom. It is unusually large and luxurious (355 x 123 cm). It was exhibited at the Anglo-Japanese Exhibition in the Kawashima pavilion. In the collection of workshop material from the Silver Studio, there is a colour reproduction of this piece cut out from a magazine. Further examination of the material in the Silver Studio Collection from that period proved fruitful as it unearthed an example of textile design, datable to 1910, which uses similar design principles of massing collections of diverse flowers in irregular flat groups on a dark ground.

LIT : *Onkiken* 1913

357
Miyako Meisho (famous places of Kyoto)
Silk damask 40 x 50 cm
(Reproduction of a detail of a design used for a screen exhibited in 1910)
Kawashima Textiles Museum, Kyoto

Kawashima Jinbei exhibited a folding screen made out of tapestry, which showed famous scenes from Kyoto. The same design, originally by Sakurai Koun, is also used for an embroidered Noh costume produced in 1900 and now in the Tokyo National Museum.

TAKEUCHI SEIHO (1864-1942)

Seiho studied Shijo-School painting under Kono Bairei (1844-1895) and became the star among the Japanese-style Kyoto painters. He travelled in Europe from 1900 to 1901 and was particularly impressed by the art of Turner and Corot. He actively experimented with the introduction of elements of Western painting into his Japanese-style paintings. He was also active in art education and became one of the most prominent painters of his generation.

LIT : Tanaka 1988

358
Moon in Venice, 1904
Sumi ink on paper
220 x 174.5 cm
Takashimaya Collection

Iida Shinshichi of the Takashimaya store was another entrepreneur who participated in the Anglo-Japanese Exhibition with his own pavilion. His speciality was velvet pictures, dyed using the Yuzen technique to reproduce paintings. He commissioned major painters to provide cartoons for these pictures. The most spectacular exhibit was the large triptych, *The Three Famous Views of the World* to which Seiho's *Moon in Venice* belonged. It is generally recognised that Seiho's source of inspiration was Turner. Seiho pays tribute to the English artist in representing Turner's favourite city in the purest medium for a Japanese-style painter, namely ink painting.

KOBAYASHI KOKEI (1883-1957)

Kobayashi was a Japanese-style painter who trained under Kajita Hanko (1870-1917). Initially he concentrated on historical genre paintings, but gradually became interested in the Yamato-e style, which developed into a major source of inspiration for him. In later life he became one of the most respected figures among the Japanese-style painters.

359
The Fire Brigade of the Kaga Clan (Kaga-tobi), 1909
Colour on silk, 85.7 x 115.4 cm
National Museum of Modern Art, Tokyo

The main task of the Edo-period Fire Brigade was not necessarily to extinguish fires but to demolish houses near a fire to prevent it spreading. Their strength and courage were admired and they were regarded as symbols of male virtue in Edo society. A combination of machismo and dandyism developed among the Fire Brigades and they often had handsome uniforms and banners. The Fire Brigade of the Kaga clan was regarded as a particularly fine example. This painting was specially commissioned for the Anglo-Japanese Exhibition by the Maeda family who had previously been feudal lords of the Kaga clan. Okakura Tenshin (1862-1913), who was instrumental in the revival of Japanese traditional art, was involved in commissioning this painting and his advice gave an important impetus to Kokei's change of direction.

OKADA SABUROSUKE (1869-1939)

Inspired to become an oil painter by seeing Hyakutake Kaneyuki's (1842-1884) paintings, Okada studied under Soyama Sachihiko (1859-1892) and was later influenced by the plein-air style of Kuroda Seiki (1866-1924) and Kume Keiichiro (1866-1934). He went to France in 1897 and stayed there until 1902. He was strongly influenced by his teacher in Paris, Raphael Collin (1850-1916). When he returned to Japan he was appointed Professor at the Tokyo School of Art. He became particularly noted for his nude paintings and portraits of women, of which *Hagi* is a fine example. This painting was exhibited at the Anglo-Japanese Exhibition as *Girl and Bush Clover*.

360
Portrait of a Lady standing against Bush Clover ('Hagi'), 1908
Oil on canvas, 124.2 x 80.3 cm
Signed and dated b.r.: S.Okada 1908
Hyogo Prefectural Museum of Art

LIT : Takashina et al. 1987, pp.210-11

ISHIBASHI KAZUNORI (1876-1928)

Ishibashi studied Japanese-style painting, but then, in 1903, he travelled to Britain, apparently because he thought, in order to master Japanese-style painting, one should also study Western-style painting. He is said to have studied first at the Kensington School but then became a student at the Royal Academy Schools. After graduating from there in 1907 he remained in Britain and became a member of the Royal Society of Portrait Painters. He returned to Japan in 1918, but came back to Britain between 1921 and 1924.

361
A Woman reading Poetry, 1906
Oil on canvas, 99.5 x 88.3 cm
Signed and dated bottom b.r.: 1906 K Ishibashi
Shimane Prefectural Museum

Ishibashi painted this work while he was in Britain, but in 1909 exhibited it at the official exhibition in Japan, *Bunten*, and won a prize. The model is said to be a famous actress. This painting was also exhibited at the Anglo-Japanese Exhibition of 1910.

Cat.355

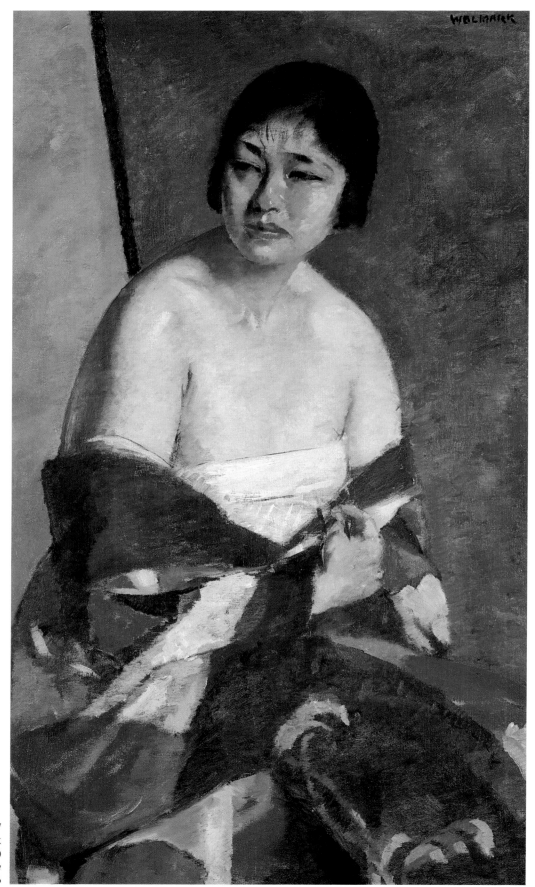

Cat.367
ALFRED WOLMARK
(1877-1961)
*Japanese Woman
in a Kimono* c.1926

XIV. THE NEW GENERATION OF ARTISTS

A. EDWARDIAN PAINTERS AND JAPAN

WILLIAM ORPEN (1878-1931)

Born at Stillorgan, County Dublin, Orpen was trained at Dublin Metropolitan School of Art and then in London at the Slade School of Art, where he met Augustus John (1878-1961), Ambrose McEvoy (1878-1927), Wyndham Lewis (1882-1957) and Spencer Gore (1878-1914). He began to exhibit at the New English Art Club in 1899. From 1902 he ran the Chelsea Art School, a private teaching studio, with Augustus John, and also began regular visits to Dublin, where he taught part-time at the Dublin School of Art between 1902 and 1914 and became involved in the Irish cultural renaissance. Orpen was a highly successful portrait painter, and became a founder-member of the National Portrait Society in 1911. He also painted a series of allegorical works, extending his Irish interest. In 1916 he joined the Army and in the following year he was sent to the Western Front as an Official War Artist. During the 1920s he had studios in Paris and London and painted war subjects as well as portraiture.

LIT : K. McConkey, p.195, pp.200-2

362
Lady on a Couch, 1900
Oil on canvas, 80 x 88.9 cm
Signed and dated b.l.: William Orpen, 1900
Leicestershire Museum and Art Gallery

LIT : Spalding 1986, ill.12

One of Orpen's early portraits. Whistler's influence is evident in the setting with an Oriental screen in the background, the asymmetrical composition with the sitter on the far right, and the loose and quick brush work.

DUNCAN GRANT (1885-1978)

Although born at Rothiemurchus, Inverness, Scotland, his early childhood was spent in India. Studied in London at the Westminster Art School and in Paris at the Ecole de la Palette. Back in London, he also attended the Slade School of Art. In 1909 he met Matisse and Gertrude Stein, and became associated with the Bloomsbury circle formed round Clive (1881-1964) and Vanessa Bell (1879-1961) and Roger Fry (1866-1934). Grant was deeply influenced by Roger Fry's Post-Impressionist exhibitions in London in 1910, and in 1912 joined the second Post-Impressionist Exhibition. He also exhibited at the New English Art Club, and was a member of the Camden Town Group. In this period, he was regarded as a leading avant-garde artist in Britain, and his work was shown with the Indépendants Anglais at the Galerie Barbazanges, Paris, in 1912.

In 1913, with Roger Fry and Vanessa Bell, Grant founded the Omega Workshop and together they were involved in decorative works until 1919.

LIT : S. Compton ed., *British Art in the 20th Century: the Modern Movement*, exh. cat., London 1987, p.431

363
James Strachey, 1910
Oil on canvas, 63.5 x 76.2 cm
Tate Gallery, London

LIT : Spalding 1986, p.39-40 with ill.24

This elegant portrait was painted early in 1910 before the first Post-Impressionist Exhibition, which was to affect Grant so deeply. The use of a Japanese screen in the background and the sitter's pose reflect the influence of Whistlerian traditions. The sitter's relaxed arm, thrown to the left, echoes the motif in the screen.

SAMUEL JOHN PEPLOE (1871-1935)

Peploe was an Edinburgh-born still-life painter, and with John Duncan Fergusson (1874-1961), George Leslie Hunter (Cat.365) and F.C.B. Cadell (1883-1937), formed a group, commonly known as the 'Scottish Colourists'. They were never a coherent group, but they all used rich, expressive colour, and had close links with French painting, especially Post-Impressionism and Fauvism. After a brief training at Edinburgh School of Art, Peploe studied in Paris from 1891 to 1894, where he attended the Académie Julian and the Académie Colarossi. In Paris he was influenced by the Impressionists, especially Manet's handling of tonal values. In 1895 he visited Amsterdam, where he saw Frans Hals' still-life works which made a deep impression on him. Back in Scotland in the mid-1890s, he painted studio interiors and small landscapes, and began a series of still-lifes, with fruit, ceramic vases, flowers and silver jugs against a dark background. By 1900 he had formed a friendship with Fergusson, with whom he painted in Brittany in 1904. In 1905 he moved to a lighter painting style: the year coincided with Whistler's memorial exhibition, and Whistler's influence is evident in a series of portraits, including *A Girl in White* (1907; The Fine Art Society). From 1910 to 1912 he lived in Paris with his family, where he began to apply Fauvist and Cubist theories to his still-life and landscape painting. His paintings from Paris were shown at the New Gallery, Edinburgh in 1913. Around 1918 he met Cadell, and in 1920 they painted together on the island of Iona. He was to return to the island almost every summer for the next thirteen years. Throughout the 1920s and 1930s, he was a successful artist, and he was elected to the Royal Scottish Academy in 1927.

He also taught part-time at Edinburgh College of Art from 1933, which subsequently ended because of his ill-health.

LIT : Billcliffe, London 1989; Hartley, 1989-1990, p.157

364
Flowers and Fruit (Japanese Background) c.1916
Oil on canvas, 40.5 x 45.5 cm
Kirkcaldy District Museums and Art Gallery

LIT : *Twentieth Century Scottish Painting*, exh. cat. Edinburgh/London 1987, pp.VIII-IX (2); Billcliffe, 1989 (62)

A Japanese woodcut is seen behind a group of objects carefully arranged on a table. The bold outlines, strong, flat colours and highly stylised forms of the print are reflected in Peploe's handling of the objects, and together they produce a decorative unity of colours and forms.

GEORGE LESLIE HUNTER (1877-1931)

Born in Rothesay, Isle of Bute, he emigrated to California with his family in 1892. He was self taught, and began working as an illustrator in San Francisco. In 1904 he visited Paris, where he was deeply affected by the Post-Impressionists and decided to become a painter. In 1906, following a brief trip to San Francisco, he came back to Scotland, where he resumed his early career as an illustrator. He continued painting, visiting Paris a number of times. Alexander Reid became his dealer and organised his first one-man exhibition in 1913 in Glasgow. His style evolved from the influences of a number of artists, including Whistler, McTaggart, Cézanne, the Fauves, and later Matisse. In 1922, he travelled extensively on the Continent, including Paris, Venice, Florence and the South of France. He exhibited with Peploe (Cat.364) and Cadell at the Leicester Galleries, London, in 1923 and 1925 (when he was joined by Fergusson), and all four exhibited together at a group show at the Galerie Barbazanges, Paris, in 1924.

LIT : Billcliffe, 1989; Hartley, 1989-1990, pp.137-8

365
Still-Life with Japanese Print, c.1922
Oil on panel, 76 x 47 cm
Signed b.r.: L Hunter
Private Collection

LIT : Billcliffe, 1989 (86)

Hunter had a small collection of Japanese woodcuts, and probably he used one of them to compose this picture. Here the frame of the print and other objects are all painted on a flat white ground, and the spatial relationships between the different objects is ambiguous.

GWEN JOHN (1876-1939)

Born in Haverfordwest, Wales, she was the elder sister of Augustus John (1878-1961). Gwen John studied at the Slade School of Art under Fred Brown and Philip Wilson Steer, and went to Paris in 1898, where she attended Whistler's new school, the Académie Carmen. Back in London in 1899, she began to exhibit at the New English Art Club in 1900. In 1903, with her friend Dorelia McNeill, she travelled to the South of France, and in the following year settled in Paris, where she was to live most of her life. While she continued painting, she earned her living by modelling. In 1904 she became a model and the mistress of Auguste Rodin, through whom she formed a friendship with the poet, Rainer Maria Rilke, who was then Rodin's secretary. In 1913 her *Girl Reading at the Window* (1911; Museum of Modern Art, New York) was included in the Armory Show in New York. In the same year, she was converted to Roman Catholicism and moved to the village of Meudon, near Paris. Gwen John's paintings are mostly small-scale portraits and still-lifes. A retrospective exhibition of her work was held in 1926 at the New Chenil Galleries, London, which included forty-four paintings and watercolours, and four albums of drawings.

LIT : C. Langdale and D.F. Jenkins, *Gwen John. An Interior Life*, exh. cat. London/ Manchester/New Haven, 1985-86

366
The Japanese Doll, 1920s
Oil on canvas, 30.5 x 40.7 cm
Ben John, London

LIT : C. Langdale and D.F. Jenkins, op. cit. (45)

The setting is Gwen John's studio at 29 rue Terre Neuve, Meudon, which appears often in her painting, such as *Girl with Cat* (late 1910s to early 1920s; Metropolitan Museum of Art, New York) and *Interior (Rue Terre Neuve)* (early to mid-1920s; Manchester City Art Gallery). Here a Japanese doll is the centre of the composition and the doll, with its black hair and bright-coloured kimono, is used to heighten the muted tones of this picture. There is another version of this composition, which was completed around 1928 (Private Collection).

ALFRED AARON WOLMARK (1877-1961)

Born in Warsaw, Wolmark emigrated to England with his family in 1883. He was brought up in London's East End, and studied at the Royal Academy Schools. He first exhibited at the Royal Academy in 1903 with the large painting of a Jewish subject, *The Last Days of Rabbi Ben Ezra*, which shows some influence of Rembrandt. In 1905 he had his first one-man exhibition at the Bruton Gallery, London. From 1911 onwards, his subject became mostly portraiture and still-life, and in this decade he established an expressionist style with pure, bright colours and solid structural forms. Wolmark was also interested in decorative work. He designed sets for the Diaghilev Ballet

in 1911, and was involved in stained-glass and pottery designs.

LIT : *Alfred Wolmark 1877-1961*, exh. cat. Ferens Art Gallery, Kingston upon Hull, 1975; K. McConkey, 1987, pp.218-19

367
Japanese Woman in a Kimono, c.1926
Oil on canvas, 88.6 x 53.5 cm
Signed t.r.: Wolmark
Victor Arwas, London

Throughout the late nineteenth and the early twentieth century, a number of Western artists painted this type of subject. However, this painting is unusual in the following respect. While the artists of older generations depicted Japanese or 'Japanese-style' girls in a highly idealised manner, reflecting either their 'cult of Japan' or aesthetic purpose, Wolmark portrayed this Japanese model in a realistic way. However, with its Mondrian-like design in the background, the shape and colour of the kimono is used to add expressive feeling rather than decorative quality.

JAMES T. SHARPE (dates unknown)

368
Masked Woman sitting against a Japanese Screen, c.1914-19
Watercolour and gouache on paper, 60.5 x 47.2 cm
Victor Arwas, London

DOROTHY WEBSTER HAWKSLEY (1884-1970)

Born in London, Hawksley studied at the Royal Academy Schools. She taught for two years at the Women's Department of King's College, London, in Kensington. She exhibited at the Royal Academy from 1909 to 1964, and also at the Paris Salon. She was a member of the Royal Institute of Painters in Watercolour and the Society of Mural Decorators and Painters in Tempera. Her painting was narrative and she evolved a flat schematic style, strongly influenced by Japanese woodcuts.

369
Japanese Fantasy (Revenge), c.1920s
Watercolour and gouache on paper,
36 x 25.5 cm, frame: 56.8 x 42.8 cm
Victor Arwas, London

B. JAPANESE ARTISTS IN BRITAIN

MAKINO YOSHIO (1869-1956)

A painter and illustrator, Makino went to America in 1892 where he studied art in San Francisco. In 1897 he moved to London where he stayed until 1942 when, after the outbreak of war, he was repatriated against his wish. He studied in

London at the Goldsmiths' Institute and at the Central School of Art, while suffering abject poverty. His illustations were accepted by the *Magazine of Art* and its editor, Marion H. Spielmann, helped him to establish a career as an illustrator. When W.J. Loftie's book *The Colour of London*, illustrated by Makino, was published in 1907, it became an overnight success. His sensitive and lyrical portrayal of misty London was acclaimed and he became a well-known personality in London society until the outbreak of World War I in 1914. He had many and varied friends, including the poet and writer Yone Noguchi, the painter Hara Busho and the suffragette, Christabel Pankhurst. He signed his name as 'Markino' to prevent mispronunciation.

LIT : Blacker 1990; Tsunematsu 1990; *Makino Yoshio Ten* 1990

370
BBC in the Rain, 1929
Watercolour on paper, 35.5 x 51 cm
Signed and dated b.r.: YM/29
Yasue Tanaka, Kagoshima

371 (Barbican only)
Buckingham Palace from Green Park, 1929
Colour print from woodblocks, 28.3 x 38.6 cm
Inscribed in Japanese b.l.
The Museum of London

372
A Night Scene in Piccadilly Circus, late 1920s
Oil on canvas, 72.5 x 60.6 cm
Signed b.r.: Yoshio Markino
Kaname Ichimura, Tokyo

The same composition appears here as in the frontispiece of *The Colour of London* (Cat.373). Makino was very fond of the London mist.

373
W. J. LOFTIE (dates unknown)
The Colour of London, 1914
Illustrated by Yoshio Makino
The Corporation of London (Guildhall Library)

374
London Pictured by Yoshio Markino, 1917
The Corporation of London (Guildhall Library)

ISHIBASHI KAZUNORI (1876-1928)
(For a short biography see Section XIII, p.109)

375
A Sculptor, 1912
Oil on canvas, 182 x 107 cm
The National Museum of Modern Art, Tokyo

According to Takeuchi Tsurunosuke, this sculptor was called 'Merifyudoru' (Merrifield?) and was using a studio which was situated in the same wing of the Royal Academy Schools as Ishibashi's. 1 Recently Oba Sadao discovered another portrait by Ishibashi also painted in England. This is the portrait of William Robert Walker, MVO and is now in Winchester Cathedral Library. 2

NOTES
1 Takeuchi Tsurunosuke, 'Ishibashi Kazunori Shi' (Mr. Ishibashi Kazunori), *Chuo Bijutsu*, vol.4, no.11, November 1918, pp.98-100; pp.99-100. We are grateful to Ms Kojima Kaoru for pointing out this source.
2 We are grateful to Mr Oba Sadao for this information.

TAKEUCHI TSURUNOSUKE (1881-1948)

Takeuchi was born in Yokohama and studied painting at the Hakubakai Yoga Kenkyusho (White Horse Society Western-Style Painting Institute). In 1908 he travelled to Britain and studied under Brangwyn (see below). He exhibited at the Royal Academy and apparently one of his works entered the Royal Collection, but this has so far not been identified. He returned to Japan in 1914 and became a leading pastel painter.

376
The Skies of England, 1908-12
Pastels, 13.7 x 24.7 cm; 18.3 x 25.4 cm; 17.4 x 25.3 cm; 16.3 x 22.7 cm
Meguro Art Museum, Tokyo

ISHIKAWA KIN'ICHIRO (1871-1945)

Born in Shizuoka, Ishikawa specialised in watercolour painting and in 1889 was taught by Alfred East who visited Japan in that year. He travelled in Europe from 1899 to 1900 and also in 1920. Ishikawa promoted the use of English-style watercolour in Japan and translated English articles and notices on this subject for the leading watercolour magazine *Mizue*. For him watercolour was the only medium in which the Japanese could compete with the West without losing their integrity. He became an important teacher of Western painting in Taiwan. [1]

NOTE
1 We are grateful to Mr Tachibana Yoshiaki of the Shizuoka Prefectural Museum of Art for the information on Ishikawa Kinichiro.

377
A View of South Kensington, c.1922
Watercolour, 27 x 18 cm
Signed b.l.: Ishikawa Kin
Koriyama City Museum of Art

C. BRANGWYN AND HIS JAPANESE FRIENDS

FRANK BRANGWYN (1867-1943)

Brangwyn, though British, was born in Belgium and also studied there. He later became one of the few British painters who were able to deal with large-scale mural paintings. In Britain he has been underrated as an artist perhaps due to his Continental background and to his 'un-British' interests. He became a close friend of the Japanese industrialist Matsukata Kojiro and apparently inspired him to start his legendary collection of Western art and Ukiyo-e prints. Brangwyn designed a gallery of Western art for the Matsukata Collection, but due to the financial collapse of Matsukata's company this came to nothing. Brangwyn seems to have taught a number of Japanese, but this needs further investigation.

LIT : *The Old Matsukata Collection 1989*

378
Portrait of Matsukata Kojiro, 1916
Oil on canvas, 73.8 x 84 cm
Signed and dated b.r.: FB/1916
Inscribed on the reverse: Painted in 1 hour/FB
Matsukata Kiyohiko, Tokyo

Apparently it took Brangwyn only an hour to paint this virtuoso portrait of his friend.

379
Designs for a Gallery of Western Art, Tokyo ('Kyoraku-kan') commissioned by Kojiro Matsukata, c.1922
Reproduction from *The Builder* (4 August, 1922)

URUSHIBARA YOSHIJIRO (1888-1953)

Born in Tokyo, Urushibara was trained in the technique of woodcut. He went to Europe and stayed there nearly thirty years until he returned to Japan in 1934. Urushibara played an important role in the dissemination of the technique and knowledge of the Japanese woodcut in the West. He was mainly active in Britain and made sensitive woodcut reproductions of paintings by other contemporary artists, but also produced his own prints of still-lifes and landscapes. He was also known as Mokuchu.

380
URUSHIBARA YOSHIJIRO AND FRANK BRANGWYN
The Béguinage, Bruges
Colour print from woodblocks, 44.8 x 56.5 cm
Signed in pencil: Y. Urushibara; Frank Brangwyn
Trustees of the British Museum, London

This is a colour woodcut by Urushibara after Brangwyn and forms part of Laurence Binyon's (1869-1943) illustrated collection of poems *Bruges*. Binyon was a poet, writer and curator of the Japanese collection at the British Museum. There is a Sharaku-like caricature of Binyon's portrait by Edmund Dulac in a private collection. [1]

NOTE
1 We are grateful to Dr Chiba Yoko for this information.

381
URUSHIBARA YOSHIJIRO AND KURIHARA CHUJI
Kew Bridge
Colour print from wood blocks, 28.8 x 22.2 cm
Signed in pencil: Y. Urushibara; C. Kurihara
Trustees of the British Museum, London

This is a print by Urushibara based on a painting by Kurihara Chuji.

382
Stonehenge in Moonlight
Colour print from woodblocks, 29.8 x 43.8 cm
Signed in pencil: Y. Urushibara
Sealed: Urushibara
Trustees of the British Museum, London

KURIHARA CHUJI (1886-1936)

Born in Mishima, Kurihara studied Western-style painting at the Tokyo School of Fine Arts. He was active in Britain from 1912 to 1924 and again from 1926 to 1927. His earlier works show the strong influence of Turner, but once in Britain, he soon came under the spell of Brangwyn and produced dynamic oil paintings. He was a member of the Royal Society of British Artists. [1]

NOTE
1 We are grateful to Mr Ushirokoji Masahiro for pointing out the achievements of this artist and to Ms Ojima Mina of the Shizuoka Prefectural Museum of Art for the help we received regarding Kurihara.

LIT : *Kurihara Chuji Ten* 1979; *Kurihara Chuji Ten* 1991

383
Richmond Bridge c.1914-16
Oil on canvas, 71 x 91.8 cm
Signed in red paint b.l.: C. Kurihara
University of Leeds Collection

In this painting Kurihara shows a Brangwyn-like masculine strength. The painting was purchased from the artist by Sir Michael Sadler in October 1916 and presented by him to the University of Leeds in 1923. There is an oil sketch of Richmond Bridge about half the size of this painting.

IAN A. J. CHEYNE (1895-1955)

A Scottish painter and print-maker, Cheyne studied at the Glasgow School of Art. He used the Japanese woodblock technique, but applied it to Scottish landscapes. [1] In his print Loch Duich he used the Ichimonji technique (the dark band at the top which fades downwards in many late Edo period prints), but ingeniously turned it sideways to depict the reflection on the water.

NOTE
1 We are grateful to Christopher Allan and Martin Hopkinson of the Hunterian Art Gallery for the information on Cheyne and Fleming.

384
Loch Duich, 1934
Colour woodcut, 27.6 x 33 cm
Studio stamp: Ian A J Cheyne
Hunterian Art Gallery, University of Glasgow

IAN FLEMING (dates unknown)

Fleming also made Japan-inspired prints. Chica Macnab was the sister of Ian Macnab and taught woodcut technique at the Glasgow School of Art.

Cat.390 A

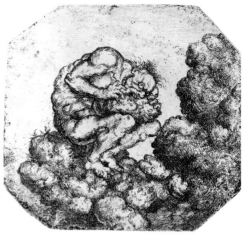
Cat.390 B

Cat.390 C

385
Kelvingrove Park (Parkscape or Landscape, Rain and Shadow), 1928
Colour print from woodblocks, 21 x 16.1 cm
Signed in pencil: Parkside 10/25 Ian Fleming
Inscribed: under the guidance of Chica MacNab
Hunterian Art Gallery, University of Glasgow

D. 'BEYOND EAST AND WEST'

WILLIAM BLAKE AND THE SHIRAKABA (SILVER BIRCH) GROUP

The arts magazine *Shirakaba* (1910-23) was the leading intellectual vehicle of the Taisho period. Among the Shirakaba group there was a very strong interest in William Blake and members shared a rather idealistic humanism. Blake featured on the cover of the magazine and the April 1914 number was a special issue devoted to Blake with articles by Yanagi Soetsu and Bernard Leach. Yanagi, one of the leaders of the Blake movement, compared him with Michelangelo and Dürer and proclaimed Blake as the only world-class painter Britain had produced! In the Bodleian Library, Oxford, there is a set of Japanese Blake literature from this time including the relevant *Shirakaba* issues, which was given to Sir Geoffrey Keynes, the Blake scholar.

386
Shirakaba (Silver Birch)
Vol. 5, April 1914
Bodleian Library, Oxford

387
Tiger, tiger, burning bright in the forests of the night
Cover designed by Bernard Leach for the *Shirakaba* magazine (July 1913)
The Japan Folk Crafts Museum, Tokyo

388
Blake and Whitman
Vol. 1, No.1, January 1931
Bodleian Library, Oxford

389
SERIZAWA KEISUKE (1895-1984)
Slipcase for 'Blake and Whitman' (vols I & II)
The Japan Folk Crafts Museum, Tokyo

It is little known in Britain that for two years, commencing in January 1931, a specialist journal on Blake and Whitman, packed with scholarly articles, was published in Japan. The slipcase was designed by Serizawa when the journal was wound up, offering all the issues in two bound volumes. Serizawa Keisuke was an active supporter of the Folk Crafts Movement (Mingei Undo) and studied Bingata, the stencil technique from the Okinawa Islands. He is the greatest exponent of stencil-dying in modern Japan.

Cat.387

KISHIDA RYUSEI (1891-1929)

One of the greatest oil painters of the Taisho period, Kishida met Bernard Leach in 1911 and became acquainted with the Shirakaba Group. He learnt the technique of etching from Leach and his experiment, *Creation*, shows the clear influence of Blake. He was then influenced by French Impressionism and Post-Impressionism. Ryusei's well-known portrait of his friend Leach is a good example of this. He became interested in the paintings of the Northern Renaissance and his style underwent another shift. The powerful landscapes of ordinary places shows that he established a realist style of his own. In 1916 he was diagnosed as having tuberculosis and, while recuperating, he concentrated on a series of intense still-lifes, for some of which he used ceramics by Leach. In 1918 he started his famous series of portraits of his daughter. In later years his paintings assumed a more Oriental nature.

390
Creation (Tenchi Sozo), 1914
Three etchings, printed by Komai Tetsuo from original plates in 1975, 12.5 x 12.5 cm each
The National Museum of Modern Art, Tokyo:

A. *Desire*

B. *Angry Adam*

C. *Man Biting a Stone*

391
Portrait of Bernard Leach
Oil on canvas, 59 x 44.2 cm
The National Museum of Modern Art, Tokyo

392
Desolate Path in Winter, 1916
Oil on canvas, 60.8 x 80.2 cm
Niigata Prefectural Museum of Art

393
Still Life (with Bernard Leach's Vase), 1918
Oil on canvas, 49.8 x 60.7 cm
Private Collection

BERNARD LEACH (1887-1979)

Born in Hong Kong, Leach studied at the Slade School of Art under Henry Tonks. Later he was taught etching by Frank Brangwyn. He went to Japan in 1909 to teach etching. However, in 1911, he was sufficiently fascinated by Raku pottery to become a pupil of Ogata Kenzan VI. In 1920 he returned to Britain and settled at St Ives. He was the most influential British studio potter of this century. His books were also important in disseminating his ideas.

394
Self-portrait
Etching, The Japan Folk Crafts Museum, Tokyo

395
Portrait of Yanagi Soetsu
Drawing, The Japan Folk Crafts Museum, Tokyo

396
Tyger, tyger, burning bright in the forests of the night .
1911, Screen, stoneware tile plate
The Japan Folk Crafts Museum, Tokyo

Cat.396

397
Taga Marsh, 1918
Etching , The Japan Folk Crafts Museum, Tokyo

398
Canal, 1919
Painted ceramic plate
The Japan Folk Crafts Museum, Tokyo

399
Vase, 1931
Stoneware with matt-white bracken glaze and painting of leaping salmon in brown
H. 32.5 cm, D. 15.3 cm
Milner White Collection, York City Art Gallery

Cat.400

HAMADA SHOJI (1894-1978)

In the West, Hamada is perhaps the best-known modern Japanese potter. He met Bernard Leach at Yanagi Soetsu's house in 1918 and travelled to St Ives with Leach in 1920. In 1923 he had two shows in London and then returned to Japan in 1924. In British eyes the collaboration between Leach and Hamada was seen as the epitome of the coming together of East and West. In 1930 he moved to Mashiko and set up his kiln. His works after his return to Japan are unsigned. In Japan he was an important member of the Folk Crafts Movement, which was heavily influenced by the ideas developed in Britain by John Ruskin and William Morris.

400
Small Jar with Patterns brushed on Glaze, 1922
H. 16.5, D. 10.5 cm
Mashiko Reference Collection

401
Dish with Floral Decoration cut thorough the Slip, 1923
Stoneware, H. 10 cm, D. 39 cm
Marked: Hamada and St. Ives Seals
University College of Wales, Aberystwyth

TOMIMOTO KENKICHI (1886-1963)

Tomimoto studied architecture and interior design at the Tokyo School of Fine Arts. In 1908 he came to Britain and studied stained glass for one term at the Central School of Art in London. He returned to Japan in 1910, met Leach there and became involved in pottery-making. He took a more independent line than the Yanagi-dominated Folk Crafts Movement circle. Some of his earlier works show sympathy with British crafts and patterns.

402
Grapevine with English Lines, 1911
Carved on wood, 65.7 x 35.0 cm
Ohara Museum of Art, Kurashiki City

403
Flower, 1912
Etching, 8.8 x 8.8 cm
Kenkichi Tomimoto Memorial Museum, Nara Prefecture

In this small etching Tomimoto evokes the designs of the early Irish illuminated manuscripts with their stylised central flower and the prominent and tightly-knit borders.

404
Grapevine-patterned Jar
(Rakuyaki Budo Monyo Tsubo), 1913
H.13.8 cm, D. 11.3 cm
Kenkichi Tomimoto Momorial Museum, Nara Prefecture

405
Old Tree, 1924
Jiki-sometsuke ceramic plate
Private Collection

302 AUBREY VINCENT BEARDSLEY (1872-1898) *The Toilet of Salomé*, 1893

SELECTED BIBLIOGRAPHY

ADBURGHAM, ALISON *Liberty's. A Biography of a Shop* London 1975

The Aesthetic Movement and the Cult of Japan exh. cat., The Fine Art Society London 1972

ALCOCK, RUTHERFORD *International Exhibition, 1862. Catalogue of Works of Industry and Art, Sent from Japan* London

ALCOCK, SIR RUTHERFORD *The Capital of the Tycoon. A Narrative of a Three Years' Residence in Japan* 2 vols., London 1863

ALCOCK, SIR RUTHERFORD *Art and Art Industry in Japan* London 1878

Sir Alfred East exh. cat., The Alfred East Gallery, Kettering n.d.

AOKI SHIGERU and HAGA TORU *Takahashi Yuichi* vol. 2 of Kanvas Nihon no Meiga (Canvas Series of Great Japanese Paintings) Tokyo 1979

AOKI SHIGERU *Takahashi Yuichi Aburae Shiryo (Documents for Takahashi Yuichi's Oil Painting)* Tokyo 1984

AOKI SHIGERU *Aburae Shogaku (The Beginnings of Oil Painting)* Tokyo 1987

Architect-Designers. Pugin to Mackintosh exh. cat., The Fine Art Society, London 1981

ASLET, CLIVE 'The Country Houses of W.E. Nesfield' *Country Life*, 16 March, pp.678-681 23 March, pp.766-769, 1978

ASLIN, ELIZABETH 'The Furniture Designs of E.W. Godwin' Bulletin of the Victoria and Albert Museum, III, no. 4, October 1967 pp.145-154

ASLIN, ELIZABETH *The Aesthetic Movement: Prelude to Art Noveau* London 1969, 1981

ASLIN, ELIZABETH 'The Oriental Influence on the Decorative Arts in France and England' *World Cultures and Modern Art* ed.Siefried Wichmann, exh. cat., Haus der Kunst, Munich 1972, pp.177-182

ASLIN, ELIZABETH *E.W. Godwin: Furniture and Interior Decoration* London 1986

ASLIN, ELIZABETH 'Japanese Influence on Nineteenth-Century Decorative Arts' *The Decorative Arts in the Victorian Period* (ed.) Susan M. Wright, The Society of Antiquaries, London 1989, pp.74-81

AYERS, JOHN, OLIVER IMPEY and J.V.G. MALLET *Porcelain for Palaces: The Fashion for Japan in Europe 1650-1750* exh. cat. Oriental Ceramic Society / British Museum London 1990

BALDRY, ALFRED LYS *Albert Moore. His Life and Works* London 1894

BARR, PAT *The Deer Cry Pavilion* London

BEASLEY, W.G. *Great Britain and the Opening of Japan 1834-1858* London 1951

BÉNÉDITE, LÉONCE 'Artistes contemporains, Whistler' *Gazette des Beaux-Arts*, XXXIII, 1905, pp.403-410, 496-511 and XXXIV, 1905, pp.142-158, 231-246

BERGER, KLAUS *Japonismus in der Westlichen Malerei 1860-1920* Munich 1980

BILLCLIFFE, ROGER *Charles Rennie Mackintosh: The Complete Furniture, Furniture Drawings & Interior Designs* Guildford and London 1979

BILLCLIFFE, ROGER *Edward Atkinson Hornel 1864-1933* exh. cat., The Fine Art Society Glasgow 1982

BILLCLIFFE, ROGER *The Glasgow Boys* London 1985

BILLCLIFFE, ROGER *The Scottish Colourists* London 1989

BLACKER, CARMEN 'Yoshio Markino: a Recollection' *The Japan Society Proceedings* no.115, March 1990, pp.27-40

BLAIR, DOROTHY *A History of Glass in Japan* Tokyo 1973

BLOOM, HAROLD *The Anxiety of Influence, A Theory of Poetry* New York 1973

BROMFIELD, DAVID 'The Art of Japan in Later Nineteenth Century Europe, Problems of Art Criticism and Theory' Ph.D. thesis, University of Leeds, 1977

BRYDON, J.M. 'William Eden Nesfield, 1835-1888' *Architectural Review*, I, 1896-1897 pp. 235-247, 283-296

BUCHANAN, WILLIAM (ed.) *Mr Henry and Mr Hornel visit Japan* exh. cat., The Scottish Arts Council, Glasgow 1978-79

BUCHANAN, WILLIAM 'Japanese influences on the Glasgow Boys and Charles Rennie Mackintosh' in Yamada 1980, pp.291-301

BURGES, WILLIAM 'The International Exhibition' *Gentleman's Magazine*, July 1862 pp.3-12

BURGES, WILLIAM 'The Japanese Court in the International Exhibition' *Gentleman's Magazine*, September 1862, pp.243-254

The Burghley Porcelains exh. cat., The Japan Society, New York 1986

BURKHAUSER, JUDE (ed.) *'Glasgow Girls': Women in Art and Design 1880-1920* Edinburgh 1990

BURTY, PHILIPPE 'Japonism' *The Academy*, 7 August 1875, pp.150-151

BURY, SHIRLEY 'The Silver Designs of Dr Christopher Dresser' *Apollo*, December 1962, pp.766-770

CALLOWAY, STEPHEN *Charles Ricketts* London 1979

Charles Rennie Mackintosh exh. cat., Japan Art and Culture Association, Tokyo 1985

Charuzu Waguman, exh. cat., Kanagawa Prefectural Museum Yokohama 1990

CHECKLAND, SYDNEY *The Elgins 1766-1917* Aberdeen 1988

CHIBA YOKO 'W.B. Yeats and Noh: From Japonisme to Zen' unpublished Ph.D. thesis, University of Toronto 1988

CHRISTIAN, JOHN and others *The Pre-Raphaelites and their Times* exh. cat., Isetan Museum of Art, Tokyo 1985

Christopher Dresser 1834-1904 exh. cat., The Fine Art Society and Haslam & Whiteway Ltd., London 1990

CLARK, JOHN *Japanese-British Exchanges in Art 1850s-1930s* privately printed, n.p. 1989

COLLINS, MICHAEL *Christopher Dresser 1834-1904* exh. cat., Camden Arts Centre, 1979

CONANT, ELLEN 'The French Connection: Emile Guimet's Mission to Japan, A Cultural Context for Japonisme' *Japan in Transition: Thought and Action in the Meiji Era* (eds.) Hilary Conroy, Sanderson T.W. Davis and Wayne Patterson, Fairleigh Dickinson University Press, Rutherford N.J. 1984

CONANT, ELLEN 'Principles and Pragmatism: The Yatoi in the Field of Art' in *Foreign Employees in Nineteenth-Century Japan* eds. Edward R. Beauchamp and Akira Iriye Boulder, San Francisco and London 1990 pp.137-170

CONDER, JOSIAH *Paintings and Studies by Kawanabe Kyosai* Tokyo 1911

CONTE-HELM, MARIE *Japan and the North East of England* London 1989

COOPER, NICHOLAS *The Opulent Eye* London 1976

CORTAZZI, SIR HUGH *Victorians in Japan: In and around the Treaty Ports* London 1987

CROOK, J. MORDAUNT *William Burges and the High Victorian Dream* London 1981

CROOK, J. MORDAUNT (ed.) *The Strange Genius of William Burges. 'Art-Architect', 1827-1881* exh. cat., National Museum of Wales Cardiff 1981

CURRY, DAVID PARK *James McNeill Whistler at the Freer Gallery of Art* New York & London 1984

DARRACOTT, JOSEPH *The World of Charles Ricketts* London 1980

DELANEY, J.G.P. *Charles Ricketts: A Biography* Oxford 1990

DENNIS, RICHARD and JOHN JESSE *Christopher Dresser 1834-1904* exh. cat.The Fine Art Society, London 1972

Design in Transition, 1868-1945 exh. cat, Crafts Gallery, the National Museum of Modern Art, Tokyo 1988

Development of Western Realism in Japan exh. cat., The National Museum of Modern Art, Tokyo 1985-86

DILLON, EDWARD *The Arts of Japan* London 1906

DOI KUMIKO 'Makie Seigan' (Portable lacquer altarpieces) *Shikkoshi*, (Journal of the Academy of Lacquer Research), (1988) pp.21-29

DRESSER, CHRISTOPHER 'Eastern Art, and its influence on European Manufactures and Taste' *Journal of the Society of Arts*, 6 February 1874, pp.211-221

DRESSER, CHRISTOPHER 'The Art Manufacturers of Japan' *Journal of the Society of Arts*, 1 February 1878, pp.169-178

DRESSER, CHRISTOPHER *Japan, its architecture, art and art manufactures* London 1882

DUFWA, JACQUES *Winds from the East. A Study in the Art of Manet, Degas, Monet and Whistler 1856-86* Stockholm and Atlantic Highlands, N.J. 1981

DURANT, STUART 'Ornament in an Industrial Civilisation' *Architectural Review* vol. 160, September 1976, pp.139-143

DURANT, STUART *Ornament. A survey of decoration since 1830* London 1986

EARLE, JOE (ed.) *The Toshiba Gallery. Japanese Art and Design* Victoria and Albert Museum, London 1986

EASTLAKE, CHARLES LOCKE *Hints on Household Taste* London 1868

EIDLITZ, DOROTHY MEIGS 'Fine Art of simplified living: Japanese rooms suggest the modern line' *Arts and Decoration* (New York), vol. 42, January 1935, pp.38-42

ETO JUN *Soseki to Asao Densetsu (Soseki and King Arthur Legend)* Tokyo 1975

EVETT, ELISA *The Critical Reception of Japanese Art in Late Nineteenth Century Europe* Ann Arbor, Michigan 1982

EVETT, ELISA 'The Late nineteenth-century European critical response to Japanese art: primitivist leanings' *Art History*, vol. 6, no. 1, March 1983, pp.82-106

FARR, DENNIS *English Art 1870-1940* Oxford 1978; 2nd ed.1984

FAS 100 exh. cat., The Fine Art Society, London 1976

La Femme: The influence of Whistler and Japanese Print Masters on American Art 1880-1917 exh. cat., Grand Central Art Galleries Inc., New York 1983

FERRIDAY, PETER 'The Peacock Room' *Architectural Review*, CXXV, 1959, pp.407-414

FLEMING, GORDON *The Young Whistler 1834-1866* London 1978

FLOYD, PHYLIS ANNE 'Japonisme in context: Documentation, Criticism, Aesthetic Reactions' Ph.D. thesis, University of Michigan 1983

FLOYD, PHYLIS 'Documentary Evidence for the Availability of Japanese Imagery in Europe in Nineteenth-Century Public Collections' *Art Bulletin* March 1986 pp.105-141

FOX, GRACE *Britain and Japan 1858-1883* Oxford 1969

FRENCH, CAL *Through Closed Doors: Western influence on Japanese Art 1639-1853* exh. cat., Meadow Brook Art Gallery Oakland University, Rochester Michigan 1977

THE FRIENDS OF RADWINTER CHURCH *A Deuce of an Uproar: William Eden Nesfield's Letters to the Rector of Radwinter in Essex* Radwinter, Saffron Walden 1988

FUJIMORI TERUNOBU *Kokka no dezain (Design for the Nation)* vol.3 of Nihon no kenchiku: Meiji Taisho Showa (West Meets East: The Japanese Introduction to Western Architecture in 19th and 20th Centuries) Tokyo 1979

FUJIMORI TERUNOBU *Meiji no Tokyo Keikaku (Planning of Tokyo in Meiji Period)* Tokyo 1982; Pb. ed. 1990

FUKUDA YOSHIKI (ed.) *Oshita Tojiro Bijutsu Ronshu (Collected essays on art by Oshita Tojiro)* Tokyo 1988

FUKUZAWA YUKICHI 'Seikoki' (An Account of a Voyage to the West) *Fukuzawa Yukichi Zenshu (Complete Works of Yukichi Fukazawa)* vol. 19, Tokyo 1962, pp.6-65

GERE, CHARLOTTE *Nineteenth-Century Decoration: The Art of the Interior* London 1989

GESTSCHER, ROBERT H. *The Stamp of Whistler* exh. cat., Allen Memorial Art Museum, Oberlin College 1977

GARNER, PHILIPPE *The World of Edwardiana* London, New York, Sydney, Toronto 1974

GIROUARD, MARK *Sweetness and Light. The 'Queen Anne' Movement 1860-1900* Oxford 1977

GIROUARD, MARK *The Victorian Country House*, New Haven and London 1979

GRAFF, C. 'Der anglo-Japanische Stil des 19. Jahrhunderts' *Österreichische Monatsschrift für den Orient*, XI, no. 2, 1885, pp.39-41

GRAUL, RICHARD *Ostasiatische Kunst und ihr Einflu auf Europa* Leipzig 1906

GRAY, BASIL letter to the editor *Burlington Magazine*, CVII, June 1965, p. 324

GREENHALGH, PAUL *Ephemeral Vistas: The Expositions Universelles, Great Exhibitions and World's Fairs, 1851-1939* Manchester 1988

GREEN, RICHARD *Albert Moore and his Contemporaries* exh. cat., Laing Art Gallery Newcastle upon Tyne 1972

GREEN, RICHARD *The Moore Family Pictures* exh. cat., York City Art Gallery 1980

GRIEVE, ALASTAIR 'Whistler and the Pre-Raphaelites' *Art Quarterly*, XXXIV, no. 2 Summer 1971, pp.219-228

GRIEVE, ALASTAIR *The Art of Dante Gabriel Rossetti* Norwich 1973-78

GRIEVE, ALASTAIR 'Whistler - The Heroism of his Modern Life, the Perfection of his Incompletion' *Art History* June 1981 pp.223

HAGA TORU *Taikun no shisetsu (The Envoy of the Taikun)* Tokyo 1968

HAGA TORU 'The Diplomatic Background of Japonisme: The Case of Sir Rutherford Alcock', in Yamada 1980, pp.27-42

HAGA TORU *Midaremgami no keifu (The Midaregami Motif and its Development)* Tokyo 1981

HAGA TORU *Kaiga no Ryobun (The Territory of Painting)* Tokyo 1984

HALÉN, WIDAR 'Christopher Dresser and Japan Observed' *Report of the Society for the Study of Japonisme*, no.4, 1984, pp.11-26

HALÉN, WIDAR *Christopher Dresser* Oxford 1990

HAMILTON, WALTER *The Aesthetic Movement in England* London 1882

HARBRON, DUDLEY *The Conscious Stone, The Life of Edward William Godwin* London 1949

HARBRON, DUDLEY 'Queen Anne Taste and Aestheticism' *Architectural Review* July 1943 pp.15-18

HARTLEY, KEITH *Scottish Art since 1900* exh. cat., National Galleries of Scotland Edinburgh and London 1989-1990

HASHIYAMA, T. *Bakumatsu Meiji Bunmei Kaika (Enlightment in the late-Edo and Meiji Period)*, Nagoya 1983

HAWKS, FRANCIS L. *Narrative of the Expedition of an American Squadron to the China Seas and Japan, Performed in the Years 1852, 1853 and 1854 under the command of Commodore M.C. Perry, United States Navy by order of the Government of the United States* Washington D.C. 1856

HEINE, WILLIAM *Graphic Scenes of the Japan Expedition* New York 1856

HICKMANN, B, (ed.) *Japanese Crafts: Materials and their Applications* London 1977

HILLIER, JACK 'The Western Taste for Japanese Prints' *Storia dell'arte*, no. 27, 1976 pp.113-120

HOLME, CHARLES *The Influence of Japanese Art on English Design* Warrington 1890

HOLME, CHARLES 'The Use of Japanese Art to Europe' *Burlington Magazine*, VIII October 1905, pp.3-10

HOLZHAUSEN, WALTER *Lackhunst in Europa* Braunschwieg 1959

HONOUR, HUGH *Chinoiserie, The Vision of Cathay* London 1961

HORNEL, E.A., *Japan* Castle-Douglas 1895

HOSLEY, WILLIAM *The Japan Idea: Art and Life in Victorian America* exh.cat., Wadsworth Atheneum, Hartford, Connecticut 1990

HOWARTH, THOMAS *Charles Rennie Mackintosh* London 1952

HUNTER, JANET E. *The Emergence of Modern Japan. An Introductory History since 1853* London and New York 1989

HUGHES, G. BERNARD 'English Cloisonné Enamels' *Country Life* 29 August 1959 pp.382-383

HUISH, MARCUS B. 'England's Appreciation of Japanese Art', *Transactions and Proceedings of the Japan Society*, vol. 7, 1906, pp.120-139

HUISH, MARCUS B. *Japan and its Art* London 1889; 3rd ed. 1912

IIJIMA, KYOSHIN *Kawanabe Kyosai o den (The Life of Kawanabe Kyosai)*, Tokyo 1984

IKEGAMI CHUJI '"Nihon shumi" kenkyu no tameni' (Towards the study of 'Japonaiserie'), in Taichiro Kobayahsi *Hokusai to Doga (Hokusai and Degas)*, Kyoto 1974, pp.392-409

IKEGAMI CHUJI 'Jemuzu Tiso no Nihonshumi' (James Tissot's Japonisme) appendix to *Ukiyo-e Shuka*, vol. 10, Tokyo 1979, pp.1-8

IKEGAMI CHUJI 'James Tissot: "Drawing Instructor" of Tokugawa Akitake' in Yamada 1980, pp.147-155

IKEGAMI CHUJI 'Jemusu Tiso no "Tokugawa Akitake zo"' ('Le Portrait du Prince japonais Akitake Tokugawa par James Tissot) *Bijutsushi. Journal of the Art History Society*, November 1980, pp.53-55

IKEGAMI CHUJI 'Bakumatsu nihon e no ryokoki' (Accounts of Travel of Late Edo Period Japan) *Yamato Bunka*, 69, September 1981, pp.15-22

IKEGAMI CHUJI 'D. G. Rossetti and Japanese Music' *Burlington Magazine*, CXXVI, no. 980, Nov. 1984, p. 699

The Illustrated Record and Descriptive Catalogue of the Dublin International Exhibition of 1865 Dublin 1866

IMPEY, OLIVER *Chinoiserie* London 1977

IMPEY, OLIVER 'Japanese Export Lacquer of the 17th Century' *Lacquerwork in Asia and Beyond*, ed. William Watson, Colloquies on Art and Archeology in Asia, University of London, Percival David Foundation of Chinese Art, School of Oriental and African Studies, London 1982, pp.124-158

In Pursuit of Beauty, Americans and the Aesthetic Movement The Metropolitan Museum of Art, New York, 1986

IONIDES, LUKE 'Memories I, Whistler in the Quartier Latin' *Transatlantic Review*, 1924, pp.37-52

IROKAWA DAIKICHI *The Culture of the Meiji period* Princeton, N.J. 1985

IRWIN, DAVID AND FRANCINE *Scottish Painters at Home and Abroad 1700-1900* London 1975

ISHIDA JUNICHIRO *Burujowaji no Soshoku (The Decoration of the Bourgeoisie)* vol.7 of Nihon no kenchiku: Meiji Taishō shôwa (West Meets East: The Japanese Introduction to Western Architecure in 19th and 20th Centuries), Tokyo 1979

JANSEN, MARIUS B. AND GILBERT ROZMAN *Japan in Transition from Tokugawa to Meiji* Princeton, N.J. 1986

Japanese Aesthetics and Sense of Space: Another Aspect of Modern Japanese Design exh. cat., Sezon Museum of Art, Tokyo 1990 (In Japanese with essays in English)

'Japanese Exhibition' *Illustrated London News*, 4 February 1854, pp.97-98

Japonisme: Japanese reflections in Western art Northern Centre for Contemporary Art Sunderland 1986

Le Japonisme Galeries nationales du Grand Palais, Paris 1988; Japanese version: *Japonisumu ('Japonisme')*, The National Museum of Western Art, Tokyo 1988

Japonisumu to Aru Nubo ('Japonismus und Art Nouveau') exh. cat., Hyogo Museum of Modern Art, Kobe 1981

JARVES, JAMES JACKSON *A Glimpse at the Art of Japan* New York 1875

JERVIS, SIMON *High Victorian Design* exh. cat., National Gallery of Canada, 1974

JERVIS, SIMON *The Penguin Dictionary of Design and Designers* Harmondsworth 1984

JOHNSON, DEBORAH 'Japanese prints in Europe before 1840' *Burlington Magazine*, CXXIV, no, 951, June 1982, pp.342-348

KEMPFER, ENGLEBERT *The History of Japan* transl. J. G. Scheuchzer, London 1727

Kaiga no Aru Nubo, Yoroppa to Nihon Ten ('Art Nouveau in Painting, Europe and Japan') exh. cat., Kokuritsu Kokusai Bijutsukan, Osaka 1980

KANAI MADOKA (ED. TRANSL..) *Egakareta Bakumatsu Meiji (Late Tokugawa and Meiji Japan Depicted)* Tokyo 1973

KANAI MADOKA *Edo seiyo jijo (Things Occidental of the Edo Period)* Tokyo 1988

KANDA TAKAO '"Nihon shumi" no tansho to kore ni taisuru nihon no hanno', ('"Japonisme" and its influence in Japan') *Hikaku Bunka Kenkyu (Comparative Studies of Culture)*, 3, Tokyo University, 1962, pp.63-83

KAWAHIGASHI YOSHIYUKI (ED.) *Josaia Kondoru kenchiku zumenshu (Architectural drawings by Josiah Conder)* 3 vols., Tokyo 1980-1981

KAWAKITA MICHIAKI *Aoki Shigeru* Tokyo 1972

KAWAMURA JOICHIRO 'Igirisu no naka no Nippon-Biazurii no <Japonesuku>' (Japan and Britain - Beardsley's "Japonesque") *Hitotsubashi Ronso*, 94, no. 6, December 1985 pp.38-63

KEENE, DONALD *Zoku hyakudai no kakaku (Japanese diaries through the ages)* 2 vols., Tokyo 1988

KENNEDY, EDWARD G. *The Etched Work of Whistler* New York 1910, (new ed. San Francisco 1978)

Kindai Nihon Bijutsu Jiten (Encyclopaedia of Modern Japanese Art) Tokyo 1989

KISHI KASHIRO *Ikeda Chikugonokami Nagaoki to Pari (Ikeda Nagaoki, the Lord of Chikugo and Paris)* Nihonjin no kokusai rikai shiriizu VI (The International Understanding of the Japanese series VI), Okayama Yunesuko kyokai (Okayama UNESCO Society), Okayama 1975

KREINER, JOSEF (ED.) *Japan-Sammlungen in Museen Mitteleuropas. Geschichte Aufbau und gegenwartige Probleme, Bonner Zeitschrift fur Japanologie* vol. 3, Bonn 1981

KUMAMOTO KENJIRO *Fijishima Takeji* Tokyo 1967

KURATA YOSHIHIRO *1885nen Rondon Nihonjin mura (A Japanese village in London in 1885)* Tokyo 1983

Kurihara Chuji Ten (Kurihara Chuji Exhibition) exh. cat., Hamamatsu City Museum of Art Hamamatsu 1979

Kurihara Chuji Ten (Kurihara Chuji Exhibition) exh. cat., Shizuoka Prefectural Museum of Art, Shizuoka 1991

LACH, DONALD F. *Asia in the Making of Europe*, vol. 1; *The Century of Discovery*, 2 books, Chicago and London 1965: vol. II; *A Century of Wonder*; book 1; *The Visual Arts*, Chicago; book 2; *The Literary Arts*, Chicago and London 1977; book 3; *The Scholarly Disciplines*, Chicago and London 1977

LAMBOURNE, LIONEL AND OTHERS *Solomon. A Family of Painters* exh. cat., Geffrye Museum, London 1985-86

LANCASTER, CLAY 'Oriental Contributions to Art Nouveau' *Art Bulletin*, XXXIV, 1952, pp.297-310

LASDEN, SUSAN *Victorian Houses* London 1981

LAUGHTON, BRUCE *Philip Wilson Steer 1860-1942* Oxford 1971

LEHMANN, JEAN-PIERRE *The Image of Japan: From Feudal Isolation to World Power 1850-1905* London 1978

LEIGHTON, JOHN *On Japanese Art* London 1863

LEIGHTON, JOHN 'On Japanese Art' *Journal of the Society of Arts*, 24 July 1863, pp.596-599

LEVER, JILL *Architect's Designs for Furniture* London 1982

LEVY, MERVYN *Liberty Style, The Classic Years: 1898-1910* London 1986

Liberty's 1875-1975 exh. cat., Victoria and Albert Museum, London 1975

LOCHNAN, KATHARINE A. *The Etchings of James McNeill Whistler* New Haven and London 1984

LOWRY, JOHN 'The Rise of the Japanese Vogue' *Country Life*, 10 April 1958, pp.752-753

McCONKEY, KENNETH *Edwardian Portraits. Images of an Age of Opulence* Woodbridge 1987

McCONKEY, KENNETH *British Impressionism* Oxford 1989

MacDONALD, MARGARET F. *Whistler. The Graphic Work: Amsterdam, Liverpool, London, Venice* exh. cat., Thos. Agnew & Sons, London 1976

MacDonald, Margaret F. 'Whistler's Design for a Catalogue of Blue and White Nankin Porcelain' *The Connoisseur*, August 1978, pp.290-295

Mackenzie, William *The Record of the International Exhibition, 1862* Glasgow, Edinburgh and London 1862

Macready, Sarah and F. H. Thompson *Influences in Victorian Art and Architecture* Society of Antiquaries, London 1985

Madsen, Stephen Tschudi *Sources of Art Nouveau* Oslo 1956

Makino Yoshio Ten (Makino Yoshio Exhibition) exh. cat., Toyota City Archives, Toyota 1990

Matsuki Bunkio (ed.) *Lotus. Special Holiday Number in Memoriam James A McNeill Whistler* Boston, December 1903

Matyjaszkiewicz, Krystyna *James Tissot* exh. cat., Barbican Art Gallery, London 1984-85

Matyjaszkiewicz, Krystyna and Michael Regan *Jemuzu Tiso ('James Tissot')* Isetan Museum of Art, Tokyo 1988

Meech-Pekarik, Julia *The World of the Meiji Print: Impressions of a New Civilization* New York and Tokyo 1986

Meech, Julia and Gabriel P. Weisberg *Japonisme Comes to America: The Japanese Impact on the Graphic Arts 1876-1925* exh. cat., The Jane Voorhees Zimmerli Art Museum, New Brunswick 1990

Meichin Roja, (Machin, Roger) *Edo jidai o mita Eikokujin (Britons who experienced the Edo Period)* Tokyo 1984

Meiji no Kyutei Gaka - Goseda Yoshimatsu (The Court Painter of the Meiji Period) exh. cat., Kanagawa Prefectural Museum, Yokohama 1986

Meiji no Soshoku Kogei (Decorative Crafts of the Meiji Period) Bessatsu Taiyo, no.70, Summer 1990

Menpes, Mortimer 'A Personal View of Japanese Art' and 'A Lesson from Khiosi' *The Magazine of Art*, April 1888, pp.255-261 pp.192-199

Menpes, Mortimer *Japan, A Record in Colour* London 1903

Menpes, Mortimer *Whistler as I knew him* London 1904

Michie, Alexander *The Englishman in China during the Victorian Era as Illustrated in the Career of Sir Rutherford Alcock* 2 vols. Edinburgh, 1900

Minami Kunzo Ten (Minami Kunzo Exhibition) Hiroshima Prefectural Art Museum, 1983

Minami Kunzo Shuga Sakuhin Ten (Exhibition of Studies by Minami Kunz>) Tokyo University of Fine Arts Museum, 1989

Miner, Earl *The Japanese Tradition in British and American Literature* Princeton 1958

Miura Atsushi 'Saron ni okeru Nihonshumi <Japonisumu> - 1850nen-1880nen no Pari no Saron ni happyo sareta Nippon o shudai to suru kaigasakuhin ni kansuru kenkyu' ('Le Japonisme au Salon: Etudes sur les oeuvres " sujets japonais dans les Salons de 1850 " 1880') *Bijutsushi-Ronso (Studies in Art History)*, Department of Art History, Faculty of Letters, University of Tokyo, no.4, 1988, pp.57-93 (with a French summary.)

Miwa Hideo *Hyakutake Kaneyuki* Tokyo 1978

Miwa Hideo 'Kaneyuki Hyakutake and His Work "Pietro Micca" *The Bijutsu Kenkyu, The Journal of Art Studies*, no.342, March 1988, pp.16-24 (in Japanese with an English summary)

Miyanaga Takashi *Bunkyu 2 nen no Yoroppa hokoku (A Report on Europe from the Year 1862)* Tokyo 1989

Miyaoka Kenji *Ikoku henro tabigeinin shimatsusho (An Account of Itinerant Entertainers in Foreign Countries)* Tokyo 1959; second ed. 1971; paper-back ed. 1978

Miyauchi Satoshi 'Dainikai Rondon Kokusaihakurankai to Nippon no shuppin-butsu ni tsuite' (The Second International Exhibition in London and the Japanese Exhibits) *Kyushu geijutsu koka daigaku kenkyuronshu (Journal of Kyushu Institute of Design)* no. 4, May 1979, pp.41-108

Montanus, Arnoldus *Atlas Japanensis* transl. John Ogilby, London 1670

Morris, Barbara *Liberty Design 1874-1914* London 1989

Morris, William 'Textiles' *Arts and Crafts Essays*, London 1893, pp.22-38

Muto Chozo *A Short History of Anglo-Japanese Relations* Tokyo 1936; new ed. 1977

Nagata Seiji 'Bakumatsu no senkaku Homma Hokuyo ni tsuite' (A Pioneer of the Late Edo Period. On Hokyo Homma) *Nihon Bijutsu Kogei (Japanese Arts and Crafts)* no. 514, July 1981, pp.15-20

Nakagawa Sensaku *Meiji no kogei (Applied Art of the Meiji Period)* Tokyo 1969

Nakamaru Seijiro to sono Jidai (Nakamaru Seijuro and his Time) Yamanashi Prefectural Museum of Art, Kofu 1988

Nakamura Giichi *Kindai Nihon bijutsu no sokumen. Meiji yoga to Igirisu bijutsu (An Aspect of Modern Japanese Art. Meiji Western Style Painting and English Art)* Tokyo 1976

Newall, Christopher *The Art of Lord Leighton* Oxford 1990

Nihon no posutashi ten (Exhibition of the history of Japanese poster) exh. cat., World Poster Museum, Nagoya 1989

1908/09 Rondon no Seishun: Zengo 1990 (Youth in London: around 1908/09) exh. cat. Fukuyama Museum, Fukuyama 1990

Nish, Ian H. *Anglo-Japanese Alliance* London 1966

Numata Jiro (ed.) *Nihon to seiyo* (Japan and the West) *Tozaibunmei no koryu (Exchange of Civilisation between East and West)* vol. 6, Tokyo 1971

The Old Matsukata Collection exh. cat., Kobe City Museum, Kobe 1989

Oliphant, Laurence *Narrative of the Earl of Elgin's Mission to China and Japan in the years, 1857, '58* 2 vols., Edinburgh and London 1859

O'Looney, Betty *Frederick Sandys 1829-1904* exh. cat., Brighton Museum and Art Gallery, Brighton 1974

One Hundred Masterpieces of Glass Work Suntory Museum of Art, Tokyo 1989 (In Japanese with a list of plates in English)

Onogi Shigekatsu *Yoshiki no Ishizue (The Foundation of style)* vol.2 of *Nihon no kenchiku: Meiji Taisho Showa (West Meets East: The Japanese Introduction to Western Architecture in 19th and 20th Centuries)* Tokyo 1979

Ormond, Richard and Leonée *Lord Leighton* New Haven and London 1975

Orpen, William (ed.) *The Outline of Art* London n.d.

Osborn, Sherard *A Cruise in Japanese Waters* Edinburgh and London 1859

Osborn, Sherard *Japanese Fragments* London 1861

Oshima Seiji *Japonisme* Tokyo 1980 (in Japanese)

Ozawa et al. *Shashin de miru Bakumatsu-Meiji (The Late Edo and Meiji Period in Photographs)*, Tokyo 1990

Pantzer, Peter 'Sadayakko. Eine Japanische Diva auf Tournee durch Österreich' *Die Japanerin in Vergangenheit und Genenwart*, vol. 17, Beitrage zur Japanologie, Vienna 1981, pp.61-91

Paris Autour De 1882: Le Développement de la peinture moderne en France et Hôsui Yamamoto exh. cat., Gifu Prefectural Museum, Gifu 1982 (In Japanese with two essays in French)

Pennell, Elizabeth and Joseph *The Life of James McNeill Whistler* 2 vols., London and Philadelphia 1908

Pevsner, Nikolaus 'Art Furniture of the 1870s' *Architectural Review*, CXI, 1952, pp.43-50

Pevsner, Nikolaus *Studies in Art, Architecture and Design,Victorian and After* London 1968

Philips, Elizabeth 'A Pagoda in Knightsbridge' *Journal of Pre-Raphaelite Studies*, IV, no. 2, May 1984, pp.37-42

Philips, George *Rudiments of Curvilinear Design*, London 1838-40

Pullan, R.P. *The Designers of William Burges* London 1885

Quam Dilecta 'Japanese Decoration Versus "The Flat Geometric"' *The Builder* 7 November 1863, pp.798-799

Reade, Brian *Aubrey Beardsley* rev. ed., London 1987

Reidemeister, Leopold *Der Japonismus in der Malerei und Graphik des 19. Jahrhunderts* exh. cat., Haus am Waldsee, Berlin 1965

Reports by the Juries, International Exhibition 1862 London 1863

Reynolds, Simon *The Vision of Simeon Solomon* Stroud, Glos., 1985

Robertson, Alexander *Atkinson Grimshaw* Oxford 1988

Rokumeikan no Yume: Kenchikuka Kondoru to eshi Kyôsai, (The Dream of Rokumeikan: The architect, Conder, and the painter, Kyôsai) Inax Booklet, vol.10, no.3 [misprinted as no.2 on back cover and colophon], Tokyo 1991

Rosetti Ten (Rossetti Exhibition) exh. cat., Bunkamura Museum of Art, Tokyo 1990-91

Roskill, Mark *Van Gogh, Gaugin and the Impressionist Circle* London 1970

Rossetti, W.M. 'The Fine Art of the International Exhibition' *Fraser's Magazine* LXVI, August 1862, pp.188-199

Rossetti, W.M. 'Japanese Woodcuts. An Illustrated Story-Book brought from Japan' *The Reader*, II, 31 October, pp.501-503; 7 November, pp.536-538, 1863

Rossetti, W.M. *Fine Art, Chiefly Contemporary* London and Cambridge 1867

Sadoya Shigenobu *Soseki to Sekimatsu Bijutsu (Soseki and the fin de siècle Art)* Tokyo 1982

Said, Edward W. *Orientalism* London 1978

Sakai Tadayasu *Umino Kusari: Egakareta Ishin (Sea Chain: Restoration Depicted)* Tokyo 1977

Sakamoto Kazumichi, Sato Ichiro, Utada Shinsuke, Miyata Junichi and Fukuda Yoshiki *Meiji Zenki Aburae Kiso Shiryoshu (Compilation of Basic Documents of Early Meiji Oil Paintings)* Tokyo 1991

Sakamoto Mitsuru 'Ishikawa Moko hitsu "Shojo aibyo zu" no genga "Misu Torinma"' ('Miss Trimmer', the original model for Ishikawa Moko's 'A Girl Cuddling a Cat') *Bijutsu Kenkyu, The Journal of Art Studies* no. 282, 1972, pp.26-8

Sandberg, John '"Japonisme" and Whistler' *Burlington Magazine*, CVI, November 1964, pp.500-507

Sandberg, John 'The Discovery of Japanese Prints in the Nineteenth Century before 1867' *Gazette des Beaux-Arts*, June 1968, pp.295-302

Sansom, G.B. *The Western World and Japan* London 1950

Sargent, Pauline *Burges* 2 parts, exh. cat., Cardiff Castle, 1977

Saris, John *The Voyage of John Saris to Japan, 1613* ed. Sir E.M. Satow, London 1900

Satow, Sir Ernest *A Diplomat in Japan* London 1921

Sawyer, Carles H. *The Theodore T. and Mary G. Ellis Collection, III: American Paintings' *Worcester Art Museum Annual*, Worcester, Mass., IV, 1941, pp.42-8

Schmutzler, Robert 'English Origins of Art Nouveau' *Architectural Review*, 1955, pp.110-115

Schmutzler, Robert *Art Nouveau-Jugendstil* Stuttgart 1962; English ed. 1978

Segi Shinichi *Nihonbijutsu no ryusutsu ('Out Flow of Japanese Art')* Tokyo 1985

Sickert, Bernard *Whistler* London and New York 1908

Shigeru Aoki and the Late Victorian Art exh. cat., Ishibashi Museum of Art, Kurume 1983 (in Japanese. Essays and listing also in English)

Shimomura Hidetoki *Shimomura Kanzan Den* Tokyo 1981

The Silk Road on the Sea exh. cat., The Kobe City Museum, Kobe 1982

Silver, J.M.W. *Sketches of Japanese Manners and Customs* London 1867

Smith, Greg and Sarah Hyde *Walter Crane 1845-1915. Artist, Designer and Socialist* exh. cat., The Whitworth Art Gallery, University of Manchester, London 1989

Spalding, Frances *Whistler* Oxford 1979

Spalding, Frances *British Art Since 1900* London 1986

SPENCER, CHARLES, (ED.) *The Aesthetic Movement (1869-1880)* exh. cat., Camden Arts Centre, London 1973

SPENCER, ISOBEL *Walter Crane* London 1975

SPENCER, ROBIN *The Aesthetic Movement: Theory and Practice* London 1972

SPENCER, ROBIN 'Whistler and Japan: Work in Progress' in Yamada 1980, pp.57-81

SPENCER, ROBIN (ED) *Whistler: A retrospective* New York 1989

STALEY, ALLEN (ED.) *From Realism to Symbolism. Whistler and His World* exh. cat., Philadelphia Museum of Art 1971

STALEY, ALLEN *High Victorian Renaissance* exh. cat., City Art Gallery, Manchester 1978

STALKER, JOHN AND GEORGE PARKER *A Treatise of Japaning and Varnishing* London and Oxford 1688; reprint London 1971

STEWART, DAVID B. *The Making of a Modern Japanese Architecture: 1868 to the Present* Tokyo and New York 1987

SULLIVAN, MICHAEL *The Meeting of Eastern and Western Art* London 1973

SURTEES, VIRGINIA *The Paintings and Drawings of Dante Gabriel Rossetti (1828-1882). A Catalogue Raisonné* Oxford 1971

SURTEES, VIRGINIA, (ED.) *The Diaries of George Price Boyce* Norwich 1980

SUTTON, DENYS *Nocturne: The Art of James McNeill Whistler* London 1963

SUZUKI HIOYUKI *Vikutorian Goshikku hokai no kenyu (A Study of the Disintegration of Victorian Gothic)* Doctoral thesis, n.p., Tokyo University 1984

SWANSON, VERN G. *The Biography and Catalogue Raisonné of the Paintings of Sir Lawrence Alma-Tadema, OM, RA* London 1990

SWINBURNE, ALGERNON C. *Poems and Ballads* London 1866

Takashima Hokkai Gashu (Paintings by Takashima Hokkai) Tokyo 1976

Takashima Hokkai Ten (Exhibition of Takashima Hokkai) Shimonoseki City Museum, Shimonoseki, 1986

TAKASHINA SHUJI *Nihon Kindai Bijutsushiron (Essays on the History of Early Modern Art in Japan)* Tokyo 1980

TAKASHINA SHUJI AND J.THOMAS RIMER WITH GERALD D. BOLAS (EDS.) *Japan in Paris: The Japanese Encounter with European Painting* exh. cat., Washington University Gallery of Art, St.Louis, Missouri 1987

Takeda Goichi: Hito to Sakuhin (Takeda Goichi: The Man and the Works) Hakubutsukan Meijimura (Meiji Village Museum) Inuyama 1987

TAKUMI HIDEO *Kindai Nihon no Bijutsu to Bungaku - Meiji Taisho Showa no Sashie (Art and Literature in Modern Japan - The Illustration of Meiji, Taisho and Showa Period)* Tokyo 1979

TANAKA HISAO *Takeuchi Seiho* Tokyo 1988

TANITA HIROYUKI 'D.G. Rosetti to Vikutoriacho no bukku dezain' (D.G. Rossetti and Victorian Book Design) *Gareria tsushin (Nouvelles de l'Estampe)* no. 22, April 1985, pp.10-17

TANITA HIROYUKI '"W.M. Rossetti's "Hokxai" (Hokusai)' *The Journal of Pre-Raphaelite Studies* November 1985, pp.89-91.

TANITA HIROYUKI 'Eikoku ni okeru <Nihonshumi - Japanisumu> no keisei ni kansuru joron, 1851-1862' (Prolegomena to the Formation of <Japanism> in Britain, 1851-1862) *Hikaku bungaku nenshi (Year Book of Comparative Literature)*, no.22, March 1986, pp.88-117

TANITA HIROYUKI 'Kodai Girishi ti Nippon - Eikoku no <Nihonshumi - Japanisumu> no ichikyokumen' (Classical Greece and Japan - An Aspect of British <Japanism>) *Sansai*, II, no. 494, 1988, pp.40-46

TANITA HIROYUKI 'Rossetti to Satsumahan Ryugakusei to - W.M. Rosetti ate no G.P. Boyce mikan shokan ittsu o megutte - (Rossetti and Two Japanese Students from Satsuma - An unpublished letter of G.P. Boyce to W.M. Rossetti) *Bijutsushi Kenkyu (Art History Studies)* December 1989 pp.69-85

TANITA HIROYUKI 'Venetsia no Bokka aruiwa Juyongen no Koto - Rosetti no The Blue Bower (1865) o megutte' (The Idyll of Venice or the 14 stringed Koto - on The Blue Bower (1865) by Rossetti) in *Rosetti Ten*, 1990-91, pp.40-46

TAN'O, YASUNORI 'Hara Busho no "Chandosu Potoreto"' ('Chandos Portrait' by Hara Busho) *Institute of Painting Technology Technical Bulletin* vol.4, (Tokyo), 1984, 12-17

TAN'O, YASUNORI '"Shisuru Gurobu wa mada kimi o matteiru..."': Koritsuseru seito - Hara Busho den' ("Thistle Grove is still waiting for you...": The Isolated Orthodoxy - The Life of Hara Busho) *E*, no.280, June, pp.20-23,-July, pp.12-15, August, pp.16-19, September, pp.16-19, October, pp.19-21, 1987.

TAYLOR, HILARY *James McNeill Whistler* London 1978

THORNTON, PETER 'John Jones, Collector of French Furniture' *Apollo*, March 1972, pp.8-21

THUNBERG, CARL PETER *Voyages au Japon* Paris 1796

TITSINGH, ISAAC *Illustrations of Japan* London 1822

TOMITA HITOSHI *Rokumeikan - Giseiyoka no sekai (The Deer Cry Pavilion - The world of pseudo-westernisation)* Tokyo 1984

Tozai bijutsu koryu ten (Mutual Influences between Japanese and Western Arts) exh. cat., The National Museum of Modern Art Tokyo 1968

TSUCHIYA YOSHIO *Satsuma Kiriko (Satsuma Cut Glass)* Tokyo 1983

TSUNEMATSU, SAMMY I (ED.) *Yoshio Markino: A Japanese Artist in London* London 1990 (in Japanese and English)

TSURUZONO SHIKIKO 'Kageki "Okikusan" o megutte - Japonisumu to gekijo ongaku' (On the Opera "Okikusan" - Japonisume and Theatre Music) *Report on the Society for the Study of Japonisme* no. 5, 1985, pp.28-39

TURNER, MARK ET AL. *A London Design Studio 1880-1963: The Silver Studio Collection* exh. cat., The Middlesex Polytechnic 1980

TURNER, MARK AND LESLEY HOSKINS *Silver Studio of Design. A Design and Source Book for Home Decoration* Exeter 1988

UNNO HIROSHI *Nihon no Aru Nuvo (Japanese Art Nouveau)* Tokyo 1978

Victorian High Renaissance exh. cat., Minneapolis Institute of Arts, 1978

WAKEFIELD, HUGH 'Der Einflu des Fernen Ostens auf die Keramik Englands' *Weltkulturen und Moderne Kunst*, ed. Siegfried Wichmann, exh. cat., Haus der Kunst, Munich 1972, pp.334-335

WALTON, KARIN 'Furniture designed by E.W. Godwin from the collections of the City Art Gallery, Bristol' *Furniture by Godwin and Breuer*, exh. cat. Bristol City Art Gallery, 1976

WARING, J.B. (ED.) *Masterpieces of Industrial Art and Sculpture at the International Exhibition 1862* 3 vols., London 1863

WATANABE TOSHIO 'Namban Lacquer Shrines : Some New Discoveries' *Lacquer work in Asia and Beyond*, ed. William Watson, Colloquies on Art and Archaeology in Asia, no. 11, University of London, Percival David Foundation of Chinese Art, School of Oriental and African Studies, London 1982, pp.194-210

WATANABE TOSHIO 'The Western Image of Japanese Art in the Late Edo Period' *Modern Asian Studies*, 18, no. 4, October 1984 pp.667-684

WATANABE TOSHIO 'Letter to the Editor' *The Journal of the Pre-Raphaelite Studies* November 1986, p.115

WATANABE TOSHIO 'Eishi Prints in Whistler's Studio? Eighteenth-Century Japanese prints in the West before 1870' *Burlington Magazine*, CXXVIII, no. 1005 December 1986, pp.873-880

WATANABE TOSHIO 'Whistler and Japan' *The Japan Society Proceedings*, 117, Spring 1991, pp.18-28

WATANABE TOSHIO *High Victorian Japonisme* Swiss Asian Studies, Research Studies vol.10 Bern 1991

WATT, WILLIAM *Art Furniture, from Designs by E.W.Godwin, F.S.A., and others* London 1877

WAY, THOMAS R. *Mr. Whistler's Lithographs* London 1896; 2nd ed. 1905

WEISBERG, GABRIEL P., PHILIPP DENNIS CATE, GERALD NEEDHAM, MARTIN EIDELBERG & WILLIAM R. JOHNSTON *Japonisme, Japanese Influence on French Art 1854-1910* exh. cat., Cleveland Museum of Art, Cleveland, Ohio 1975

WEISBERG, GABRIEL P. *Art Nouveau Bing. Paris Style 1900* New York 1986

WEISBERG, GABRIEL P. AND YVONNE M.L. WEISBERG *Japonisme. An Annotated Bibliography* New York and London 1990

WENTWORTH, MICHAEL 'Tissot and Japonisme' in Yamada 1980, pp.127-146

WENTWORTH, MICHAEL *James Tissot* Oxford 1984

WILKINSON, NANCY BURCH 'Edward William Godwin and Japonisme in England' Ph.D. University of California, Los Angeles Ann Arbor, MI, 1987

WHISTLER, J.M. *The Gentle Art of Making Enemies* London 1890, reprinted New York 1967

WHITFORD, FRANK *Japanese Prints and Western Painters* London 1977

WICHMANN, SIEGFRIED, (ED.) *Weltkulturen und moderne kunst* exh. cat., Haus der Kunst, Munich 1972 (the English edition - also 1972 - includes revisions)

WICHMANN, SIEGFRIED *Japonismus. Ostasien-Europa. Begegnungen in der Kunst des 19. und 20. Jahrhunderts* Herrsching 1980, English edition, London and New York 1981

WILLIAMSON, G.C. *Murray Marks and His Friends* London and New York 1919

WILSON, SIMON *Beardsley* rev. ed. Oxford 1983

WOOD, CHRISTOPHER *The Dictionary of Victorian Painters* 2nd ed., London 1978

WORSWICK, CLARK *Japan. Photographs 1854-1905* London 1980

YAMADA CHISABURO *Ukiyo-e to Inshoha (Ukiyo-e and the Impressionists)* Tokyo 1973

YAMADA CHISABURO, F. (ED.) *Dialogue in Art. Japan and the West* London, Paris and Tokyo 1976

YAMADA CHISABURO, F. (ED.) *Japonisme in Art. An International Symposium* Tokyo 1980

YOKOHAMA KAIKO SHIRYOKAN (Yokohama Archives of History)(ed.) *F. Beato Bakumatsu Nihon Shashinshu (Photographs of the Late Edo Period Japan by F. Beato)* Yokohama 1987. Also published in hardback as *Bakumatsu Nihon no Fukei to Hitobito: Ferikkusu Beato Shashinshu (The Landscape and People of the Late Edo Period: The Photographs of Felix Beato)*, Tokyo 1987

YOKOTA YOICHI (ED.) *Yokohama Ukiyoe* Yokohama 1989

YOKOYAMA TOSHIO *Japan in the Victorian Mind: A study of stereotyped images of a nation, 1850-80* Basingstoke and London 1987

YONEMURA, ANN *Yokohama: Prints from Nineteenth-Century Japan* exh. cat., Arthur M. Sackler Gallery, Washington, D.C. 1990

YOSHIDA MITSUKUNI *Bankoku Hakurankai (International Exhibitions)*, Tokyo 1970 (rev. ed. 1985)

YOSHIDA MITSUKUNI *Ryoyo no me. Bakumatsu Meiji no bunka sesshoky (Mutual Vision of East and West. Cultural Contacts during the Last Days of the Tokygawa Shogunate and the Meiji Period)* Tokyo 1970

YOSHIDA MITSUKUNI, (ED.) *Zusetsu Bankoku Hakurankaishi 1851- 1942 (The Illustrated History of International Exhibitions 1851-1942)* Kyoto 1985

YOSHIDA MITSUKUNI (ED.) *Bankoku Hakurankai no kenkyu (The Study of International Exhibitions)* Kyoto 1986

YOSHIKAWA SEIICHI & MIZUNO SHINTARO (EDS.) *The Tokyo Station and Kingo Tatsuno* exh. cat., Tokyo Station Gallery, Tokyo 1990 (in Japanese, partly with English translations)

YOUNG, ANDREW MCLAREN *James McNeill Whistler* exh. cat., Arts Council of Great Britain, London and the English-Speaking Union of the United States New York 1960

YOUNG, ANDREW MCLAREN *Glasgow University's Pictures* exh. cat., P & D. Colnaghi & Co. Ltd., London 1973

YOUNG, ANDREW MCLAREN, MARGARET MACDONALD, ROBIN SPENCER AND HAMISH MILES *The Paintings James McNeill Whistler* 2 vols., New Haven and London 1980

ZATLIN, LINDA GERTNER *Aubrey Beardsley and Victorian Sexual Politics* Oxford 1990

LIST OF ARTISTS

LIST OF LENDERS

FRANCE

MUSEE BARON MARTIN, GRAY 87

MUSEE DES BEAUX-ARTS, NANTES 88

GERMANY

PETER PANTZER, BONN 288, 352

JAPAN

BANK OF JAPAN, TOKYO 121

CHIBA PREFECTURAL MUSEUM OF ART 333

HIROSHIMA PREFECTURAL MUSEUM OF ART 251

HYOGO PREFECTURAL MUSEUM OF ART 360

ICHIMURA KANAME, TOKYO 372

IMPERIAL COLLECTION, TOKYO 248

ISHIBASHI MUSEUM OF ART, KURUME 323, 326

JAPAN FOLK CRAFTS MUSEUM, TOKYO 387, 389, 394, 395, 396, 397, 398

GALLERY ART KAMIGATA, KYOTO 151, 152, 153, 154, 155, 156, 159, 160

KANAGAWA PREFECTURAL MUSEUM, YOKOHAMA 142, 227, 228, 236, 237, 238, 239, 240, 241, 242, 243, 244

KATAKURA COLLECTION, SHIROISHI 136

KAWANABE KYOSAI MEMORIAL MUSEUM 267, 268, 269, 270, 271

KAWASHIMA TEXTILES MUSEUM, KYOTO 356, 357

KOBE UNIVERSITY (DEPT. OF ARCHITECTURE) 342, 343, 344, 345, 346

KOJUN-SHA (KEIO UNIVERSITY), TOKYO 256

KONOIKE-GUMI COLLECTION, OSAKA 350

KORIYAMA CITY MUSEUM OF ART 247, 377

KOTOHIRA SHRINE MUSEUM 246

KYOTO UNIVERSITY (DEPT. OF ARCHITECTURE) 123, 124

KYOTO UNIVERSITY OF INDUSTRIAL ART AND TEXTILES 162

MASHIKO REFERENCE COLLECTION 400

MATSUKATA KIYOHIKO, TOKYO 378

MEGURO ART MUSEUM, TOKYO 376

MUSEUM OF MODERN JAPANESE LITERATURE, TOKYO 328, 329, 330, 331, 332

NABESHIMA HOKOKAI, SAGA 134, 135

NATIONAL MUSEUM OF MODERN ART, TOKYO 359, 375, 390, 391

NIIGATA PREFECTURAL MUSEUM OF ART 392

OHARA MUSEUM OF ART, KURASHIKI 402

OTANI MEMORIAL ART MUSEUM, NISHINOMIYA 252, 253, 254, 255

PAPER MUSEUM, TOKYO 165

PRIVATE COLLECTION 141, 245, 324, 325, 393, 405

SHIBAKAWA MATAHIKO, NISHINOMIYA 347, 348

SHIMANE PREFECTURAL MUSEUM 361

SOCIETY OF JAPANESE ARCHITECTS, TOKYO 132

SUGIURA TOKIKO 334, 335

SUNTORY MUSEUM OF ART, TOKYO 137, 138, 139, 140

SUNTORY WHISKY MUSEUM, YAMANASHI PREFECTURE 161

TOBACCO AND SALT MUSEUM, TOKYO 158

TAKASHIMAYA COLLECTION 358

TANAKA YASUE, KAGOSHIMA 370

TOCHIGI PREFECTURAL MUSEUM OF ART 226, 231

TOKYO NATIONAL MUSEUM 122, 259

TOKYO UNIVERSITY OF FINE ARTS 225, 235, 249, 250, 257

TOKYO UNIVERSITY LIBRARY 258

TOMIMOTO KENKICHI MEMORIAL MUSEUM, NARA PREFECTURE 403, 404

WASEDA UNIVERSITY THEATRE MUSEUM, TOKYO 338, 339, 340, 341

YAMAGUCHI EIICHI, YOKOHAMA 261

YAMATO BUNKAKAN MUSEUM, NARA 15, 16

YAYOI ART MUSEUM, TOKYO 336, 337

YOKOHAMA CITY ART MUSEUM 260, 276, 277, 278, 279

LIECHTENSTEIN

MARLBOROUGH INTERNATIONAL FINE ART 67

UNITED KINGDOM

VICTOR ARWAS, LONDON 174, 296, 311, 313, 314, 367, 368, 369

ASHMOLEAN MUSEUM, OXFORD 73, 78, 310, 355

BIRMINGHAM CITY MUSEUMS AND ART GALLERY 80

BLACKBURN MUSEUM AND ART GALLERY 89

BODLEIAN LIBRARY, OXFORD 25, 144, 157, 163, 164, 166, 320, 321, 386, 388

BRISTOL CITY MUSEUMS AND ART GALLERY 101

TRUSTEES OF THE BRITISH MUSEUM, LONDON 24, 27, 62, 72, 74, 76, 229, 230, 262, 302, 380, 381, 382

MR AND MRS BROUGHTON 265

BURGHLEY HOUSE STAMFORD 6, 7, 8, 12

BURRELL COLLECTION, GLASGOW 70

SYNDICS OF CAMBRIDGE UNIVERSITY LIBRARY 306

CHELSEA COLLEGE OF ART AND DESIGN LIBRARY 304

SIR HUGH AND LADY CORTAZZI 2, 3, 5, 23, 26, 28, 29, 30, 31

TOM CRAIG 107, 108, 109

JOHN CULME 212, 216, 217, 218, 221, 222, 223

CITY OF EDINBURGH ART CENTRE 94

LORD ELGIN 19, 20, 21, 22

DAVID ELLIOTT, OXFORD 297

SYNDICS OF THE FITZWILLIAM MUSEUM, CAMBRIDGE 307

GLASGOW ART GALLERY AND MUSEUM 282, 283, 285, 287, 291

GLASGOW SCHOOL OF ART 315, 316, 317, 318

GROSVENOR MUSEUM, CHESTER 82

GUILDHALL ART GALLERY (CORPORATION OF LONDON) 95

GUILDHALL LIBRARY (CORPORATION OF LONDON) 60, 219, 312, 351, 373, 374, 379

NICHOLAS HARRIS GALLERY, LONDON 168, 169, 175, 177, 178, 179, 180, 181, 182, 183, 191, 193

HASLAM AND WHITEWAY LTD., LONDON 170, 171, 172, 173, 176, 184, 187, 188

HORESH COLLECTION, LONDON 50, 52, 53, 54, 57, 58, 143, 146, 147, 148, 149, 185, 190, 192, 224

E. A. HORNEL TRUST, KIRKCUDBRIGHT 292

HUGH LANE MUNICIPAL GALLERY OF MODERN ART, DUBLIN 65, 84

HUNTERIAN ART GALLERY, UNIVERSITY OF GLASGOW 66, 71, 75, 77, 272, 284, 319, 384, 385

KEN AND JENNY JACOBSON 33, 34, 35, 36, 37, 38, 39, 40, 41, 42, 43, 44, 45, 46, 47, 48, 49, 51, 55, 56, 59

MRS C. A. JAMIESON, 145B, 145C

JAPAN SOCIETY, LONDON 1, 4, 17, 18

PETER JEFFS AT NICHOLAS HARRIS GALLERY, LONDON 186

BEN JOHN, LONDON 366

KIRKCALDY DISTRICT MUSEUMS AND ART GALLERY 364

UNIVERSITY OF LEEDS COLLECTION 383

LEICESTERSHIRE MUSEUM AND ART GALLERY 362

LIBERTY'S ARCHIVES 203, 205

LIVERPOOL LIBRARIES AND ARTS (HORNBY LIBRARY) 195, 196, 197, 198, 199

LONDON LIBRARY 61

ANDREW MCINTOSH PATRICK 92, 114, 115, 116, 167, 189, 201, 204, 275, 281, 289, 295

MIDDLESEX POLYTECHNIC (SILVER STUDIO COLLECTION), LONDON 206, 207, 208, 209, 210, 211

BARBARA MORRIS, BRIGHTON 202

MUSEUM OF LONDON 371

NATIONAL GALLERIES OF SCOTLAND, EDINBURGH 93, 290

NATIONAL TRUST (ELLEN TERRY MEMORIAL MUSEUM) 106

ROSEMARY NEWALL 280

PRIVATE COLLECTION 112, 113, 266, 274, 365

READING UNIVERSITY LIBRARY 299, 305

ROYAL ALBERT MEMORIAL MUSEUM, EXETER 309

ROYAL INSTITUTE OF BRITISH ARCHITECTS (BRITISH ARCHITECTURAL LIBRARY DRAWINGS COLLECTION), LONDON 98, 99, 100, 102, 110

COLLECTION OF THE LATE BRIAN READE 301

MRS VICTORIA SCARBOROUGH 81

SHEFFIELD UNIVERSITY LIBRARY 327

TRUSTEES OF THE TATE GALLERY, LONDON 64, 68, 69, 79, 96, 363

UNIVERSITY COLLEGE OF WALES, ABERYSTWYTH 83, 401

TRUSTEES OF THE VICTORIA AND ALBERT MUSEUM, LONDON 9, 10, 11, 13, 14, 97, 103, 104, 105, 111, 194, 200, 213, 214, 215, 220, 286, 308, 353, 354

MRS D. WALLIS 145A

TOSHIO WATANABE, OXFORD 322

EARL OF WEMYSS AND MARCH 90

WALKER ART GALLERY (TRUSTEES OF THE NATIONAL MUSEUMS AND GALLERIES ON MERSEYSIDE) 294

MICHAEL WHITEWAY 273

E. I. WIRGMAN, LONDON 232, 233, 234

WORSHIPFUL COMPANY OF MAKERS OF PLAYING CARDS, LONDON 150

YORK CITY ART GALLERY 85, 293, 399

UNITED STATES OF AMERICA

DOBRA COLLECTION, NEW YORK 86

FREER GALLERY OF ART, SMITHSONIAN INSTITUTION, WASHINGTON D.C. 263, 264

MANNEY COLLECTION, NEW YORK 91

METROPOLITAN MUSEUM OF ART, NEW YORK 32

PRINCETON UNIVERSITY LIBRARIES 298, 300, 303

WORCESTER ART MUSEUM, WORCESTER, MASSACHUSETTS 63

ACKNOWLEDGEMENTS

We are indebted to the following individuals for our research, selection of exhibits, as well as for compilation of the catalogue. Without their support, the exhibition and publication would have never been materealised. (TS/TW)

ABE NOBUO
PROFESSOR ADACHI YUJI
CHRISTOPHER ALLAN
VICTOR ARWAS
TABITHA BARBER
THOMASINA BECK
TERRY BENNETT
ROGER BILLCLIFFE
DR NICOLA GORDON BOWE
THE HON. JAMES BRUCE
WILLIAM BUCHANAN
DR CHIBA YOKO
JOHN CHRISTIAN
DR JOHN CLARK
TIMOTHY CLARK
PROFESSOR ELLEN P. CONANT
SIR HUGH CORTAZZI
TOM CRAIG
JOHN CULME
JON CULVERHOUSE
JOSEPH DARRACOTT
RUSSELL DENWOOD
PROFESSOR DOMYO MIHOKO
LORD AND LADY ELGIN
BETTY ELZEA
ENDO NOZOMI
ANTHONY J. FARRINGTON
RUPERT FAULKNER
JOHN FISCHER
FUJIGUCHI ETSUKO
FUJIIWA KAZUFUMI
PROFESSOR FUJIMORI TERUNOBU
FUKUDA YOSHIKI
FUKUI YOSHIHISA
MIREILLE GALINOU
KENNETH GARDNER
RICHARD GREEN
CATHERINE HAILL
C.M. HAINES
NICHOLAS HARRIS
MR AND MRS HILLELSON
HASHIMOTO HIROKI
RICHARD HOLLIS
MARTIN HOPKINSON

MR AND MRS HORESH
CLIVE HURST
RALPH HYDE
PROFESSOR IKEGAMI CHUJI
DR OLIVER IMPEY
ALAN IRVINE
ITO HISAKO
KEN JACOBSON
PETER JEFFS
KAMON YASUO
KAMBA NOBUYUKI
PROFESSOR KAWAMURA JOICHIRO
DR KAWANABE KUSUMI
VIVIEN KNIGHT
KOJIMA KAORU
KOKATSU REIKO
KOMATSU TAISHU
LIONEL LAMBOURNE
MATSUMOTO SEIICHI
KRYSTYNA MATYJASZKIEWICZ
ROBERT MEYRICK
DR GOS MICKLEM
MIWA HIDEO
BARBARA MORRIS
MURATA TETSUO
NAKAJIMA HIROMITSU
CHRISTOPHER NEWALL
DAVID NEWMAN
NIIKURA-MATSUMURA ERI
NOGAWA MUNEYUKI
OBA SADAO
OBIKATA NAMIKO
OCHI YUJIRO
OKA YASUMASA
OJIMA MINA
OYAMA MIZUYO
OZAKI TAKAFUMI
PROFESSOR PETER PANTZER
ANDREW MACKINTOSH PATRICK
SIMON REYNOLDS
TOM RICHARDS
ALEXANDER ROBERTSON
SAKAI TADAYASU
SAKURAI TAKESHI
SATO DOSHIN
JOHN SCOTT
SHIGA HIDETAKA
SHIMIZU MASAKO
SHIMOYAMA HAJIME

JEREMY SMITH
HUGH STEVENSON
LINDSEY S. STEWART
PROFESSOR SUZUKI HIROYUKI
SUZUKI KANJI
TACHIBANA YOSHIAKI
PROFESSOR TAKEUCHI TSUGUO
PROFESSOR TANITA HIROYUKI
AILSA TANNER
PROFESSOR TAN'O YASUNORI
SIMON TAYLOR
DR CHRISTOPHER THACKER
TOMIYAMA HIDEO
PETER TROULES
TSUCHIYA YOSHIO
TSUNEMATSU IKUO
MARK TURNER
IZUMI K. TYTLER
UEKI TOSHIKO
USHIROKOJI MASAHIRO
UTAGAWA TAKASHI
UTAGAWA TOYOKUNI
DR CLIVE WAINWRIGHT
DR HELEN WATANABE-O'KELLY
MICHAEL WHITEWAY
EMMA WIRGMAN
DR STEPHEN WILDMAN
JULIE ANNE WILSON
DR ANDREW WILTON
CHRISTOHER WOOD
YAMANASHI EMIKO
YOKOTA YOICHI
YU-YING BROWN

The publishers of the catalogue, Barbican Art Gallery and the Setagaya Art Museum would like to thank all the lenders of works from both private and public collections who have kindly supplied photographic material for the catalogue and exhibition, or who have given permission for its use.

We are also most grateful to the following photographers who undertook considerable photographic work for catalogue reproduction use:

A.C. COOPER LIMITED
FUJIKAWA KIYOSHI
GREEN & RUSSELL
HIBI SADAO
MASUDA AKIHISA 125-9, 131
MIYAHARA KANAE
JONATHAN MORRIS-EBBS
RODNEY TODD-WHITE & SON
UENO NORIHIRO

Our thanks also must be extended to the following individuals and organisations:

ARCHITECTURAL INSTITUTE OF JAPAN, TOKYO
BRIDGESTONE MUSEUM OF ART, TOKYO
THE FREER GALLERY OF ART, SMITHONIAN INSTITUTION, WASHINGTON, D.C.
GIFU MUSEUM OF FINE ARTS
KAWAHIGASHI YOSHINORI
MEIJIMURA MUSEUM
MIYOSHI HAJIME
NATIONAL INSTITUTE OF JAPANESE LITERATURE, TOKYO
ORIENTAL CERAMIC SOCIETY, LONDON
OTSUKA KOGEI-SHA
PHILADELPHIA MUSEUM OF ART
SAGA PREFECTURAL MUSEUM
SEZON MUSEUM OF ART, TOKYO
SHUEI-SHA, TOKYO
SOKEI ACADEMY OF FINE ARTS (INSTITUTE OF PAINTING TECHNOLOGY), TOKYO
SOTHEBY'S, NEW YORK
TAN'O YASUNORI
TOKUSHIMA MODERN ART MUSEUM
TOYOTA CITY MUSEUM
WASEDA UNIVERSITY LIBRARY, TOKYO
ART YOMIURI
YUNIKA COMANY LIMITED

SPONSORS

Barbican Art Gallery and the Setagaya Art Museum
acknowledge with grateful thanks the support of
the following:

THE BRITISH PETROLEUM COMPANY PLC

THE YASUDA FIRE & MARINE INSURANCE
COMPANY LIMITED

ASAHI BREWERIES, LTD.

THE DAI-ICHI KANGYO BANK, LTD.

THE FUJI BANK, LTD

THE MEIJI MUTUAL LIFE INSURANCE CO.

THE MITSUBISHI BANK, LTD.

THE MITSUBISHI TRUST AND BANKING
CORPORATION

NIPPON LIFE INSURANCE CO.

ORIENT CORPORATION

THE SUMITOMO BANK, LTD

THE SUMITOMO TRUST AND BANKING CO., LTD.

SUNTORY LIMITED

YAMATANE CORPORATION

with the assistance of NIKKEI and the Japan Foundation